VINCENT ADEJUMO

THE RETURN OF BLACK NATIONALISM AND THE DEATH OF WHITE SUPREMACY

9781627311625

FERAL HOUSE
1240 WEST SIMS WAY
SUITE 124
PORT TOWNSEND, WA 98368
WWW.FERALHOUSE.COM
INFO@FERALHOUSE.COM
DESIGN BY DANTE CARLOS

TABLE OF CONTENTS

To the late great Dr. Gary L. Lemons,

Your inspiration and support have been invaluable to me throughout this entire writing process. Your encouragement and love shaped me and this book.

I deeply appreciate your belief in me even when I had none, the uplifting laughter, and the constant support that was provided.

This book humbly represents the values that you have added to my life. This is, and always will be, a gift to our people made possible by you.

Rest in Peace, Doc.

FOREWORD

BY DR. ADEYEMI DOSS

As a scholar of African American Studies, I have long witnessed how Black nationalism provides a vital framework for understanding and addressing the persistent challenges facing our communities. Black nationalism represents hope, self-determination, and collective power—principles that become increasingly relevant as we confront ongoing racial oppression in America. In my years of studying and teaching Black political thought, I have seen how the dream of integration has fallen short of delivering true liberation. The continued assault on Black lives, dignity, and opportunities demands solutions beyond the traditional civil-rights approach.

This is why Dr. Vincent Adejumo's *The Return of Black Nationalism and the Death of White Supremacy* arrives at such a critical moment in our history.

In an era marked by the resurgence of overt white supremacy and racial capitalism, the question of Black liberation remains as urgent as ever. The continuation of systemic racism, economic exploitation, and political marginalization of Black communities demands not just analysis but actionable solutions. It is within this context that Dr. Adejumo's vital work emerges, offering a clear-eyed examination of Black nationalism as a framework for collective advancement and self-determination. Black nationalism, at its core, represents more than just a political ideology—it embodies a comprehensive vision for Black empowerment and autonomy. As Dr. Adejumo masterfully demonstrates, it encompasses economic self-reliance, political self-determination, and cultural sovereignty. These principles become increasingly relevant as we witness the persistent wealth gap, political disenfranchisement, and cultural appropriation that continue to impact Black communities across America. The systemic barriers to Black wealth creation, from discriminatory lending practices to redlining's lasting effects, underscore the urgent need for economic independence and community-based solutions that Black nationalism advocates.

The escalation of white supremacist rhetoric and policies during the Trump era serves as a stark reminder that the structures of racial oppression remain deeply embedded in American society. From the violent insurrection at the Capitol to the ongoing attacks on Critical Race Theory and Black history in schools, this period exposes how quickly decades of perceived racial progress can be undermined, revealing the fragility of incremental reforms within a system fundamentally built on racial hierarchy. Dr. Adejumo's call for a Black nationalist party emerges not from separatist ideology but from a clear-eyed assessment of political reality and the limitations of existing political structures in addressing the specific needs and aspirations of Black communities.

The Return of Black Nationalism and the Death of White Supremacy focuses sharply on the economic and political dimensions of Black nationalism. As wealth inequality continues to grow along racial lines, with the median white family holding eight times the wealth of the median Black family, the need for economic solidarity and collective development becomes increasingly apparent. The COVID-19 pandemic further exposed these disparities, as Black businesses and communities faced disproportionate economic impacts. Dr. Adejumo's analysis demonstrates how Black nationalism offers practical strategies for building economic power through cooperative economics, support of Black-owned businesses, and the development of independent financial institutions.

Politically, the book makes a compelling case for why traditional two-party politics has failed to deliver substantive change for Black communities. The systematic voter suppression efforts, gerrymandering, and the dilution of the Voting Rights Act reveal the limitations of working solely within existing political structures. Dr. Adejumo's argument for a Black nationalist party represents not just a critique of these structures but a bold vision for how Black political power might be organized and exercised more effectively. This is not presented as a panacea but as a strategic option for advancing Black interests in a political system that has historically subordinated them.

The strength of this work lies in its ability to bridge theoretical analysis with practical application. While grounded in the historical traditions of Black nationalist thought—from Marcus Garvey to Malcolm X—it remains firmly focused on contemporary challenges and opportunities. Dr. Adejumo's examination of how Black nationalism can serve as a counter to white supremacy is particularly nuanced, avoiding both naive optimism and defeatist pessimism. His analysis draws important lessons from past movements while adapting their insights for modern challenges.

As we continue to witness the limits of liberal integrationism and the persistence of structural racism, this book offers crucial insights into alternative paths forward. The failed promises of the post-civil-rights era, coupled with ongoing police brutality, mass incarceration, and economic marginalization, demand new approaches to Black liberation. Recent movements like Black Lives Matter demonstrate the continued relevance of collective Black resistance and the need for systemic change. Dr. Adejumo reminds us that Black nationalism remains a powerful framework for addressing these contemporary challenges.

The Return of Black Nationalism and the Death of White Supremacy arrives at a critical moment in American history, as questions of racial justice, economic inequality, and political representation take center stage in national discourse. The ongoing movement for Black lives, coupled with growing awareness of systemic racism, creates an opportunity for radical reimagining of social, economic, and political structures. Through rigorous analysis and bold vision, Dr. Adejumo provides an invaluable resource for understanding both the theoretical foundations and practical applications of Black nationalism in our current context. His work challenges us to think beyond conventional political frameworks and imagine new possibilities for Black liberation and self-determination.

The urgency of Dr. Adejumo's message resonates deeply in our current political climate, where the backlash against racial-justice movements has intensified. From the banning of books about Black history to the criminalization of protest, we are witnessing renewed attempts to suppress Black political consciousness and organizing. Yet paradoxically, these very attempts at suppression highlight the transformative potential of Black nationalist thought. As my own students increasingly question the efficacy of traditional civil rights strategies, Dr. Adejumo's analysis offers them a powerful alternative framework for understanding both their oppression and their liberation.

This book stands as a beacon for future generations of activists, scholars, and community leaders who seek to build Black power beyond the limitations of electoral politics. It provides not just critique but concrete strategies for building autonomous Black institutions, developing economic power, and creating new political structures. Dr. Adejumo's work will undoubtedly inspire readers to move beyond performative allyship and symbolic gestures toward the serious work of dismantling white supremacy and building genuine Black power. For anyone committed to the project of Black liberation, this book is not just recommended reading—it is essential.

Dr. Adeyemi Doss
Assistant Professor of African American Studies
Saint Louis University

THE OLD PLANTATION (SLAVES DANCING ON A SOUTH CAROLINA PLANTATION), CA. 1785–1795.
WATERCOLOR ON PAPER, ATTRIBUTED TO JOHN ROSE, BEAUFORT COUNTY, SOUTH CAROLINA.
(COURTESY OF THE ABBY ALDRICH ROCKEFELLER FOLK ART MUSEUM.)

VINCENT ADEJUMO

INTRODUCTION TO BLACK NATIONALISM

1

The concept of race in America has been and continues to be a complicated, yet chaotic aspect of the country's history. America's racial hierarchy, as well as the very fabric of its institutional systems, is responsible for its ascension as the hegemonic power of the planet. Since the founding of this country, the havoc that race causes in America is systemically designed to ensure whites remain in a supreme position in society while Blacks remain in servitude. The only solution for this pattern to be broken is for Black Americans to make a conscious effort to return Black nationalism to the forefront of its consciousness and kill white supremacy. In Malcolm X's 1964 address "The Ballot or the Bullet," he declared,

> *The philosophy of Black nationalism means that the Black man should control the politics and the politicians in his own community.... The economic philosophy of black nationalism is pure and simple. It only means that we should control the economy of our community. Why should white people be running all the stores in our community? Why should white people be running the banks of our community? Why should the economy of our community be in the hands*

> *of the white man? Why? If a black man can't move his store into a white community, you tell me why a white man should move his store into a black community.... The philosophy of Black nationalism involves a re-education program in the Black community in regard to economics.... So, the economic philosophy of Black nationalism means in every church, in every civic organization, in every fraternal order, it's time now for our people to become conscious of the importance of controlling the economy of our community. If we own the stores, if we operate the businesses, if we try and establish some industry in our own community, then we're developing to the position where we are creating employment for our own kind. Once you gain control of the economy of your own community, then you don't have to picket and boycott and beg some cracker downtown for a job in his business.*[1]

These words on Black nationalism from Malcolm X were a powerful soliloquy in 1964 when a variation of this speech was given after he left the Nation of Islam. Each iteration of the speech has arguably gained relevance with each passing generation. Malcolm X's "Ballot or the Bullet" speech provides a relevant foundation for this book because it highlights the core themes of education, economics, and politics, which are central to his Black nationalist philosophy. These key themes serve as a platform for arguing for Black nationalism as well as the death of white supremacy as the solution for the unique problems that Black Americans face. These problems include racial disparities between Blacks and non-Blacks, especially whites, in areas such as wealth, education, health, labor, criminal justice, social capital, and political capital. Black-led civil rights organizations believed that the Civil Rights Act of 1964 and Voter Rights Act of 1965 would bring liberation to Black people in America and rebalance the relationship with whites in a few decades. As readers will discover, contemporary data suggest that African Americans are still at the bottom of every measurable category mentioned.

For example, according to the Federal Reserve, in 2019, the average net worth of an African American family was $142,500, compared to $983,400 for white families. In the 2017–2018 academic year, 195,014 bachelor's degrees were awarded to African Americans and 1,189,619 were awarded to whites, as per the National Center for Education Statistics. The Centers for Disease Control found that 13.6% of African Americans in 2019 were uninsured while only 9.8% of whites were. There are very few African American–centered Political Action Committees and lobbying organizations to advocate for policies to remedy these disparities. However, other ethnic minorities such as Jews, Hispanics, and Asians deploy numerous lobbying organizations and Political Action Committees centered on the cultural norms of their heritage and an affinity for their countries to advance their political and economic interests while in America and, ultimately, address their own problems.

Black nationalism in and of itself is not singular. It encompasses a multitude of concepts which include Black empowerment, Black Radicalism, nation within a nation, separatism, Pan-Africanisms, and African Internationalism. The enduring legacy of Black resistance, from the era of slavery to Reconstruction and the civil rights movement, makes these concepts essential for pushing forward the argument for Black nationalism. For example, during the period of slavery (1619 to 1865), enslaved Africans would often use spirituals and songs to convey coded messages to each other. These messages often indicated plots for rebellious activities, such as causing an insurrection on the plantation, escaping, or killing the slave master.

The communications theorist Kerran L. Sanger, in a 2009 essay titled "Spirituals as Strategy," notes that slave spirituals were also used to counter the slave-master narrative that enslaved Africans were not human:

> *The spirituals, both in the act of singing and in the words of the songs, became a critical part of countermanding the master's ideology about slaves. This was a form of rhetorical resistance that both*

> *limited the slaves' worth to their masters and, more importantly, enabled slaves to refute the very definitions and assumptions on which this psychological oppression was based. As they refuted those definitions, they replaced them with ones of their own making.*[2]

These spirituals conjured a culture of resistance that was succinctly articulated by David Walker, a free Black man who was also an abolitionist, in an 1829 publication titled *An Appeal to the Coloured Citizens of the World*. Within this manuscript, Walker promoted the idea of enslaved Africans liberating themselves from the institution of slavery, contributing to the radicalization of the emerging abolitionist movement in the 1820s. Walker argued for a more radical approach to abolition when he wrote,

> *[T]hey want us for their slaves and think nothing of murdering us in order to subject us to that wretched condition—therefore, if there is an attempt made by us, kill or be killed. Now, I ask you, had you not rather be killed than to be a slave to a tyrant, who takes the life of your mother, wife, and dear little children? Look upon your mother, wife and children, and answer God Almighty; and believe this, that it is no more harm for you to kill a man who is trying to kill you than it is for you to take a drink of water when thirsty; in fact, the man who will stand still and let another murder him is worse than an infidel, and, if he has common sense, ought not to be pitied.*[3]

Walker's rhetoric in *Appeal* set the blueprint for the Black radical tradition that would be carried on by leaders and insurrectionists such as Nat Turner, Robert Smalls, Harriet Tubman, and John Brown. These leaders thought of themselves in a nationalist framework, not as an American but as Black. To be Black in America at this time was to be part of a nation within a nation because of the vastly different experiences that enslaved and freed Africans had compared to white Americans. Different treatment forced Blacks in the period of slavery to understand their world differently from whites, based on race, class, lineage, and economic and social standing. Many Black leaders, whether enslaved like Nat Turner or free like the journalist and physician Martin Delany, would eventually use their experiences to pledge allegiance to their race, not to the country where they were held captive or relegated to second-class citizenship.

Radical Black leaders' devotion to their race made so-called allies uncomfortable. For example, William Lloyd Garrison, editor of the *Liberator* who was considered a radical thanks to his fierce opposition to slavery, vehemently disagreed with Walker's *Appeal*. Garrison was a devout Quaker, which informed his belief in nonviolence. The basis of his disagreement was that enslaved Africans who were interested in their freedom should not engage in the same violent tactics that the white slave master used upon them. Garrison wrote in the pages of the *Liberator* in 1831,

> *Believing, as we do, that men should never do evil, that good may come; that a good end does not justify wicked means in the accomplishment of it; and that we ought to suffer,*[4] *as did our Lord and his apostles, unresistingly—knowing that vengeance belongs to God, and he will certainly repay it where it is due;—believing all this, and that the Almighty will deliver the oppressed in a way which whey know not, we deprecate the spirit and tendency of this Appeal.*

Garrison then goes on to lament that "Mr. Walker but pays them in their own coin, but follows their own creed, but adopts their own language. We do not preach rebellion—no, but submission and peace."

Garrison's notion of submission and peace, with its Christian undertones, was a common theme for many contemporary so-called "allies" who opposed Black nationalism. It was Delany's Black nationalist vision, centering Black people's freedom, that Garrison objected to. Garrison was opposed to Black emigration to South America or West

Africa to establish a separate country and self-governance. This was in contrast to their contemporary Frederick Douglass. Many whites did not view Black emigration itself as a serious threat to American society. Whites—both non-slave-owners who wanted to protect their jobs as skilled tradesmen and slave-owners who wanted to rid the country of meddlesome free Black abolitionists, especially those from Northern states who might stir up insurrections—advocated and supported emigration to a foreign country, as evidenced by the prominence of the American Colonization Society, which established in 1822 the colony that would become Liberia.

However, what distinguished Delany from the American Colonization Society is that he believed an independent nation should be established by Black people from America, not benevolent white people like the creators and funders of the ACS. Readers will meet many leaders and activists who embodied different tenets of Black nationalism and faced opposition to their ideology, not only from benevolent-in-name-only whites but also from a contemporary rival organization that was also Black.

In facing opposition, whether from rival organizations or from society at large, Black nationalists by default adopt some features of what has been called "oppositional culture." Oppositional culture is created when a community or group develops behaviors and norms that challenge the ideals of the mainstream culture that is dominating it. Oppositional culture as a coping mechanism or as a tool of resistance for African Americans is a common theme that will be reiterated throughout this book to illustrate why Black nationalism is essential for addressing racial inequality. Successful Black nationalists often used the tactics of oppositional culture to galvanize their audiences.

The sociologist Michael Hecter argues that ethnic groups that are identified as subordinate draw upon cultural resources endemic to their community to resist systemic oppression. Another sociologist, Theresa Martinez, notes that modern sociologists take this concept of oppositional culture a step further by surmising that

> *Non-European groups in the United States draw on their own cultural resources to resist oppression under oppressive circumstances. These groups will develop an oppositional culture or "culture of resistance" that embodies "a coherent set of values, beliefs, and practices which mitigates the effects of oppression and reaffirms that which is distinct from the majority culture."*[5]

Black Nationalism conceptualized from Martinez's framework of oppositional culture and resistance casts a larger spotlight on those in power who may subscribe to white supremacist ideology with respect to race using the economic, legal, and social systems and norms using culture as a tool to dominate Black Americans.

Enslaved Africans, who were considered chattel, were taught a strand of white Anglo-Christian culture to ensure that they would always think of themselves as subservient to the slave master and the plantation. In modern times, the purpose of education has not changed since the days of chattel slavery. For instance, according to data from as early as the 1950s, Black Americans have the lowest rate of pursuing self-employment in the United States.

The low rates of self-employment in the African American community creates a system of dependency and reliance on either white-owned corporations or white-managed institutions to supply them with a means for living and survival. Therefore, the education system promotes political and economic inequality because it does not teach African Americans how to solve their economic and political problems or remedy economic and political disparities between Blacks and whites. Additionally, an "Afrocentric" educational curriculum created by Blacks to solve African Americans' financial and policy problems may be the most effective way to teach African Americans to solve the problems that are byproducts of white supremacy in general and the public education system specifically.

Many have argued that it is up to government institutions and elected officials to remedy the inequalities between African Americans and whites. Prominent scholars and activists such as Ta-Nehisi Coates argue that the most effective remedy would be reparations for African Americans. Others, including Representative Ayanna Presley, argue that student-loan forgiveness would particularly benefit Black women, who hold the largest amount of student debt in the country.

Can policies such as reparations and student-loan forgiveness correct resource inequities between African Americans and whites? Despite representation of Black Americans at all levels of government, government policies have been ineffective in remedying inequitable access to finite resources between Black and white Americans.

Therefore, it is argued throughout this book that a return of Black nationalism to the forefront of the consciousness of African Americans is the most effective ideology for addressing racial inequalities in economics, politics, and education. A byproduct of bringing Black nationalism back into the consciousness of African Americans is that embracing the concepts and practices will lead to the death of the psychodynamic effects of white supremacy. The belief in white supremacy, from the founding of this country, has played a significant role in ensuring that Black Americans do not dare challenge the system that has ensured its subjugation to white-owned institutions. It is also the same system that Black people consciously and subconsciously participate in not only to survive but to seek equality with their oppressors. Black nationalist ideology offers an alternative to assimilationist strategies and builds upon the idea of creating opportunities and resources to be shared among all African Americans. Assimilationist strategies since the 1960s have not elevated Black Americans either economically or educationally and, in some respects, they have fallen even farther behind. Anti-assimilationism should hold a greater appeal for Black Americans because the dominant society has not been willing to address the inequities between Black and white America.

In his 1963 "Message to the Grassroots" speech, Malcolm X proclaimed,

> *When you want a nation, that's called nationalism. When the white man became involved in a revolution in this country against England, what was it for? He wanted this land so he could set up another white nation. That's white nationalism. The American Revolution was white nationalism. The French Revolution was white nationalism. The Russian Revolution too—yes, it was—white nationalism. You don't think so? Why do you think Khrushchev and Mao can't get their heads together? White nationalism. All the revolutions that are going on in Asia and Africa today are based on what?—Black Nationalism. A revolutionary (today) is a Black Nationalist. He wants a nation . . . If you're afraid of Black Nationalism, you're afraid of revolution. And if you love revolution, you love Black Nationalism.*[6]

Here he illustrates the urgent need for African Americans to think of themselves as a nation. Asian, Jewish, and Latin American groups in America have adopted nationalist beliefs centered on their native cultures to control the economic resources of their community. Movements in the Trump era, such as Black Lives Matter, have shown that there is an appetite for revolution in the African American community. Revolutionary tactics like organized marches, sit-ins, and forceful appeals to elected officials have been a consistent theme in this era.

However, revolutionary tactics alone are not enough. As Malcolm X states, only a nationalist approach can remedy these inequities. In the era of Trump, African Americans do not leverage any power because they do not think of themselves from a nationalist standpoint. W. E. B. Du Bois argued in the early twentieth century that African Americans are faced with seeing themselves from two perspectives in America: as a Negro and as an American. This constant warring between the two perspectives that African Americans exhibit in the Trump era may be a barrier for progressing past the Civil

Rights Era tactics that were centered on assimilating African Americans with whites.

Since the 1960s, assimilationist policies have given the illusion of fairness between African Americans and whites, because people are generally unaware of the inequalities, fixated as they are on their immediate realities and not the bigger picture. Ultimately, as will be pointed out throughout this book, returning to a Black nationalist framework with the result of killing white supremacy is the most effective solution in the era of Trump and beyond for African Americans to lift the veil and solve their problems.

W. E. B. DU BOIS, 1907. (JAMES E. PURDY, NATIONAL PORTRAIT GALLERY, CREATIVE COMMONS LICENSE.)

CHAPTER ONE

HISTORY AND FUNDAMENTALS OF BLACK NATIONALISM

Amos Wilson, arguably the most influential scholar and practitioner of Black nationalism, argues that "Nationalism is an ideology of a thousand faces. While we all may have a similar sense of what it involves, we cannot all agree on any one definition of it." Wilson defines a nation as being made up of people who share language, territory, economic ties, and behaviors. The U.S. population's diversity of race, lineage, and culture is a characteristic dating back to its colonial era. This diversity, however, is dominated by whites of European descent and Blacks of sub-Saharan African descent. Since the colonial era, whites have placed themselves in the dominant position culturally, politically, and economically, while Blacks were brought to the colonies from various African tribes by whites to serve white interests, first as chattel, then as second-class citizens, and now as economic serfs, constrained to a system that creates and maintains economic inequality. This relationship has been the focus of racial conflict in the United States. Racism and white supremacy are in the very DNA of the United States and have led to racial conflicts such as the Civil War, which ultimately led to two different forms of nationalism in America: white nationalism and Black nationalism.

DR. AMOS WILSON, C. 1980S

In the wake of the 2016 election of Donald Trump, white nationalist discourse became common in mainstream media and social media. In August 2019, in Dayton, Ohio, and El Paso, Texas, massacres committed by white men left numerous Black and brown citizens dead. Politicians such as Beto O'Rourke, a native of El Paso and former candidate for the 2020 Democratic Party nomination, proceeded to blame Trump for "White Nationalist" rhetoric that set the conditions for the gunmen to act. CNN's Jake Tapper in an interview after the shootings asked O'Rourke, "Do you think President Trump is a white nationalist?" O'Rourke replied, "Yes. I do."

At different points in American history, ethnic minorities have pursued self-determination to counter white nationalism and advance their communities in areas such as education, politics, society, and economics. Asian immigrants in the United States exemplified nationalistic principles of self-determination by establishing Chinatowns in San Francisco and other large cities. Latin immigrants in Florida exhibited nationalistic principles by establishing Ybor City in Tampa and Little Havana in Miami. Irish immigrants settled in America during colonial times as indentured servants and after immigration from Ireland to the U.S. became more prevalent during the Irish Famine in the mid-nineteenth century. Many of those immigrants settled in the South Boston ("Southie") and Dorchester neighborhoods of Boston, Hell's Kitchen and Woodlawn neighborhoods of New York City, and the Fishtown and Northeast neighborhoods in Philadelphia at the start of the twentieth century and in a short time consolidated political power for their benefit.

Those ethnic groups, upon arrival in the United States, experienced discrimination not only in laws that were enacted by the local municipalities that they settled in, but also in social standing. Discrimination against these groups by the larger dominant hegemonic society reinforced the nationalistic principles of self-determination and independence that were already present in their culture. Their cultures, in turn, helped to create the communities they later established in their chosen settlements.

African Americans did not have the choice of migrating to North America as other ethnic groups did. African Americans experienced discrimination and subjugation at greater levels than other ethnic groups, first under a system of chattel slavery and then as second-class citizens. Free Black groups arose later in the period of chattel slavery, and within those groups, leaders developed the foundations of Black nationalism. The debates over what it meant to be a free Black person in North America occurred parallel to the debates around the concepts that would define American independence. These foundational ideas about what it meant to be Black in this new country grew more critical when free Blacks realized that they—unlike the white indentured servants from Europe and their descendants—would be denied full citizenship in the new United States.

Discrimination against African Americans has resulted in them having the least wealth, the worst health, the lowest outcomes in primary and secondary education, highest rate of death at the hands of law enforcement, and the highest rate of imprisonment. These issues have remained consistent, even during and after the Barack Obama presidency. The solutions put forth by politicians and activists have not been effective in addressing these issues.

White nationalism in America is not a new concept. The political scientist and sociologist Dean Robinson argues that

> *White American nationalism reflected a sentiment that the United States was, or ought to be, the domain of the white man. This idea, in turn, rested upon a set of notions concerning innate traits that white people in the United States supposedly had, the different traits that blacks (and others) allegedly had, and the appropriate station or social status these traits demanded.*

White nationalist ideology influenced race relations in America from the beginning. Several of the Founding Fathers were white nationalists because they marginalized Native

Americans and tried to enslave them to claim the lands they had cultivated for centuries before Europeans came. The founders rebelled against British rule and were white nationalists who believed white men had rights to land they took, disregarding original ownership and their colonial standing.

The founders' attitudes toward the lands and Native Americans was evident in the white supremacist rhetoric used in the arguments for the colonies' independence. The founders put white nationalism and white supremacy into practice through laws that protected chattel slavery in the declarative documents leading up to independence and the system of governance established in the Articles of Confederation of 1783 and the Constitution of 1789. Nowhere is the white nationalist ideology of the founding fathers more evident than in the paradox of enslaving Africans themselves while objecting to their own "enslavement" by the British Crown.

European colonizers in sixteenth- and seventeenth-century North America prioritized economic expansion and the ongoing exploration of foreign territories. British colonists attempted to distance themselves from the control of the authoritative hold of their king. The British policies to pay for the French and Indian War, such as the Sugar Act and Stamp Act, triggered the struggle for American independence. The colonists realized that Britain was prolonging its control over the colonies by enforcing the collection of taxes without the colonists having representation in Parliament. The American colonists compared British policies to those of a slave owner.

However, this "taxation without representation" was hardly the worst atrocity in colonial society, compared to the barbaric act of enslaving Africans. Colonial leaders such as Thomas Jefferson and George Washington attempted to justify slavery by claiming that Africans were naturally suited to the harsh landscape and arrived with agricultural skills. They also argued that the increased labor demand for crops such as cotton required them to investigate alternatives, since there were issues with using Native Americans and indentured European servants for intensive labor. These issues included Native Americans being more susceptible to European diseases and white indentured servants violating their contracts by escaping. Colonists justified using enslaved Africans for agricultural labor by claiming their supposed disease resistance and easily identifiable skin color made escape less likely.

Colonial leaders such as Jefferson, Washington, and James Madison were among those who advocated for the colonies' independence and freedom from Britain while also maintaining personal cadres of enslaved Africans. In 1776, when the Declaration of Independence was signed, a significant number of its signers—forty-one out of fifty-six—had slaves. Most colonial leaders were from the Virginia colony, where 40% of the nation's slaves were located during the 1770s and '80s.

Other reasons were created to justify slavery. For example, in Jefferson's view, the liberation of enslaved Africans would result in their destitution and displacement in a foreign country. Therefore, he assumed they would steal from the American colonists and have to be sent back to Africa. Jefferson tried to introduce measures to abolish slavery in the Virginia constitution while serving in the House of Burgesses. During his presidency, his 1806 State of the Union address urged Congress to abolish the importation of Africans for the purposes of enslaving them. This culminated in the 1807 Act

UNDATED, UNATTRIBUTED PAINTING OF SALLY HEMINGS BASED ON CONTEMPORARY DESCRIPTIONS.

Prohibiting the Importation of Slaves. Yet, while he enacted anti-slavery laws, Jefferson himself still owned slaves until his death in 1826, including the now-famous Sally Hemings.

The contradictory ideas of thinkers such as Washington, John Adams, and John Locke also influenced strategy in the Revolutionary War. The colonists allowed many of the enslaved Africans to enlist with colonial forces with the promise that they would be freed. However, the promise of freedom did not materialize for the majority, as they were still enslaved by their owners after the war. This again furthered the contradiction of colonists equating enslavement of Africans with British taxation. However, abolitionists such as Anthony Benezet, Benjamin Rush, Nathaniel Appleton, and Thomas Paine rejected the equation of colonial grievances with slavery. Paine argued in *Common Sense* and "African Slavery in America" that slavery was unethical and inhumane.

The American historian Edmund Morgan argues that, desperately needing more soldiers to fight the British, the American colonists struggled during the Revolutionary War. Unquestioned loyalty and fortitude were demonstrated by enslaved Africans who, though denied the freedom promised for their service and permitted to enlist by their masters, served with distinction. This motivated more individuals to promote the ideology of abolitionism. John Jay and Alexander Hamilton established the Manumission of Slaves Society in 1785 in New York. Their advocacy and lobbying on the issue of chattel slavery in New York through their organization led to revisions of New York colonial and state laws on slavery. These revisions ultimately resulted in the end of slavery in New York in 1827, marking the largest liberation of Africans in bondage in the U.S. before the Civil War. Manumission of enslaved Africans in New York would eventually spark more discussion on the morality of slavery across the country and deepen the divide between Northern and Southern states on the issue.[7] Pennsylvania became one of several northern states to abolish slavery after the American Revolution by establishing laws that

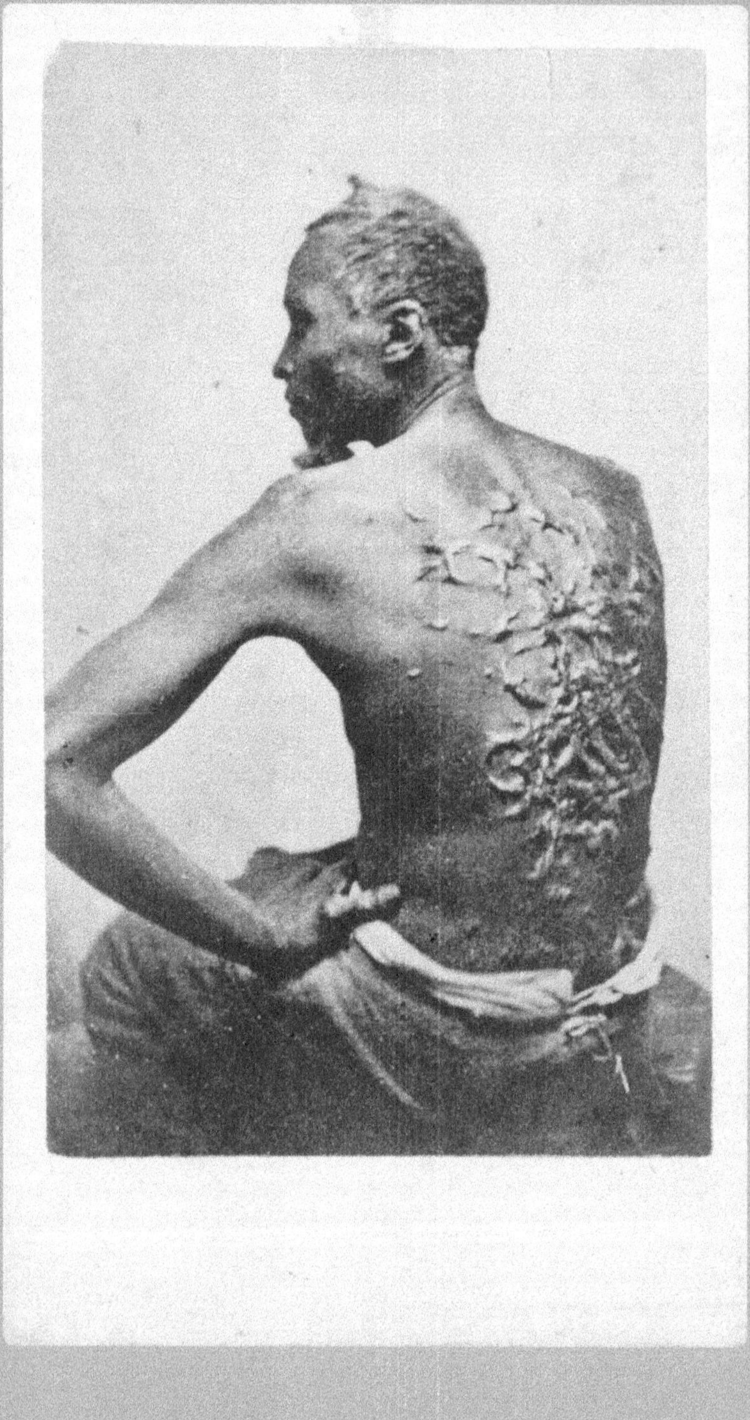

"WHIPPED PETER," OR "GORDON." CARTE DE VISITE BY MCPHERSON AND OLIVER OF BATON ROUGE, LOUISIANA, ON APRIL 2, 1863. (LIBRARY OF CONGRESS.)

liberated enslaved Africans who came to the state wanting to live there; furthermore, enslaved Africans could not be taken from the state without the state's consent, thus abolishing slave imports.

Slavery in Southern states was eventually abolished via the Emancipation Proclamation in 1863, the Confederate surrender to the Union in April 1865, and the ratification of the 13th Amendment in December 1865. However, long before this, some colonists, mainly Quakers in Pennsylvania, had advocated for the reform of the social norms and policies that were the foundation of slavery. Their advocacy, along with that of free blacks such Martin Delany, David Walker, and Harriet Tubman, contributed to the Emancipation Proclamation and eventually to the enforcement of the 13th, 14th, and 15th Amendments from 1865 to 1870. The American Paradox remained part of the white citizens' worldview, as evidenced by the questionable actions of colonists and citizens, continued disputation of taxes, and negative attitudes toward enslaved Africans despite the official eradication of a system that justified the bondage of Black people.

To achieve global economic power, the burgeoning American nation increased its demand for African slaves in both its northern and southern regions, aiming to secure the necessary capital and production for independence. The drive for hegemonic dominance for newly minted white Americans also meant that they had to become more entrenched in their nationalistic and white supremacist principles for the foreseeable future. The principles of white nationalism established during the British colonial era remain part of America's foundation.

The sociologist Elizabeth Martinez defines white supremacy as

> *an historically based, institutionally perpetuated system of exploitation and oppression of continents, nations, and peoples of color by white peoples and nations of the European continent, for the purpose of maintaining and defending a system of wealth, power, and privilege.*[8]

White supremacy allows white nationalists to believe that whites should naturally rule over nonwhites and their homelands. That is not to say that all white people consciously subscribe to white nationalism or nationalist rhetoric. However, all whites in some way, shape, or form have built-in privileges from the system of white supremacy.

Amos Wilson argues that

> *Black nationalism is ideally a mass or people's movement. It seeks to encompass the Afrikan masses and involve them intimately in their own liberation from oppression and in the determination of their own political destiny. The chief opponents of Black nationalists have traditionally been bourgeois, assimilationist, liberal, and conservative intellectuals, both Black and white.*[9]

Assimilationism here means a preference to intertwine with the dominant society rather than establish systems of organization or governance independently. But a Black nationalist does not necessarily have to be an anti-assimilationist. However, anti-assimilationists are often Black nationalists. As Dean Robinson notes,

> *Numerous studies have labeled political leaders like Booker T. Washington, W. E. B. Du Bois, and Marcus Garvey as "nationalist." However, while each activist understood Blacks to share a common destiny, and while each encouraged Blacks to work together toward common political and economic goals, only one, Garvey, wanted a separate state.*

J. Herman Blake, the first Black professor at the University of California, Santa Cruz, who worked with Eldridge Cleaver and studied the Black Panthers and other Black empowerment groups, describes Black nationalism as

> *a consequence of the duality of the experience of Afro-Americans, a people who are identified*

> *by racial characteristics as different from the "typical" American and denied full participation in this society for that reason, while, at the same time, they are expected to meet all the responsibilities of citizen.*[10]

Blake identifies three pillars of Black nationalism: politics, economics, and culture. But what does Black political nationalism look like?

PATHBREAKER A CARTE DE VISITE OF MARTIN R. DELANY AS MAJOR OF THE 104TH UNITED STATES COLORED TROOPS, C. 1865. (NATIONAL PARK SERVICE.)

Political nationalism originated in the pre–Civil War era, with free Blacks such as Delany expressing the desire to emigrate from the U.S. and establish their own nation of both indigenous Blacks of that land and descendants of enslaved Africans in America. Delany first developed this idea in response to his experiences growing up as a free Black in the early nineteenth century. Although he was technically free, Martin experienced racism as a boy and as a young man. For example, after co-founding the *North Star* newspaper in 1847 with Douglass and Garrison, Martin went on a "Western tour" to recruit subscribers.

While in Ohio in 1848, Delany was chased down by a white mob intent on lynching him. In his own words,

> *A torch was brought, and the tar barrel set in a flame, when store boxes were piled upon it, which produced a fire that must have been seen several miles around. The fire was built in the middle of the street, directly opposite the hotel in which we stayed. Then came the cry, "Burn them alive!— kill the niggers!—they shall never leave this place!—bring them out!—rush in and take them!—Which is their room? Niggers! come out, or we will burn down the house over your heads!" A consultation was held, the result of which was that they would rush into our room, drag us out, tie and hand-cuff us, and take us immediately to the South and sell us! declaring that I would bring "fifteen hundred dollars, cash!"* [11]

Delany escaped from the hotel the next day. In 1850, he went on to pursue medical training at Harvard Medical School. However, he was expelled because white students didn't approve of him being there on account of his race. The white students passed a motion which stated, "We have no objection to the education and evaluation of blacks but do decidedly remonstrate against their presence in college with us."[12] In that same year, the Fugitive Slave Act was signed into law by President Millard Filmore. This act was the result of a compromise between the free states and slave-holding states and levied fines of up to $1,000 ($31,000 in 2025 dollars) against officials who did not report a runaway slave and allowed slave owners to only supply an affidavit to a federal marshal to procure a Black person that they believed, rightly or wrongly, had escaped.

A recaptured slave was not permitted a trial by jury and whoever assisted the runaway could be jailed or fined. In many cases, "slave patrols" were compensated either monetarily or with legal immunity. This set of laws and procedures became the basis of the American criminal justice system—based initially on the capture of Black bodies. Many Blacks who were either born free or received manumission were falsely accused of being runaway slaves. They, in turn, were either re-enslaved or pressed into slavery for the first time. The Fugitive Slave Act and other experiences with racism motivated Delany over the next decades of his life to advocate for free Blacks and then newly emancipated African Americans to emigrate to South America and Africa.

In 1852, Delany published *The Condition, Elevation, Emigration, and Destiny of the Colored People of the United States*, which advocated for emigration as a solution to ensure the survival of people of African descent in America, noting that oppressed people throughout history had benefited from emigration. He wrote,

> *That there have been people in all ages under certain circumstances, that may be benefited by emigration, will be admitted; and that there are circumstances under which emigration is absolutely necessary to their political elevation cannot be disputed. This we see in the Exodus of the Jews from Egypt to the land of Judea; in the expedition of Dido and her followers from Tyro to Mauritania; and not to dwell upon hundreds of modern European examples—also in the ever memorable emigration of the Puritans, in 1620, from Great Britain, the land of their birth, to the wilderness of the New World, at which may be fixed the beginning of emigration to this continent as*

> *a permanent residence. This may be acknowledged; but to advocate the emigration of the colored people of the United States from their native homes is a new feature in our history, and at first view, may be considered objectionable, as pernicious to our interests. This objection is at once removed, when reflecting on our condition as incontrovertibly shown in a foregoing part of this work.*[13]

Delany also broke with mostly white abolitionist colleagues such as James G. Birney, a member of the American Colonization Society, by rejecting the notion that Blacks who were free should emigrate to Liberia. Delany wrote,

> *Liberia is no place for the colored freemen of the United States; and we dismiss the subject with a single remark of caution against any advice contained in a pamphlet, which we have not seen, written by Hon. James G. Birney, in favor of Liberian emigration.... Liberia is not an Independent Republic: in fact, it is not an independent nation at all; but a poor miserable mockery—a burlesque on a government—a pitiful dependency on the American Colonizationists, the Colonization Board in Washington city, in the District of Columbia ...*
>
> *The advantages of this continent* [meaning here the Americas as a whole] *are superior, because it presents every variety of climate, soil, and production of the earth, with every variety of mineral production, with all kinds of water privileges, arid ocean coast on all sides, presenting every commercial advantage. Upon the American continent we are determined to stay, in spite of every odds against us.*

His attention to the resources available on the continent will continue to be a theme in the advocacy of Black nationalists.

Delany argued that Central and South America would be the best place for free Blacks to emigrate to. He wrote,

> *Central and South America, are evidently the ultimate destination and future home of the colored race on this continent; the advantages of which in preference to all others, will be apparent when once pointed out.... In the productions of grains, fruits, and vegetables, Central and South America are also prolific; and the best of herds are here raised. Indeed, the finest Merino sheep, as well as the principal trade in rice, sugar, cotton, and wheat, which is now preferred in California to any produced in the United States—the Chilian flour—might be carried on by the people of this most favored portion of God's legacy to man. The mineral productions excel all other parts of this continent; the rivers present the greatest internal advantages, and the commercial prospects, are without a parallel on the coast of the new world.*

In referring to the natural resources and means of production in Central America, Delany established a foundation for emigrating free Blacks to build a nation. Every nation must also have allies, which Delaney addressed by stating,

> *This vast number of people, our brethren—because they are precisely the same people as ourselves and share the same fate with us, as the case of numbers of them have proven, who have been adventitiously thrown among us—stand ready and willing to take us by the hand—nay, are anxiously waiting, and earnestly importuning us to come, that they may make common cause with us, and we all share the same fate.*

The manuscript was well received immediately after its release to the free Black community. However, after the Civil War, the idea of mass emigration lost its appeal to the newly freed African Americans. Leaders such as Douglass now turned their attention to civil rights. The civil rights movement of that time led to the ratification of the 14th and 15th Amendments to the United States Constitution. Naturalized citizenship and the doctrine of equal protection under the law were established by the 14th Amendment. The 15th established the right of Black men to vote. Although this was the case, very few Black men voted, especially in the South. Laws such as poll taxes and grandfather clauses, enacted by states and municipalities, aimed at preventing people from voting.

The oppression of Blacks that followed the Civil War led to African American leaders focusing on economic uplift of the community based on the self-help model. Self-help here entails the community attempting to overcome systemic racism and white supremacy by putting itself on an equal footing economically and politically with other groups in the United States. Economic nationalism was developed out of this model when it became clear that emigration en masse was not feasible, and that African Americans would remain second-class citizens for the foreseeable future despite being freed from slavery. Economic nationalism, in the words of J. Herman Blake, "called for racial solidarity and economic co-operation as the solution to the problems of the African American."

The main proponent of this form of nationalism was Booker T. Washington, who developed it in the late nineteenth century in response to the growing number of immigrants from northern European countries. Washington's ideas were also influenced by his experiences, first as a slave growing up in the South and then as the Tuskegee Institute's first president. Economic nationalism was borne out of the debate between Washington and Du Bois in what is famously dubbed the "Atlanta Compromise" at the International Convention in Atlanta in 1895. In his remarks, Washington expressed that the best way forward for African Americans was to focus more on economic security by way of practical occupations and living peacefully around white people than on social mobility:

> *Our greatest danger is that in the great leap from slavery to freedom we may overlook the fact that the masses of us are to live by the productions of our*

> *hands and fail to keep in mind that we shall prosper in proportion as we learn to dignify and glorify common labor, and put brains and skill into the common occupations of life.*[14]

In return for the loyalty that Blacks showed whites, Washington argued that it was the duty of whites to help Blacks because Blacks continue to serve whites "without strikes and labor wars, tilled your fields, cleared your forests, build your railroads and cities, and brought forth treasures from the bowels of the earth, and helped make possible this magnificent representation of the progress of the South." To solidify his point, Washington argued, "In all things that are purely social we can be as separate as the fingers, yet one as the hand in all things essential to mutual progress." Washington's message in the Atlanta Compromise speech suggested to hostile Southern whites and supportive Northern whites that Blacks could improve their social standing by embracing their inferior positions. They should also, he argued, focus on developing skills geared toward the industrial field to be as self-sufficient as possible.

Whites in every socio-economic category tacitly approved of Washington's approach because it allowed them to stay in power both economically and socially. Additionally, it motivated Black individuals in the South to enhance their abilities and achieve a sense of autonomy. Whites found it easier to adjust to Blacks being free from slavery so long as they remained in servitude to them. The granting of privileges, such as dining with the president, to Blacks such as Washington fueled white anger out of fear that their social dominance was under threat. Black intellectuals such as Du Bois agreed with some of Washington's ideals but opposed his focus on economic pursuits over political and social mobility.

Du Bois supported Washington's focus on uplifting African Americans. However, while Du Bois originally commended Washington for his ability to sway white audiences, he found flaws in Washington's ideology. Du Bois did not believe that Blacks should only be taught to work jobs in the industrial sector. He believed that a liberal-arts curriculum was vital for Blacks to thrive because Black schools relied on teachers with higher education. Du Bois also believed that Black people should not remain silent, because doing so would prevent them from being able to attain equality with white citizens or claim any rights they had to their property or livelihood. *In The Souls of Black Folk*, Du Bois argued against the accommodationist ideology that Washington had deployed in the Atlanta Compromise. He wrote,

> *This "Atlanta Compromise" is by all odds the most notable thing in Mr. Washington's career. The South interpreted it in different ways: the radicals received it as a complete surrender of the demand for civil and political equality; the conservatives, as a generously conceived working basis for mutual understanding. So both approved it, and today its author is certainly the most distinguished Southerner since Jefferson Davis, and the one with the largest personal following.... Mr. Washington represents in Negro thought the old attitude of adjustment and submission; but adjustment at such a peculiar time as to make his programme unique. This is an age of unusual economic development, and Mr. Washington's programme naturally takes an economic cast, becoming a gospel of Work and Money to such an extent as apparently almost completely to overshadow the higher aims of life.*[15]

In *Up from Slavery*, Washington responded to such criticism, stating,

> *I tried to emphasize the fact that while the Negro should not be deprived by unfair means of the franchise, political agitation alone would not save him, and that back of the ballot he must have property, industry, skill, economy, intelligence, and character, and that no race without these elements could permanently succeed.*[16]

Despite the valid critiques of the Atlanta Compromise as too accommodating to white Southern racists, it also laid out the blueprint for economic nationalism in the American South. Washington also rejected Delany's brand of nationalism by way of emigration in the Atlanta Compromise:

> *To those of my race who depend on bettering their condition in a foreign land or who underestimate the importance of cultivating friendly relations with the Southern white man, who is their next-door neighbor, I would say: "Cast down your bucket where you are"— cast it down in making friends in every manly way of the people of all races by whom we are surrounded.*
>
> *Cast it down in agriculture, mechanics, in commerce, in domestic service, and in the professions. And in this connection it is well to bear in mind that whatever other sins the South may be called to bear, when it comes to business, pure and simple, it is in the South that the Negro is given a man's chance in the commercial world, and in nothing is this Exposition more eloquent than in emphasizing this chance. Our greatest danger is that in the great leap from slavery to freedom we may overlook the fact that the masses of us are to live by the productions of our hands and fail to keep in mind that we shall prosper in proportion as we learn to dignify and glorify common labor and put brains and skill into the common occupations of life.*

Washington firmly believed that the Deep South had the resources, capital, and industry needed to sustain Black Americans. He understood that Southern white nationalists held positions of power politically and economically and that Blacks did not have the economic infrastructure to effectively challenge the white power establishment. His call for Blacks to focus more on "property, industry, skill,

OFFICERS OF THE NATIONAL NEGRO BUSINESS LEAGUE, AT INDIANAPOLIS IN 1904.

OFFICERS OF THE INDIANAPOLIS NEGRO BUSINESS LEAGUE, 1904.

economy, intelligence, and character" was not because he thought Blacks were inferior. He wanted Blacks to build an economic base because he understood that living under apartheid conditions in the American South roughly forty years after chattel slavery meant that Blacks had to use every inch of their time and capital wisely. Black people in this period, especially in the South, did not have the political or economic apparatus to challenge whites. For Washington, the Black community had to develop the economic base first via entrepreneurship, land ownership, and tangible skills. After this was achieved, he believed that Blacks would be in a better position to challenge for more political and social rights.

Washington put economic principles of Black nationalism into practice in the curriculum that he implemented at the Tuskegee Institute and the organizations that he founded, such as the National Negro Business League. At Tuskegee, the students were taught, as Washington described,

> *practical knowledge of some one industry, together with the spirit of industry, thrift, and economy, that they would be sure of knowing how to make a living after they had left us. We wanted to teach them to study actual things instead of mere books alone.*

The emphasis on industry, thrift, and economy in the early curriculum of the Tuskegee institute prepared students for the legal barriers that would come. The "separate but equal" principle legally justified racial segregation following the Supreme Court's *Plessy v. Ferguson* ruling of 1896. However, before the ruling, there were several events that led to the decision. The white Southern historian Comer Vann Woodward noted in 1966,

> *The first genuine Jim Crow law requiring railroads to carry Negroes in separate cars or behind partitions was adopted by Florida in 1887. Mississippi followed this example in 1888; Texas in 1889; Louisiana in 1890; Alabama, Arkansas, Georgia, and Tennessee*

> *in 1891; and Kentucky in 1892. The Carolinas and Virginia did not fall into line until the last three years of the century.*
>
> *Negroes watched with despair while the legal foundations for the Jim Crow system were laid and the walls of segregation mounted around them. Their disenchantment with the hopes based on the Civil War amendments and the Reconstruction laws was nearly complete by 1890. The American commitment to equality, solemnly attested by three amendments to the Constitution and by elaborate civil rights acts, was virtually repudiated. The "compromise of 1877" between the Hayes Republicans and the southern conservatives had resulted in the withdrawal of federal troops from the South and the formal end of Reconstruction. What had started then as a retreat had within a decade turned into a rout. Northern radicals and liberals had abandoned the cause: the courts had rendered the Constitution helpless; the Republican party had forsaken the cause it had sponsored. A tide of racism was mounting in the country unopposed.*[17]

With Jim Crow "separate but equal" laws at the federal and state level being enacted at the turn of the twentieth century, hopes for African Americans to not be treated as second-class citizens throughout the country dwindled. Conditions that African Americans contended with in the Jim Crow South included lynchings, segregation, and deprivation of formal education. Faced with these developments, Washington responded by founding the Negro Business League in 1900 to enhance economic opportunities for African American businesses and work toward social equality. Small business owners, farmers, doctors, lawyers, craftspeople, and other professionals made up the league's membership. The business league maintained directories of African American businesspeople in major U.S. cities.

Because Jim Crow segregation was entrenched in the culture of the South, building an economic program based on self-help became vital for Blacks to survive. Not only did Washington achieve this with the curriculum at Tuskegee and the agenda set forth by the National Negro Business league, but he also endorsed entrepreneurs outside of his NNBL network. For example, after a few rebuffs, he allowed Sarah Breedlove, a.k.a. Madam C. J. Walker, to speak at an NNBL convention in 1913 at the Tuskegee Institute. The Netflix TV Series *Self Made* (2020) depicted Booker T. Washington's original hesitation to invite Madam Walker to speak at the National Negro Business League as misogynistic. To this point, there are no official records to support the notion that Washington was misogynistic. Nevertheless, Washington introduced Walker at the NNBL conference, calling her "a striking example of the possibilities of Negro womanhood in the business world." What this shows is that, although it took a bit of time, Washington was committed to ensuring that Black people, regardless of gender, understood the importance of using economics to be self-sufficient.

Washington was more amenable to the idea of civil rights by the turn of the century. For example, starting in 1900, Washington secretly funded court cases in which African Americans filed lawsuits for their civil rights. In the first of these suits, in New Orleans, Washington challenged racist grandfather voting clauses in Louisiana via the Afro-American Council. He helped raise and contribute much of his own funding for the case to move forward. Listed as "X. Y. Z." in the council records, he also raised money from white liberals to fund the case. Disagreements among the attorneys, Afro-American Council leaders, and local contributors led to the case's failure. The subsequent court cases involving civil rights of African Americans that Washington helped fund were *Giles v. Harris* in 1903 and *Giles v. Teasley* in 1904. Both involved an African American plaintiff named Jackson Giles from Montgomery, Alabama, filing suit against the State of Alabama for violation of civil rights. Giles contended in *Giles v. Harris* that the Alabama constitution breached the U.S. Constitution by refusing Blacks the right to vote and equal protection under the laws.

In *Giles v. Teasley*, Giles again filed suit against the State of Alabama, charging that he was "refused the right to vote for, as he alleged, no reason other than his race and color, the members of the board having been appointed and having acted under the provisions of the state constitution of 1901."

As in Louisiana, Washington concealed his contributions to the trial, although there were major differences in how he did it. Instead of contributing through an organization as he did in Louisiana, Washington funded the Giles trials directly by corresponding with his personal lawyer Wilford H. Smith through his secretary Emmett J. Scott. They invented code words to use in their letters and continued to exchange "money, news, and advice." In the end, both court cases involving Giles were thrown out in the Supreme Court on technicalities. This role was at odds with the accommodationist policies he espoused publicly.

This illustrates how Washington exemplified Du Bois's concept of "double consciousness." Publicly, he supported accommodationist ideology and policies that aligned with racial segregation. In a sense, Washington addressed civil rights from an external view, separate from African Americans. This allowed him to be comfortable in public supporting policies that structurally preserved the institutions that oppressed African Americans.

However, Washington's covert support of lawsuits and work with his rivals, first through the Afro-American council and then directly with W. E. B. Du Bois, affirmed his ability to contextualize the problems of African Americans from a Black nationalist perspective. If Washington had not funded these cases covertly or if he had not publicly espoused accommodationists rhetoric, he might not have been able to secure funding for Tuskegee from wealthy whites such as Andrew Carnegie and John D. Rockefeller or, worse, there could have been threats on his life. For this reason, Washington governed himself accordingly by conforming to social norms of Blacks set forth by whites publicly but privately engaged in activity to "uplift the race." Whether it was the curriculum at the Tuskegee Institute, the founding of the National

Negro Business League, or funding of civil rights cases, Washington did pursue a Black nationalist agenda rooted in self-sufficiency.

By the time of Washington's death in 1915, Black nationalism had begun to develop a cultural perspective. Cultural nationalism was developed during the Jim Crow era by advocates such as Du Bois, Arthur Schomburg, and Carter G. Woodson. This form of nationalism encouraged African Americans to study the contributions of Black people to society in order for them to maintain a positive image of themselves as well as prove to whites that Black people were not savages and should be accepted. Under no circumstances did Du Bois think that Blacks should remain inferior to whites.

CARTER G. WOODSON IN THE LIBRARY OF HIS WASHINGTON, D.C., HOME, C. 1948. (SCURLOCK STUDIO RECORDS, ARCHIVES CENTER, NATIONAL MUSEUM OF AMERICAN HISTORY, SMITHSONIAN INSTITUTION.)

He believed culture was key in emphasizing the humanity of African Americans and advocated for their equal rights with whites. He believed Blacks should be free to vote, attain higher education, and have their individual freedom just like any other citizens. His philosophy of cultural nationalism stressed the importance of cultural as well as economic and political contributions of African Americans.

Woodson was a contemporary of Du Bois's: he was the second Black person to graduate with a Ph.D. from Harvard, Du Bois having been the first. He corresponded frequently with Du Bois and even asked him to collaborate on projects for Negro History Week in the mid-1920s. However, Woodson disagreed with Du Bois later and thus went on to create his own brand of cultural nationalism as an academic scholar, activist, and practitioner. Woodson first began his pursuits of cultural nationalism academically at Harvard, where he earned a Ph.D. in history. His dissertation, according to the historian Charles Harris Wesley, "had few references to Negroes, while slavery was treated as a political and economic issue." However, after 1912, Woodson immersed himself in the cultural history of African Americans. He began in 1915 by establishing the Association for the Study of Negro Life and History (ASNLH) in 1915 at the Wabash Avenue YMCA in Chicago. Now called the Association for the Study of African American Life and History (ASALH), the ASNLH was crucial in advancing the study and promotion of African American culture. Through the organization, Woodson in 1916 established the *Journal of Negro History* to publish studies on Black culture and history and various interdisciplinary topics, both in the U.S. and globally.

The first studies published in the *Journal* include "The Negroes of Cincinnati Prior to the Civil War" by Woodson, "The Story of Maria Louise Moore and Fannie M. Richards" by W. B. Hartgrove, "The Passing Tradition and the African Civilization" by Monroe N. Work, and "The Mind of the African Negro as Reflected in His Proverbs" by A. O. Stafford. These studies focused on either African American or Black diaspora culture. After establishing the *Journal of Negro History*, Woodson went on to join the history department at Howard University, where, as dean and head of graduate faculty, he created a liberal arts and sciences curriculum centered on the history of Europe, Africa, Asia, and Latin America. After leaving Howard and committing fully to the ASNLH, Woodson created Negro History Week in 1926. This idea stemmed from combining the birthdays of Abraham Lincoln and Frederick Douglass in February. The African American studies scholar Jarvis R. Givens states that the week was sponsored by the ASNLH and was designed to diffuse "counterhegemonic ideas about Black life and culture into school communities."[18]

Negro History Week became popular as a grassroots movement, thanks to Black primary and secondary educators. According to Givens, over 80% of Black high schools participated by the early 1930s. It became a vehicle for aligning curricular content with African Americans' political desires and their critiques of American education. Furthermore, it cultivated a learning aesthetic centered on Black humanities, carving out formalized space in schools for Black cultural expression and intellectual ideas about the world. Woodson's brand of oppositional culture influenced future Black leaders and inspired Black cultural movements in the 1960s and '70s that centered on the reawakening of Black history. Woodson's 1933 book *The Mis-Education of the Negro* argues that African Americans can use knowledge of their history and culture to build and maintain their own institutions in opposition to the larger dominant hegemonic society. He writes that "It is very clear that if African-Americans got their conception of religion from slaveholders, libertines, and murderers, there may be something wrong about it." African American culture at that time was rooted in religion, specifically Judeo-Christian culture, and Woodson argues that the problem with this for African Americans is that this conception of religion came directly from white men of European descent, meaning that African Americans were destined for servitude. Whether that servitude was via slavery or second-class citizenship at the time Woodson wrote *Mis-Education*, religion played a huge role in how African Americans conceptualized themselves and their culture. This conceptualization put white people, and especially white-owned institutions, squarely above African Americans economically, politically, and socially.

Woodson challenged African Americans to recognize that the brand of Christianity they practiced derives from the psychology of the oppressor. The negative stereotypes of African Americans as lazy, shiftless, violent, docile, or sexually promiscuous were born of white people's interpretations of the Bible using preconceived notions. Woodson observed that Blacks re-enact these stereotypes that whites had created, and thus Black culture goes from opposing the white power structure to willingly participating in its own destruction. The re-enactment of these stereotypes is so ingrained, Woodson argues, that African Americans have come to behave as expected by white society without being compelled to do so. Within the framework Woodson lays out in *Mis-Education,* the docility came directly from Judeo-Christian values. The New Testament passage urging slaves to submit to their masters (Ephesians 6:1) had detrimental consequences for African American social and cultural progress, including African Americans placing the interests of whites over their own; relying upon white-owned institutions and businesses for basic needs instead of developing Black-owned institutions and businesses that put the economic interests of African Americans first; and African Americans being docile in the presence of whites but not showing respect for themselves. Elsewhere in *Mis-Education,* Woodson writes:

> *If you can control a man's thinking you do not have to worry about his action. When you determine what a man shall think you do not have to concern yourself about what he will do. If you make a man feel that he is inferior, you do not have to compel him to accept an inferior status, for he will seek it himself. If you make a man think that he is justly an outcast, you do not have to order him to the back door. He will go without being told; and if there is no back door, his very nature will demand one.*[19]

This is why nationalism from a cultural perspective should be the basis of any Black nationalist platform. Unless economic, political, and educational equity is tackled with a nationalist approach, the subordinate group will remain inferior to their oppressors. Whites have determined since the days of slavery how exactly African Americans should think and behave. Whites have used a range of tools, including religion, popular culture, education, and policies, to create and maintain systems of control, creating a system in which whites don't need to actively impose their will. Because of this, Woodson argued, African Americans will behave in ways that serve whites' interests due to the established power dynamic.

The sociological and economic practices of African Americans that are not conducive to their uplift are enacted without the permission of whites. What ultimately happens is that African Americans put whites at more of an advantage than they were previously. Woodson succinctly summed up his point regarding Black culture in *Mis-Education* by stating, "History shows that it does not matter who is in power . . . those who have not learned to do for themselves and have to depend solely on others never obtain any more rights or privileges in the end than they did in the beginning." With that said, if African Americans do not put the interest of their culture at the forefront, as history shows, the result is a never-ending cycle of not being able to elevate beyond the status of subservience to their oppressors. Woodson's call to critically examine culture from a nationalist perspective so that African Americans can rise above their subservient status aligns with Marcus Garvey's agenda of making Blackness an integral part of society at large.

How much does Marcus Garvey figure into Black nationalism in early-twentieth-century America? Research shows intersection between New York–based Black nationalists and the spiritual and religious practices of people of African descent in Jamaica, which was then a colony of the British empire. Does the same hold true for political ideas? J. Herman Blake calls Garvey's form of nationalism "integral nationalism" and differentiates it from other forms, emphasizing its deviation from the dualistic nature of previous nationalist thought. Blackness was fully embraced by this philosophy, which simultaneously and forcefully rejected white America. Not only was the notion of "Black-centered" essential to Garvey's lectures and publications, but it also guided his business and political operation. Garvey translated his integral nationalist vision into action by establishing the Universal Negro Improvement Association (UNIA) and the African Communities League. This agenda resulted in annual publication of *The Negro World*; the creation of Booker T. Washington University located in the Phyllis Wheatley Hotel in New York; a UNIA delegation presenting at the third assembly of the League of Nations in Geneva; and the enrollment of over one million members in the UNIA and the African Communities league combined in 1920 with various chapters across the nation.

Throughout Garvey's time in the United States, he articulated his desire for African Americans to emigrate to Africa. In January 1922, on the eve of his arrest for mail fraud on J. Edgar Hoover's orders, Garvey stated,

> *I come to the people in the role of the reformer and say to them, "Awake! the day is upon you, go forth in the name of the race and build yourselves a nation, redeem your country Africa, the land from whence you came and prove yourselves men worthy of the recognition of others." This is the offence I have committed against the selfish Negro preachers and politicians who have for more than half a century waxed fat at the expense of the people.*

Here Garvey echoes the call Martin Delany had made a generation earlier for African American emigration to Africa.

In the late nineteenth century Africa was partitioned among major European powers without any input from either native Africans or those in the diaspora. By 1914, 90% of the continent had been divided among seven European countries.

Ethiopia and Liberia were the only remaining countries that were independent from European dominance.

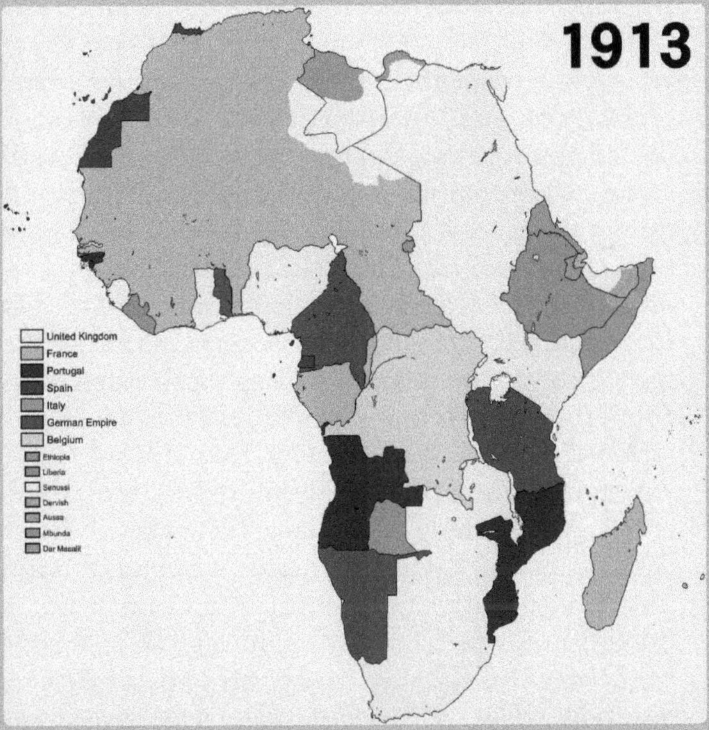

THE CONTRASTING MAPS OF AFRICA FROM 1880 AND 1913 VISUALLY DEMONSTRATE THE DRAMATIC TERRITORIAL CHANCES AND COLONIAL EXPANSIONS THAT RESULTED FROM THE BERLIN CONFERENCE AND THE SUBSEQUENT SCRAMBLE FOR AFRICA BY EUROPEAN POWERS.

Faced with the realities of the colonization of Africa, the UNIA put Garvey's rhetoric into practice by deploying a delegation of executive members to the third Assembly of the League of Nations in Geneva in 1922 and requesting that the League give the former German colonies in East Africa and Southwest Africa to the Black race.

It was the first time a primarily Black nongovernmental organization had participated in a globally recognized summit. What was powerful about it was the UNIA's boldness in facing the conglomerate of colonizers on their own turf and attempting to exert their own power. Germany had lost World War I, leaving the League of Nations with the job of transferring their overseas territories to new authorities. German East Africa and Southwest Africa thus became League of Nations "Mandates' divided among some of the war's victors, namely Britain, France, Belgium, and South Africa. Though this situation was intended to be temporary, most of the territories did not achieve independence until the pan-Africanist movements of the 1960s (and Namibia not until 1990). This was by design, so the colonizing powers could continue to exercise their dominance over the native Africans and extract resources without any regulation. Pan-Africanists such as Kwame Nkrumah, who became Ghana's first prime minister after British colonialism ended in 1957, spearheaded the movement for African independence through organized protests, writing, and lectures. German Southwest Africa is now Namibia, and German East Africa included what are today Burundi, Rwanda, and parts of Tanzania and Mozambique. While seeking to establish a temporary governing body controlled by the UNIA, they faced opposition from a contingent of League of Nation members advocating for their rule over Germany's former colonies in Africa. The most prominent UNIA member was Eliezer Cadet, a Haitian national who had garnered the attention of Garvey's associates after writing them to condemn America's meddling in Haiti. Cadet had represented the UNIA at the Paris Peace Conference of 1919, where he presented a UNIA document that included nine points in a proposal for Black people educated in western society to manage not only the former German colonies but also all of Africa. These points were:

> 1 *The right of self-determination will be applied to Africans and to every European colony where the African race predominates;*
>
> 2 *The abolition of every economic obstacle injurious to the industrial development of Africa;*
>
> 3 *The enjoyment by Negroes of the right to travel and to reside in any part of the world, all the while possessing the same prerogatives as the Europeans in the enjoyment of these rights;*
>
> 4 *The right for Negroes to receive the same standard of education accorded to Europeans;*
>
> 5 *The expulsion of all Europeans who oppose or violate African customs;*
>
> 6 *The repeal in all countries of all proscriptive ordinances leveled against Negroes. Furthermore, complete political, industrial, and social equality ought to be granted to them (Negroes) in all countries where they live side by side with members of other races;*
>
> 7 *The repeal of the laws restricting land-ownership leveled against the natives of South Africa, and the restitution of the land to the original owners;*
>
> 8 *The enjoyment by negroes of the right of proportional representation in every system of government in the world;*
>
> 9 *The return to the natives of Germany's African colonies, which will be governed by Negroes educated in Eastern and Western Countries.*[20]

The ninth point highlights the difference between Garvey's Black nationalism and Du Bois's brand of Pan-Africanism. In the Du Boisian model, native Africans in the German colonies would be gradually granted incremental power in shared governance with African Americans. In the UNIA Black nationalist model, the former colonies would be governed by Blacks educated outside Africa without any plan of natives participating in governance.

A downside to both proposals is that they wrongly assume that Black people, whether African American, African, or from some other foreign land who received a higher education in countries other than the continent of Africa, are inherently more intellectually fit to govern that country than the native Blacks of that land or of Blacks, whether native or foreign, who were educated on the continent. Also, the second point assumes that colonist-owned corporations based in Africa will just pick up and leave without conflict. Marcus Garvey himself affirmed these ideals of native Africans in an exposé published in 1924 titled *Aim and Objects of Movement for Solution of Negro Problem Outlined*, in which he states,

> *To establish a Universal Confraternity among the race; to promote the spirit of pride and love; to reclaim the fallen; to administer to and assist the needy; to assist in civilizing the backward tribes of Africa; to assist in the development of Independent Negro Nations and Communities; to establish a central nation for the race; to establish Commissaries or Agencies in the principal countries and cities of the world for the representation of all Negroes; to promote a conscientious Spiritual worship among the native tribes of Africa; to establish Universities, Colleges, Academies and Schools for the racial education and culture of the people; to work for better conditions among Negroes everywhere.*[21]

Marcus Garvey, the UNIA, and pan-Africanists in general were fighting hegemonic powers at that time but at the same time reinforcing the hegemonic and colonizer assumption that native African peoples were "backwards" and needed education reform according to western standards. Despite these shortcomings, the demands made by the UNIA at the Paris Peace Conference and League of Nations Assembly laid the groundwork for a nationalist agenda rooted in Blackness. History, culture, and economics encompassed every facet of Garvey's program. As he wrote in the *Negro World* in 1918,

> *Nationhood is the only means by which modern civilization can completely protect itself. Independence of nationality, independence of government, is the means of protecting not only the individual but the group. Nationhood is the highest ideal of all peoples. The evolutionary scale that weighs nations and races, balances alike for peoples; hence we feel sure that someday the balance will register a change for the Negro.*[22]

Garvey's vision recognizes that Black Americans have their own unique history, culture, and economic circumstances and should not think of themselves as an isolated and fragmented group but instead create co-dependent economic, political, and educational institutions solely owned and operated by people of African descent. Only when this is accomplished will the community be able to lift itself socially, compete with other groups for equitable resources, and begin the process of killing the psychodynamics of white supremacy.

After Garvey's prison sentence was commuted by President Calvin Coolidge in 1928, several Black nationalist groups began to gain traction. The Movement to Establish a 49th State was established by Oscar Brown, Sr., in 1936, during Franklin Delano Roosevelt's New Deal era, when there were only forty-eight states in the union. The group sought to establish a forty-ninth state within the contiguous United States occupied and governed strictly by African Americans. The movement's ambition was thwarted by insufficient funding, leading to its demise within three years and limiting its impact beyond Chicago. Brown pointed out that, "Like a lot of good ideas, it failed because of a lack of funds. We just couldn't communicate the idea well enough."

A similar proposal was made by the Nation of Islam, which was founded in 1930, using faith as a foundation for political and economic principles of Black nationalism. Its political and economic strategies were directly influenced by Garvey's brand of Black nationalism. For example, the Nation bought property, owned and operated businesses, and started educational centers around the country. It also openly called for the founding of a Black-only state. Elijah Muhammed, the "Messenger" and spiritual leader of the Nation, in *Message to the Black Man*, established the separate-state philosophy:

ELIJAH MUHAMMAD AT CHICAGO COLISEUM, ILL., ON FEB. 26, 1966. (ASSOCIATED PRESS.)

> *We want our people in America whose parents or grandparents were descendants from slaves, to be allowed to establish a separate state or territory of their own—either on this continent or elsewhere. We believe that our former slave masters are obligated to provide such land and that the area must be fertile and minerally rich. We believe that our former slave masters are obligated to maintain and supply our needs in this separate territory for the next 20 to 25 years—until we are able to produce and supply our own needs.*

Garvey's influence on Malcolm X, a leading figure in the Nation during the 1950s and '60s, stemmed from Malcolm X's father's affiliation with the Garvey movement. He routinely echoed Elijah Muhammad's doctrine before his Hajj in 1964 for African Americans to receive plots land in the United States to establish a separate state. In a speech given in 1963 at the University of California, Malcolm X specifically stated,

> *We must have a permanent solution. A temporary solution won't do. Tokenism will no longer suffice. The Honorable Elijah Muhammad has the only permanent solution. Twenty million ex-slaves must be permanently separated from our former slave master and placed on some land that we can call our own. Then we can create our own jobs. Control our own economy. Solve our own problems instead of waiting on the American white man to solve our problems for us.... He says that we can dig the natural resources from the earth once we are in our own land. Land is the basis of all economic security. Land is essential to freedom, justice, and equality. Land is essential to true independence.*

With the Nation of Islam gaining headway in the 1960s with its Black nationalist message and programs, other groups with similar ideologies also had begun to take shape. The Black Panther Party was formed in 1966 by Huey P. Newton and

Bobby Seale as a self-defense organization. The geographer James Tyner argues that "the Black Panther Party, therefore, did not emerge as a cultural nationalist group, nor a variant of Pan-Africanism; rather, the Party was a founded initially as a grassroots organization formed to address local concern." Although this was the case, the Panthers left a little room for a Black nationalist approach in their ten-point program that was revised in 1972. The specific points that aligned with political nationalist principles include:

> POINT 1. WE WANT FREEDOM. WE WANT POWER TO DETERMINE THE DESTINY OF OUR BLACK AND OPPRESSED COMMUNITIES. *We believe that Black and oppressed people will not be free until we are able to determine our destinies in our own communities ourselves, by fully controlling all the institutions which exist in our communities.*

> POINT 3. WE WANT AN END TO THE ROBBERY BY THE CAPITALISTS OF OUR BLACK AND OPPRESSED COMMUNITIES. *We believe that this racist government has robbed us, and now we are demanding the overdue debt of forty acres and two mules. Forty acres and two mules were promised 100 years ago as restitution for slave labor and mass murder of Black people. We will accept the payment in currency which will be distributed to our many communities. The Germans are now aiding the Jews in Israel for the genocide of the Jewish people. The Germans murdered six million Jews. The American racist has taken part in the slaughter of over fifty million Black people; therefore, we feel that this is a modest demand that we make.*;

> POINT 10. WE WANT LAND, BREAD, HOUSING, EDUCATION, CLOTHING, JUSTICE, PEACE AND PEOPLE'S COMMUNITY CONTROL OF MODERN TECHNOLOGY. *When, in the course of human events, it becomes necessary for one people to dissolve*

> *the political bands which have connected them with another, and to assume, among the powers of the earth, the separate and equal station to which the laws of nature and nature's God entitle them, a decent respect of the opinions of mankind requires that they should declare the causes which impel them to the separation.*[23]

From the Black Panther Party's origins in focusing on local issues through chapters across the country, it took on nationalist and eventually internationalist rhetoric and agendas. These transformations ranged from local grass-roots and cultural nationalism to revolutionary nationalism to internationalism to intercommunalism. Tyner notes "that many Panthers in New York disagreed with Newton's ideological shift away from black nationalism; very few understood his abstract theory of imperialism." Charles E. Jones, author of *The Black Panther Party Reconsidered*, argues that the rapidly advancing character of Newton's and the Panthers' thinking proved problematic. He states, "Often ideological shifts were not accompanied by sufficient political education so that rank-and-file Panthers could understand fully the new set of ideas." Newton defended the ideological shift from Black nationalism to intercommunalism, which he contextualized as local communities connected via economic and political systems across the globe to challenge capitalism and imperialism, by arguing, in an unpublished manuscript in 1970 titled "Intercommunalism: A Higher Level of Consciousness," that Black nationalism "fails to encompass the unique situation of Black Americans since Black Americans have only the cultural and social customs that have evolved from centuries of oppression."[24]

Despite Newton's arguments against a nationalist approach, Black nationalist groups continued to form. In the ethnic-studies scholar Dan Berger's view, New Afrikan political thought integrated long-existing strands of Black nationalism, including cultural pride, anti-imperialism, spirituality, self-defense, self-governance, land ownership,

T-SHIRT WITH IMAGE AND TEXT "IN PURSUIT OF HUMAN RIGHTS, FREE THE REPUBLIC OF NEW AFRIKA 11," 1971 (KEN LAWRENCE COLLECTION, SPECIAL COLLECTIONS LIBRARY, PENNSYLVANIA STATE UNIVERSITY.)

IN PURSUIT OF
HUMAN RIGHTS
FREE THE RNA 11 NOW!
POLITICAL PRISONERS OF WAR IN AMERIKA
FREE THE
REPUBLIC of NEW AFRIKA 11
NATIONAL RNA-11 DEFENSE COMMITTEE
NATIONAL HEAQUARTERS
P.O. Box1184New York, New York 10027

and economic betterment. Self-determination, as an individual and collective right, guided the formation of the Republic of New Afrika. The RNA was originally formed in 1968 in Detroit at a national conference attended by upwards of 500 Black nationalists. The attendees chose Robert Williams, a noted Black nationalist at the time, as its national president. However, he was living in China, and the brothers Richard Henry, who changed his name to Imari Abubakari Obadele, and Milton Henry, who changed his name to Gaidi Obadele, along with Betty Shabazz, widow of Malcolm X, led the organization. Functionally, the RNA's contribution to the Black arts cultural renaissance mirrored the Black Panther Party's revolutionary approach and the Nation of Islam's spiritual worldview. The RNA's "New Afrikan creed," like the Nation of Islam, lauded Black excellence, mandated personal standards of dress and hygiene, and centered the traditional nuclear family as the core of their political organization.[25]

In 1970, the brothers disagreed about the direction of the Republic. Gaidai favored a more political strategy while Imari favored a more military approach. Imari won and guided the Republic to a more militaristic ideology. Following a partial payment to Lofton Mason, a Black farmer, Imari founded the Republic of New Afrika's capital in Hinds County, Mississippi, on twenty acres of his land.

The legal scholar Robert Tsai notes,

> *"The New Afrikans' plan to control territory and subvert the constitutional order from within provoked efforts by agents of conventional sovereignty to reverse that triumphant image of black nationalism. Apparently, members had gone ahead with the consecration ceremony even before the land deal had been finalized. Mason announced on May 3 the cancellation of the land sale agreement. Though the owner had accepted a partial down payment in good faith and allowed RNA members to begin making improvements on the land, he now had second thoughts."*[26]

Alleged pressure from the FBI ultimately led Mason to reverse the sale. Because the land sale was stalled, the group moved to a house near Jackson State University. Meanwhile, several RNA members, including Imari, were charged in the murder of a police officer who died in a shootout in Detroit in 1971 during an attempt to apprehend a murder suspect. Imari was convicted and sentenced to three years in prison. During his imprisonment, the Republic was once more split, and this division led to the rise of Chokwe Lumumba, who became minister of justice, vice president, and ultimately president of the Republic.

Lack of unity in the 1970s led to a decline in the group's influence. However, individual members continued to make an impact in the larger dominant hegemonic society with their advocacy for reparations. Imari joined the National Conference of Black Lawyers in forming N'COBRA (National Coalition of Blacks for Reparations in America). It was a proposal from N'COBRA that prompted Representative John Conyers of Michigan to propose a bill in 1989 to study the idea of reparation programs and policies for African Americans, and Imari's influence in N'COBRA was instrumental in achieving this. It also marked the first time since the 1860s that a major proposal involving reparations for African Americans made its way to the House floor for introduction.

Imari Obadele went on to earn a doctorate in political science and develop a Black history curriculum at Temple University. Following his departure from the Republic of New Afrika, Gaidi Obadele, who changed his name back to Milton Henry, established the Christ Presbyterian Church, where he championed Black nationalism informed by his personal experiences. Lumumba, who had sworn allegiance to the Republic of New Afrika as a law student and was a part of their early history, became known as the "people's lawyer" for his work in civil rights and criminal law. In June 2013, he was elected mayor of Jackson, Mississippi, winning 85 percent of the electorate. After his death in 2014, his son Chokwe Antar Lumumba was elected mayor of Jackson in 2017.

As the saga of New Afrika echoes the rhetoric of foundational Black nationalists such as Delany, Garvey, and Malcolm X regarding land and space as fundamental components of Black nationalism, Black Americans cannot build a nation, much less bring Black nationalism back to the forefront or bring an end to white supremacist thinking, without building toward the ownership and control of their own land. The next chapter will examine the history of African Americans not only owning land but establishing thriving self-governing enclaves in the United States.

CHAPTER TWO

BLACK ENCLAVES

During the period of Reconstruction, African Americans developed a communal-based lifestyle to survive the bleak prospects of second-class citizenship. Using the skills that they acquired during the period of slavery as slave intrapreneurs by innovating more effective techniques to manage the plantation and as entrepreneurs by hiring themselves out to other plantation owners, African Americans after emancipation utilized the natural resources around them and relied on social capital to enforce policies in their communities. This was done in African American communities from sections of towns to official townships that were majority African American and used formal and informal processes and relationships to maintain the social order in their society. This led to majority-Black communal districts and townships including Greenwood in Tulsa, Oklahoma; Rosewood and Ocoee in Florida; Seneca Village, New York; Africatown, Alabama; and Mound Bayou, Mississippi.

These Black enclaves contained political, business, and educational institutions that were owned and operated solely by African Americans. As these collectives were developing, laws passed at all governmental levels worked to exclude newly freed African Americans from mainstream society. "Black Codes," for instance, enacted by state governments in the aftermath of the Civil War, disenfranchised Black citizens, prohibited firearm ownership, and mandated apprenticeships for Black orphans, frequently under the control of their former owners. A few states required Blacks to register annually for labor contracts; if they refused, they could be forced into labor without wages.

However, before the rise of Black enclaves after Reconstruction, most Black-run communities were forts and freedmen's towns. The first Black-majority community in North America, Gracia Real de Santa Teresa de Mosé, or Fort Mosé, was founded in 1738 two miles north of St. Augustine, the capital of Spanish Florida, which at the time stretched from what is now eastern Alabama to all of today's Florida. Fort Mosé was the only free Black town in what is now the southern United States to be founded and financially supported by a European colonial power. The settlement was pivotal to the Spanish Empire in North America for two reasons: 1) it enticed enslaved Africans in the British colonies of Georgia and South Carolina, who were critical to amassing wealth for their owners and the British Empire, to run away and provide labor to a rival empire; and 2) the town served as a buffer between the British whenever they attempted invade St. Augustine. What also made Fort Mosé attractive to enslaved Africans looking to run away from the British Empire is that the Spanish government made them citizens. As early as October 1687, St. Augustine was welcoming fugitives from the English colonies.

Diego de Quiroga y Losada, who was the governor of Florida at that time, reported that a group of Black people from St. George, Carolina (in what is today South Carolina), including two females and a nursing child, arrived in his territory. The English records documented their names as Robi, Jesse, Conano, Gran Domingo, Cambo, and Jacque, along with a three-year-old child. Quiroga tasked the two men with working on building a fort to protect St. Augustine. He employed the two women as domestic servants. The historian Jane Landers noted that former Carolina slaves working for Quiroga received wages, highlighting the uncertainty of their legal status. The Florida governor refused to return the formerly enslaved fugitives from Carolina to an English sergeant-major who arrived the next fall, arguing they had become Catholic, married, and found jobs. Quiroga offered to buy the formerly enslaved people, who claimed to fear for their lives. Consequently, a policy regarding fugitive slaves developed, creating serious diplomatic and military problems for Spain. The governor and royal treasury officials repeatedly petitioned King Charles II of Spain for assistance with the matter. Eventually, Charles issued a royal cedula (decree) on November 7, 1693, regarding the former slaves, "Giving liberty to all the men as well as the women so that by their example and by my liberality others will do the same." This decree laid the legal basis of Fort Mosé as occupied exclusively by refugee Africans.

FLORIDA A&M COLLEGE.
(2C2K PHOTOGRAPHY, CREATIVE COMMONS LICENSE.)

In 1738, approximately forty free Black people established and settled in Fort Mosé, which was led by a seasoned African-descended war veteran named Francisco Menéndez. Menéndez had fought in the Yamasee war in 1715 while enslaved in South Carolina and was released from Spanish imprisonment in 1737. In the spring of 1740, British troops led by James Oglethorpe invaded Florida and captured Fort Diego, which was a little north of Fort Mosé. When residents of Fort Mosé heard the news of the capture of Fort Diego, they fled south to St. Augustine thereby leaving Fort Mosé unprotected and vulnerable to the British. However, on June 14th, Menéndez and his men recaptured Fort Mosé on what became known as "Bloody Mose" but returned to St. Augustine, which was majority Spanish descent at that time, to live in that city. The Governor of Florida ordered the Black occupants, again led by Menéndez, to rebuild and resettle in Fort Mosé. Negotiations following the French and Indian War resulted in Spain ceding Florida to Britain in 1763, culminating in the abandonment of the second Fort Mosé. After this, a significant portion of its population fled to Cuba and thus remained Spanish subjects.

Although Fort Mosé was short-lived, it is a powerful example of how Black bodies were used as chess pieces between empires and why the ownership of land is an integral part of Black nationalism. For example, Menéndez's honorable service to the Spanish Empire as head of the Black militia, culminating in his manumission, did not shield him from racism; he had to repeatedly petition for his liberty. Landers reports that Menéndez, along with ten other enslaved Africans, fled to Florida from South Carolina in 1724, hoping to gain freedom as promised in Charles II's 1693 edict. He was sold back into slavery and his petition was rebuffed not only when he first arrived in 1724 but also again in 1735. Spain's official regulations for enslaved Africans who escaped from colonies established by Britain, France, and the Netherlands in the late 1730s caused diplomatic tensions among these empires, especially concerning the escapees and their leader. However, what if they had escaped to a different territory, such as French Louisiana. Would they have been sold back into slavery? Would they have received freedom? We will never know. However, the point here is that, without their own territory, enslaved Africans from any territory were subject to bondage to European empires. Responding to this reality, several groups of escaped enslaved Africans formed maroon communities in the late eighteenth and early nineteenth centuries. From small, short-lived groups of a few members to large, powerful states lasting centuries, maroon communities—called *palenques* in the Spanish colonies and *mocambos* or *quilombos* in Brazil—varied greatly in size and longevity. The initial application was to livestock that had escaped to the woods and were living freely. The term *cimmaron* was also applied to Native Americans and subsequently imported African slaves who, as personal property, escaped Spanish plantations for remote mountain areas.[27]

Maroons in general were not a new concept in the western hemisphere before 1700; they came into existence a few decades after Christopher Columbus made landfall in the western hemisphere in 1492. On July 13, 1571, King Philip II of Spain authorized the Audiencia of Santo Domingo (which encompassed modern-day Venezuela, the Guyanas, the Greater Antilles, and Florida) to conquer a maroon settlement about thirty-six miles outside Santo Domingo, in what is today the Dominican Republic. As compensation for their participation in the raid, the king gave the participants the captured *cimarrones* as slaves.[28]

This was only one of many such examples. Beginning in the 1520s, runaway African slaves established maroon communities in remote areas bordering Spanish territories, including present-day Jamaica, Haiti, Dominican Republic, Panama, and Mexico. Just as Florida became the first North American colony to grant enslaved Africans who escaped bondage their own sanctioned municipality, it also was the site of major maroon activity in the eighteenth century. Spain's refugee policy for escaped Africans contributed to this. Records show that numerous early escapees integrated into Spanish society in colonial cities such as St. Augustine, but others founded their own settlements within established Native American groups following Britain's transfer of

Florida to Spain in 1783. A sizeable number of enslaved Gullahs (an African American population of the Georgia and Carolina Sea Islands and nearby mainland, with a large amount of preserved African language and tradition) managed to escape from coastal South Carolina and Georgia into the Florida peninsula. According to the historian Joseph Opala, Gullah communities were creating independent settlements in the Florida wilderness by the late eighteenth century. They built separate villages of thatched-roof houses, encircled by corn and swamp rice fields, and also kept cordial relations with the diverse Native American population.

With the passage of time, a single, loosely organized tribe emerged, uniting the two groups, with Black people in significant leadership positions. It is this conglomerate of Native American nations that adopted the name "Seminole" by 1822. In proximity to Native American settlements, independent Black and maroon villages, towns, and settlements arose. Angola was the first town to be documented. Near modern-day Tampa Bay, it was situated by the Manatee River, adjacent to a substantial Seminole settlement.[29] By the beginning of the Second Seminole War in 1835, the Black Seminole population was largely concentrated across five separate settlements: Pilaklikaha, King Hadjo's Town, Bucker Woman's Town, Mulatto Girls' Town, and Minatti.

The Black Seminoles became a point of contention when the United States government decided to remove the Seminole Nation from Florida to Oklahoma. Removing Native Americans from their lands became a priority for the administration of President Andrew Jackson. The removal of Seminoles resulted in land acquisition in large parts of north and central Florida as well as the recapture of enslaved Africans for sale or forced labor under government orders.[30] The war highlighted not only the symbiotic relationship between Black Seminoles and Native Americans but also the relationship between Black Seminoles and enslaved Africans on nearby plantations. Black Seminoles offered both friendship and acceptance to other Black people in the territory. The historian Anthony Dixon states that Black Seminoles often crossed the boundaries and establish relationships with those who were enslaved on nearby plantations.

General Thomas Jesup of the U.S. Army attempted to negotiate an end to the second Seminole war, but because of the Black Seminoles' influence, he changed his mind about the terms: "Major General Jesup, on behalf of the United States, agrees that the Seminoles and their allies who come in, and emigrate to the West, shall be secure in their lives and property; that their negroes, their bona fide property, shall accompany them to the West by 'their allies.' The Seminoles understood the Negroes living among them, and since before the war an estimated four-fifths of the Seminole Negroes . . . were runaway slaves—and during the war the Seminole had been joined by several hundred more runaways—the Seminole 'allies' numbered far more Negroes than the Seminole 'slaves.'"[31]

ATTACK BY THE SEMINOLE INDIANS ON A FORT ON THE WITHLACOOCHEE RIVER IN DECEMBER 1835. (GREY & JAMES, 1837, LIBRARY OF CONGRESS.)

Jesup made a secret deal with Coi Hajo and other chiefs on April 8, 1837, to give up the captured slaves from the war. Jesup wrote to General R. Jones,

> *It was easier, however, to make such an agreement than carry it out. Some of the "captured Negroes," to be sure, had been taken against their will and were glad to be returned to their masters, but others, when they heard of the new arrangement, banded together for defense whether against white men or Indians. They were supported by more militant Indians like Osceola, who, when Coi Hajo announced in council that the runaways were to be returned, rose in a rage, declaring that so long as he was in the Nation it should never be done. When several Floridians arrived in the emigration camp to search for slaves the Negroes and many Indians fled. On June 2 the young militants, Osceola, Philip's son Wild Cat, and John Cavallo* [John Horse], *seized and carried away the Seminole hostages given under the terms of the truce. All is lost, and principally by the influence of the Negroes.*

The Seminole force remained largely intact. Lieutenant-Colonel W. S. Harney numbered the Seminole forces at 2,500, "not including as well as the best of them." The fierce resistance of the Black Seminoles and escaped slaves in the Second Seminole War deeply disturbed Jesup, prompting him to plan for a retreat. He wrote,

> *The two Indian are rapidly approximating; they are identified in interests and feelings. Plantation slaves had been prominent in depredations, and one had occupied a ship. Should the Indians remain in this territory, the negroes among them will form a rallying point for runaway negroes from the adjacent states; and if they remove, the fastnesses of the country will be immediately occupied by negroes.*

Nevertheless, Jesup erroneously believed that the Seminoles would surrender all runaway slaves if allowed to live in a small district close to Florida Point.[32] Enslaved Africans on various plantations in central Florida fought bravely in the Second Seminole war from 1835 to 1842. They were admired for their ferocity and ability to navigate the heavy Florida swampland and forest. Many of them also fled to the British during the American Revolution and the War of 1812 and to the Spanish before the United States purchase of Louisiana in 1804 and Florida in 1821. In Florida during the Seminole Wars, enslaved Africans escaped to join the Seminole Indians, assisting them in their resistance against white settlers and later accompanying them in their forced removal to Oklahoma and Mexico by the U.S. government. The Seminole War in Florida was a fight by the Seminoles to remain on their land in Florida. However, for the enslaved Africans that escaped from the plantation, the war in part was a slave revolt and a fight for freedom.

Regarding the tenacity and leadership of the Black Seminoles Jesup wrote, "This, you may be assured, is a negro and not an Indian war." White American leaders viewed the escaped slaves fighting with the Seminoles as challenging the full military might of the United States. The officers were reluctant to hand back the Black Seminoles to their masters after the army managed to capture them, as they were concerned that these experienced warriors, who were used to their freedom, might incite turmoil on the Southern plantations, like the Black Haitians rebelling against the French. The United States spent more than $20 million fighting the Seminoles. The war left more than 1,500 soldiers and uncounted American civilians dead.

Had the Black Seminoles not established alliances and networks throughout Florida and the southern Atlantic, they would have not been positioned to sustain the costly rebellion against the American government. The person most prominent in leading the Black Seminole rebellion and later free Black settlements was Juan Caballo, also known as John Horse, Juan Cavallo, and Gopher John.

The Seminole Nation note in their official archives

JOHN HORSE, A.K.A. GOPHER JOHN, ENGRAVING PUBLISHED IN JOSHUA REED GIDDINGS, *THE EXILES OF FLORIDA; OR, THE CRIMES COMMITTED BY OUR GOVERNMENT AGAINST THE MAROONS: WHO FLED FROM SOUTH CAROLINA AND OTHER SLAVE STATES, SEEKING PROTECTION UNDER SPANISH LAW*, COLUMBUS, OHIO, FOLLETT, FOSTER AND CO., 1858.

that John Horse was born into slavery in 1812 in Florida. His father, Charley Cavallo, was a Seminole with Creek and Spanish ancestry, while his mother, who was Charley Cavallo's slave, had direct lineage from sub-Saharan Africa. In the United States, John Horse accomplished great things as a Black freedom fighter. He participated in the Second Seminole War as a sub-chief, served with distinction in the Mexican military, and was introduced to President James K. Polk of the United States. He defended free Black settlements on three frontiers and spent much of his life on a quest to secure a free homeland for his people in Mexico. Horse and approximately 289 supporters established their own communities in the Wewoka Creek bottomlands and its branches in the Western Creek Nation, in what is today Oklahoma, in 1849. There they cleared land, built homes, and cultivated crops. The modern city of Wewoka, Oklahoma, is located south of one of the original settlements. Horse became the de facto leader of the Wewoka Creek group and kept them well armed, independent, and free from slaving activities. Deeply concerned for his people's well-being in Indian Territory, Horse reluctantly left the West.

In the fall of 1849, accompanied by the Seminole chief Coacoochee (Wild Cat) and around 100 followers, Horse departed the Wewoka Creek settlement to establish a long-held dream of a new nation in Mexico. Settling in Coahuila, many of the immigrants served as border guards for the Mexican government. After valiantly fighting in many battles and border skirmishes, they were granted land for their people. Thus, Horse was able to accomplish one of the defining goals of Black nationalism, the establishment of a Black state and also one outside of the U.S., as Delany was later to advocate.

Major Black enclaves outside of Florida also emerged in the late eighteenth and early nineteenth centuries. In the nineteenth century, Seneca Village, located in Manhattan, New York, became the most prominent Black-run community in the Northeast. Seneca Village's origins begin with a wealthy white couple named John and Elizabeth Whitehead.

They purchased 200 acres of farmland in northwestern Manhattan in 1824. Between 1825 and 1832, approximately half the Whiteheads' land was sold to fellow African Americans. The Central Park Conservancy recorded that Andrew Williams, a twenty-five-year-old African American shoe-shiner, bought the first three lots for $125. Twelve lots were purchased by Epiphany Davis, a store clerk, for $578, with six more lots bought by the African Methodist Episcopal Zion Church. From those origins, a thriving Black community developed. Approximately ten residences existed in the Village around the early 1830s, growing to over 1,600 Black residents by the 1850s.

To alleviate the densely populated and unpleasant urban environment in lower Manhattan, New York City was planning a sizable municipal park during this time. Most of this land was used for farming and was home to Seneca Village. However, the city of New York's city council wanted this land to be part of what was planned to be the country's largest state park, to match the grand parks of Europe. Eminent domain allowed the city to seize the land, leading to compensation disputes and claims of undervaluation. (Eminent domain seizures were a common practice in the nineteenth century and had been used to develop the grid of streets decades earlier.) Ultimately, all residents had to leave their homes in Seneca Village by the end of 1857. Central Park was officially opened to the public in 1876.

Although Blacks in Seneca Village had the right to vote in the state and lived in a separate enclave away from New York's everyday perils of racism and poor health conditions, in the end their space was still taken away from them. Although Fort Mosé, the five major Black enclaves created by the Black Seminoles, and Seneca Village were examples where land was either swindled legally by a governmental agency or taken through force from communities of Blacks, there are two examples of successful Black enclaves that still exist today: Africatown and Mound Bayou.

Africatown, in Mobile, Alabama, was established by Africans who were forcibly taken from their homeland and enslaved and later established a self-governing community while preserving their African cultural roots. Even after more than 140 years since the *Clotilda*, the final ship in American history to transport unwilling Africans, docked in Mobile Bay, this sense of heritage and community remains strong.

The story of Africatown began in 1860, when the *Clotilda*'s owner, Timothy Meaher, dispatched Captain William Foster to West Africa and successfully smuggled 110 enslaved Africans from Dahomey, in present day Benin, into Mobile, with one person perishing during the Middle Passage.[33] Following the end of the Civil War and emancipation in 1865, the formerly enslaved Africans from the *Clotilda* established themselves as free Americans while retaining their African heritage.

ABACHE AND CUDJOE KAZOOLA LEWIS, TWO SURVIVORS OF THE *CLOTILDA* TRAFFICKING SHIP, PHOTO TAKEN IN 1914. (LIBRARY OF CONGRESS.)

Their initial settlement was established in 1866 just three miles north of present-day downtown Mobile, Alabama. They settled in the woods and marshes in this area, where they built simple homes and a school, founded a church, planted gardens, tended livestock, hunted, fished, and farmed. From their efforts arose a strong, self-supporting community despite the threat of violence from ex-Confederate soldiers who were still active during the initial settlement. While in their original settlement, they attempted to raise funds to sail back to their homeland in the immediate aftermath of the Civil War but failed, prompting Cudjoe Lewis, the de facto leader of the enclave, to ask Timothy Meaher for a plot of land that he owned. Timothy refused to deed them land so the now refugees as well as formally enslaved Africans decided to continue to raise money by working at the local lumber mill and selling produce to purchase their own land in the vicinity. The refugees finally raised the money and through Cudjoe Lewis purchased two acres of land for $100 near present-day Magazine Point, which was about a mile south of the original Africatown settlement. For decades after the final settlement, they continued speaking their native tongue, known as Tapa, which originates from the Nupe ethnic group in present-day Nigeria, and lasted until the 1950s. They also had disputes arbitrated by their tribal chieftain, Charlie Poteete, and had their illnesses treated by the African doctor, Jabez. [34]

Prior to World War II, Africatown was a unique community in Mobile County. However, throughout the twentieth century the once-thriving enclave began to decline. In 2021, descendants of Meaher sold a former credit union building to the city for $50,000, far below the $300,000 appraisal, and a food bank now operates there. It is also the headquarters of the Africatown Redevelopment Corporation, Africatown in 2022 had a population of about 2,000, with more than 100 being descendants from the enslaved Africans that were aboard the *Clotilda*. Although Africatown is not as prominent as it once was, it is still a national treasure that exemplifies the Black nationalist spirit of Black people using available resources to build and maintain institutions.

Another all-Black enclave founded over 100 years ago that is still in existence today is Mound Bayou, Mississippi, not far from Africatown in Alabama. It was founded by two cousins, Isaiah Montgomery and Benjamin Green, former slaves who had been owned by Joseph Davis, the brother of the former president of the Confederacy, Jefferson Davis.

Isaiah Montgomery was born on Hurricane Plantation near Vicksburg, Mississippi, and raised by Joseph Davis, who envisioned the possibility of educated slaves with a degree of self-rule in an idealistic environment. Benjamin T. Montgomery, Isaiah's father, was a well-educated and successful slave who was also friends with Davis, and Benjamin, with Davis's consent, owned a store. With the profits, Benjamin Montgomery hired a tutor for his and Davis's children, who were taught together. In the wake of the Civil War, the plantation was purchased by the elder Montgomery, who then created the cooperative Black community known as Davis Bend. Low crop prices, floods, insects, and a labor shortage all contributed to the venture's downfall. Isaiah Montgomery took note of the factors that led to the failure of Davis Bend, which led to the formation of Mound Bayou.

From its founding, Mound Bayou immediately prospered, producing cotton on a larger scale than had been known in the Delta region. New settlers were attracted to the fertile lands and built factories to accommodate growing industry. In 1893, a successful petition by citizens led to the community's incorporation as a village. In 1912, Mound Bayou petitioned the governor to raise it to the status of a town. It was granted at once, and Mound Bayou was on its way to being the crown jewel of the Delta region.The progress of Mound Bayou caught the attention of Booker T. Washington, who subsequently worked with Isaiah Montgomery in developing Mound Bayou's legal and government framework. A photograph from circa 1900 depicts Washington leaning into a crowd gathered on an outdoor platform during the Mound Bayou Oil Mill and Manufacturing Company's dedication, an event that drew 16,000. Washington visited Mound Bayou in 1907 and observed its inner workings in person:

Between the Mississippi and the Yazoo Rivers, Mound Bayou is the centre of a Negro population more dense than can be found anywhere else outside of Africa. The Negroes outnumber the whites seven to one throughout the Delta. There are whole sections of these rich bottom-lands where no white man lives. Mound Bayou and the territory for several miles around it on every side is one such section—a Negro colony, occupying 30,000 acres, all of which is owned by Negroes, most of them small farmers who till 40 and 80-acre tracts. Mound Bayou is a self-governing community. That is one of the interesting things about it. It has had, since it was incorporated in 1898, a mayor, three aldermen, a constable, and a town marshal, all of them Negroes. This was unavoidable, as the community, since its founding, had only one white resident—the man who installed the telephone system. He stayed only long enough to train the townspeople on its operation. One morning in the fall of 1887, a northbound train stopped in the midst of this wilderness, a party of Negroes stepped off, and the train went its way. The leader of the group, a small, slender man, with strongly marked features and a deliberate and thoughtful manner, held in his hand a plot, which he looked at from time to time. This was Isaiah T. Montgomery and the men with him were the first contingent of prospective settlers. It was not easy, as I have often heard Mr. Montgomery say, to find settlers in that early day. The task of taming this wild country seemed hopeless to men with so few resources and so little experience. On this morning, Mr. Montgomery thought it best to make a little speech before proceeding with the work that had brought them thither. "You see," he said, waving his hand in the direction of the forest, "this is a pretty wild place." He paused, and the men looked hesitatingly in the direction he had indicated but said nothing. "But this whole country," he continued, "was like this once. You have seen it

> *change. You and your fathers have, for the most part, performed the work that has made it what it is. You and your fathers did this for someone else. Can't you do as much now for yourselves?" The men picked up their axes and attacked the wilderness.*

With a population of 1,328 in 2020, Mound Bayou is Mississippi's 136th-largest city. Its population had dropped by 13.37% since the previous census in 2010, with an annual decline rate of 1.56%. In Mound Bayou, the average household income is $28,896, and almost half of the residents are living in poverty. In the 2020s the average monthly rent hovered near $465, and the median home price has been approximately $81,900. Mound Bayou's median age is 29.1 years—25.2 for males, 33.7 for females—and its population is 100% Black.

While Africatown and Mound Bayou remain, other Black communities like Black Wall Street, Rosewood, and Ocoee have been destroyed or gentrified by white violence. Since the dawn of the new century, much has been written and produced in various formats about Black Wall Street. Ta-Nehisi Coates wrote in depth about Black Wall Street in 2014 in the widely read article "The Case for Reparations." Home Box Office (HBO) produced two award-winning series, *Watchmen* in 2019 and *Lovecraft Country* in 2020, that fictionalize not only the destruction of Black Wall Street itself but also the landscape of the community in that time.

The 2001 Tulsa Race Riot Report states that some African American riot victims were the offspring of enslaved Blacks who journeyed alongside the Creeks, Cherokees, and Choctaws during the Trail of Tears. The rest were offspring of escaped slaves who found safety among Native American tribes before and during the Civil War. Yet most of Tulsa's Black citizens arrived in Oklahoma during the period of rapid growth around the time it achieved statehood, at a time when many whites were arriving as well. They moved to Oklahoma because they were looking to improve their lives by taking advantage of the opportunity that the oil industry provided. The late nineteenth century saw a significant migration of residents from Missouri, Kansas, Mississippi, and Georgia to all-Black towns in Oklahoma, driven by a desire to escape the racist customs prevalent in the South. The resurgence of white supremacist groups like the Ku Klux Klan in the early twentieth century prompted the development of Black Wall Street on Greenwood Avenue in Tulsa, Oklahoma.

The Black towns in Oklahoma, especially the Black Wall Street section in Tulsa, and the numerous self-sufficient towns throughout the western plains existed as a territory where Black people could create their own realities free from the system of white supremacy. O. W. Gurley and J. B. Stradford were two of the men searching for opportunities. Gurley's vision for Black Wall Street began in Perry, Oklahoma:

> *Driven by entrepreneurial ambition, Gurley, at age 25, joined the Cherokee Outlet Opening on September 16, 1893, running fifty miles to claim a plot of prairie grass. Standing on a plot of land with his wife Emma Gurley, he staked claims in what would soon become Perry, Oklahoma, one of many towns advertised to Blacks in the new territory. Gurley envisioned Oklahoma as the start of a new life for Black Americans decades after emancipation, and he was ambitious. He ran for county treasurer, was made principal at the town's school, and ultimately opened a successful general store, which he ran for a decade. By the turn of the century, Gurley and his fellow homesteaders heard tales of giant oil fields in the nearby boomtown of Tulsa. A gusher well called the Ida Glenn Number 1, the first find in the massive Mid-Continent Oil Field, was making local Tulsans rich, and eventually turned no-name wildcatters Harry Ford Sinclair and J. Paul Getty into oil barons. O. W. Gurley wanted to take advantage of that opportunity. He sold his store and land in Perry and moved about 80 miles to Tulsa in 1905, taking the second major risk of his young life.* [35]

Gurley bought more than forty acres of land in 1906 and ensured that only African Americans could purchase plots. In the early twentieth century, Gurley sheltered African Americans seeking refuge from the oppressive system of white supremacy in Mississippi. He also created opportunities for any Black person to start their own business. He lent money to people and encouraged them to further their entrepreneurial endeavors as he had done since his youth. After a while, Greenwood Avenue became self-contained and self-sufficient as more and more businesses were founded.

Stradford also came from humble beginnings. Stradford was born in 1861 to a freed slave named Julius Caesar Stradford, who had been emancipated in Stratford, Ontario, and named his son J. B. for John the Baptist. Stradford's career path took him from Oberlin and Indiana Law School to St. Louis and Lawrenceburg, Kentucky, where he opened a diverse range of businesses: pool halls, shoeshine parlors, bathhouses, and boarding houses. However, like Gurley, he took major financial risks in his younger years as an eventual investor in the development of Black Wall Street. His move to Tulsa in 1899, prompted by a failed hotel venture, marked the beginning of his efforts to build a Black community on the city's outskirts. Upon Gurley's 1906 arrival, they collaborated on Greenwood's development. Like Gurley, Stradford specialized in real estate, developing rental properties.

Despite prioritizing wealth accumulation, Stradford actively championed Black rights by lobbying regularly against Oklahoma's Jim Crow laws. His portfolio included many properties, most notably the Stradford Hotel, which was the nation's biggest and most thriving Black-owned hotel at the time. With fifty-four rooms plus a casino, dining room, saloon, and pool hall, the Stradford occupied 301 Greenwood Avenue.[36] In the end, Stradford believed that Blacks could achieve economic advancement by pooling their resources, collaborating, and backing each other's businesses.

At its zenith, the Greenwood district of Tulsa, Oklahoma, was known as "the promised land," especially to Black Oklahomans. This was because it offered Black people a sanctuary from the racism in the rest of the city. Although Black people in Tulsa in the early twentieth century could work in primarily white areas, their money could not be spent in white businesses because of segregation and racism. Consequently, the Black community had to create its own businesses for necessities and entertainment, so more money generated in the district circulated and remained in the district than was the case with other enclaves. A dollar in the Greenwood district could go through 36 to 100 transactions and stay in Greenwood for close to a year before exiting. Over seventy businesses operated in Greenwood in one-to-three-story red brick buildings, many of them Black-owned. The area encompassed four hotels, a cabaret, two newspaper presses, a cigar shop, eight physicians, seven barbers, nine restaurants, and approximately six professional offices (real estate, dental, and legal).

Loula and John Williams, a Black couple, owned a confectionery at 102 Greenwood Avenue and the East End Garage around the corner on Archer Street. The Williamses also owned the 750-seat Williams Dreamland Theatre located at 129 Greenwood Avenue, which booked original Black theatrical performances through the Theatre Owners Booking Association, as well as showing the latest releases of Black-produced silent films for the city to enjoy.[37] It featured live entertainment and served as a community meeting place. The office of Dr. R. T. Bridgewater, who also owned seventeen housing units, was in the Woods Building at 101-105 Greenwood Avenue. His opulent North Detroit Street home was dubbed a palace by the *Tulsa Star*, a Black-owned newspaper. The newspaper *Tulsa World*, which was owned by whites, recognized Black Wall Street as a bastion of prosperity for Blacks in the city, remarking, "Residents in the Negro section of the city have proven themselves no less enterprising than the white people. In all of the Negro additions numerous dwellings are to be seen."[38] These achievements of wealth-building led to Booker T. Washington himself declaring the Greenwood district "the Negro Wall Street of America." By 1921, Tulsa's Black population was estimated at 10,000 of a total population of 100,000. It's been estimated that, during its prime, Black Wall Street hosted over 600 businesses, with a particularly busy period from Thursday to Sunday, including both legitimate and illicit enterprises. At least three Black business owners each had a net worth of $1 million. But these achievements could not prevent the white supremacist attack that was forthcoming.

According to the Tulsa Riots Report of 2001, the massacre began on May 30, 1921, when Dick Rowland, a Black man, unintentionally stepped on the foot of a white woman named Page in an elevator. Having screamed, she caused him to quickly leave the premises. The following day's afternoon newspaper featured a provocative front-page story alleging Rowland tried to rape Page. Even more alarmingly, a missing editorial which is suspected to be titled "To Lynch Negro Tonight" may have suggested Rowland, then in police custody, would be lynched by white people that evening. The May 31, 1921, edition of the *Tulsa Tribune* rolled off the press at three o'clock and within the hour the streets of Tulsa resounded with talk of lynching. As expected, before sunset a white crowd started assembling outside the jail where Rowland was being held and soon grew into the hundreds as word spread.

Three white men arrived at the courthouse at 8:20 p.m. and demanded Rowland from the authorities, but they were denied. Over a thousand people in the white mob became highly charged as soon as the Black men arrived at the courthouse.[39] White people who lacked guns went back home to fetch them. Some white people tried forcing their way into the jail to get the weapons inside. However, a small group of National Guardsmen, prepared to shoot, forced the angry white people to leave. Following the initial gunshot, African Americans began "a retreating fight" back toward Black Wall Street. The initial phase resulted in multiple casualties, though the exact count remains unclear. For the next few hours, downtown Tulsa experienced scattered instances of fighting. Meanwhile, local law enforcement assisted white residents in preparing an armed response and deputized around 500 men.[40] Witnesses reported hearing sirens, whistles, and other signals around

5:00 a.m., indicating the arrival of organized, angry white mobs into the Greenwood district later. The *Tulsa World* noted that prominent white businessmen were among those driving cars loaded with armed whites into the Greenwood area. Besides the multitude of white supremacists invading the Black Wall Street district, at least six airplanes were deployed, some reportedly firing on African Americans.

Ultimately, over 1,250 Black households were demolished along with various commercial establishments. The estimated property damage was between $1.5 million and $2 million, surpassing $25 million in present-day value. In the accounting of the deaths, the Department of Health's Bureau of Vital Statistics estimated ten white and twenty-six Black deaths; however, the Red Cross records showed a total of 300 people being killed. The *Tulsa Tribune* reported conflicting casualty numbers, citing sixty-eight and 175 in separate articles.

There were attempts to revive Black Wall Street's legacy in Greenwood in the 1940s and '50s. Around 10,000 residents called Black Wall Street home in the 1950s. The massacre threatened Black residents' generational wealth, but many businesses contributed to its rebuilding. America's socioeconomic system, when controlled by white elites, can be, as Black Wall Street's fate shows, used to enforce white supremacy. As a further example of this, the once-promising financial recovery of Black Wall Street was thwarted by highways built through it under eminent domain. Already in 1957, Tulsa's Comprehensive Plan envisioned an encircling four-highway ring road, known as the Inner-Dispersal Loop (IDL). Completed in 1971, the IDL replaced Greenwood and Kendall-Whittier's dense, varied, mixed-use, mixed-income, pedestrian-friendly, and transit-oriented sections, particularly to the north (I-244) and east (U.S. 75). Though they rebuilt following the 1921 massacre, Mabel Little's family suffered multiple losses of their home and businesses in 1970. Little told the *Tulsa Tribune* in 1970, "You wiped out all that was ours." Hughes Van Ellis, one of the last known living survivors of the massacre, stated that "It sticks in my mind. I wake up about four times a night, you know. Some nights, I'll stay woke, say, 30, 40 minutes till I can lay back down. I

CAPTURED MEN FORCIBLY MARCHED TO THE TULSA CONVENTION CENTER ON JUNE 1, 1921. (COLLECTION OF THE SMITHSONIAN NATIONAL MUSEUM OF AFRICAN AMERICAN HISTORY AND CULTURE.)

WAY TO
-DURING TULSA RACE RIOT
JUNE 1st 1921.

can't sleep at night. I have to have light. I love light. When I got old enough to marry and raise a family, that's when, yeah, dawned on me so much." Viola Ford Fletcher, the oldest known survivor of the massacre, recalled that "I'm a survivor of the Tulsa Race Massacre. I'm here seeking justice, and I'm asking my country to acknowledge what happened in Tulsa in 1921. The night of the massacre, I was awakened by my family, my parents and five siblings were there. I was told we had to leave, and that was it. We lost everything that day. Our homes, our newspaper [The *Tulsa Star*], our theaters, our lives. Greenwood represented all the best of what was possible for Black people in America. This Congress must recognize us and our history."

The massacre of Black Wall Street would reverberate around the country, with other majority-Black enclaves experiencing the full weight of violent white supremacist attacks. During the summer of 1919, dubbed "Red Summer," numerous race riots erupted nationwide, notably in Chicago; Washington, D.C.; Knoxville, Tennessee; and Omaha, Nebraska. From 1918 to 1923, 362 riots were officially recorded. The violence against Blacks would continue throughout the 1920s, not only against individuals in the form of lynchings but against entire Black enclaves.

Florida experienced both high-profile lynchings and the erasure of Black enclaves during this time period. In Macclenny, Florida, four innocent Black men—Fulton Smith, Ray Field, Ben Givens, and Sam Duncan—were lynched by a white mob on October 5, 1920. The *New York News* on December 15, 1922, reported,

> *Two negros were captured here for the murder of a white school teacher but only one was burned at the stake tonight. Before he died, Charles Wright, age 21, confessed that he alone had committed the murder of Miss Ruby Hendry, exonerating Albert Young who was also captured by a party of whites. Following the burning of Wright, Young was turned back to the authorities, and all hands scrambled for souvenirs of the remains.*

Two others were hanged as well, and the town's Black church, school, and Masonic lodge were set on fire and destroyed. The Perry, Florida, lynchings and subsequent razing of the town's Black establishments happened less than a month before the Rosewood, Florida, massacre and approximately two years after the riot and slaughter of Black residents in Ocoee, Florida.

Ocoee, in central Florida, is a mostly quiet Orlando suburb. The 100th anniversary of its 1920 massacre brought back painful memories for the descendants of survivors. In 2008, the film *Ocoee: Legacy of the Election Day Massacre* was released, and on November 1, 2020, a local Orlando network premiered *Ocoee Massacre: A Documentary Film* on its station. The events were ignited by the attempt by a Black man, Julius "July" Perry, to vote in the 1920 election.

Understanding the Ocoee massacre requires an understanding of the origins of the city of Ocoee itself: it was founded in the 1850s by Dr. J. D. Starke, who brought twenty-three enslaved Africans with him to do the heavy lifting of developing the area, which at the time was mostly swamp and forest. At Starke's request, these people worked tirelessly under the scorching central Florida sun from morning until night to bring his dream of a township to life.

After the Civil War, numerous Confederate veterans moved there and employed Black workers to toil on their farms for meager pay in the harsh conditions of the Florida landscape. Since 1888, a significant number of these laborers purchased the very plots they toiled on from their white supervisors, thus securing wealth and stability largely absent in the Jim Crow South for Black individuals. Census data from 1920 show roughly one-third of Ocoee's 800 residents were Black.[41] The Black and white population numbers were a major factor in the massacre, which was not the first clash between whites and Blacks in Ocoee. Two months before the November 1920 riot, many whites left Ocoee to go to a dance in nearby Clarcona. According to reports, in their absence, a group of Black men intimidated the white people who remained at home. Sam Salisbury, who would later play a major role in the Ocoee massacre, threatened the gang with a pistol, yet, by his account, ultimately chose inaction. There were also reports that a white man was on two separate occasions run off the road by a young Black man called Ronnie Petsey. As punishment, he received a bullet to the leg. Moreover, white Ocoee residents claimed that Blacks regularly gathered at the local grocery stores, blocking white individuals from going inside. Salisbury further asserted that "Black men, in groups, would visit white farmers' homes to create an atmosphere of intimidation."[42]

There were whispers of a Black scheme to stockpile ammunition and seize control. The KKK sent a threatening letter to two prominent Republican white leaders, an attorney named W. R. O'Neal and Judge John Cheney, a month before the election. The letters mailed to the men proclaimed, "We shall always enjoy WHITE SUPREMACY in this country and he who interferes must face the consequences."[43] The daughter of a prominent white Ocoee official recalled nearly fifty years later that "90 percent of all law enforcement officers, judges, public servants and lawyers in Winter Garden and Ocoee were Klan members."

The presidential election of 1920 between the Republican candidates Warren G. Harding and Calvin Coolidge and the Democratic candidates James Cox and Franklin D. Roosevelt represented important transitions at that time. World War I had just concluded, and the nation and its industries were shifting back to pre-war activities. The women's suffrage movement had reached its apex that year with the ratification of the 19th Amendment, which gave women the right to vote. However, in its enforcement Black women as well as Black men were not allowed to vote at this time, especially in Florida. The Red Summer violence had occurred a year before and the lynchings of Black people as well as the resurgence of the Klu Klux Klan continued into 1920.

Ocoee was not an incorporated area of Orange County in November 1920 but a part of the county's Precinct 10. In the 1920 Census, Ocoee's population was recorded as 255 African Americans and 560 whites. There were two areas in Ocoee where a great deal of African Americans lived: the

Northern or Methodist Quarters near the northwestern part of Starke Lake and the Southern or Baptist Quarters near the southwestern and south-central parts of Starke Lake. This background provides the context for arguably the most violent election day to ever occur in this nation's history. In the two Black communities of Ocoee, the night before the 1920 election, the Klan paraded in their robes and crosses. As the historian Carlee Hoffman recounts, "Megaphones blared warnings that Black voting was forbidden, with severe consequences promised to anyone who disobeyed. At the polls in Orange County on Election Day, a group of Black voters attempted to cast their ballots." However, entry to polling stations was prohibited for Blacks. White authorities positioned around polling centers instructed poll workers to bar Black voters.

On November 2, 1920, Moses Norman went to the polls in Ocoee to cast his ballot. Norman, a prominent Black landowner, owned a thriving citrus grove among his Ocoee properties. With their 100-acre family orange grove providing a comfortable income, he and his wife Elisa enjoyed a lavish lifestyle. Downtown's brick streets provided the setting for his impressive drive in a luxurious six-cylinder Columbia convertible, complete with whitewall tires, silver spokes, and stylish storm curtains.

When he attempted to vote, he was denied and told to go home because he had failed to pay his poll tax. Following this, Norman drove thirteen miles east to Orlando to meet John M. Cheney, a leading Orlando lawyer, Rollins College trustee, and Republican candidate for U.S. Senate. Advising Norman to go back to Ocoee to vote, Cheney stated it was his constitutional right. He then told Norman to record the names of all African American voters who were denied their right to vote, as well as the names of the poll workers who denied them. Motivated by the risk of a lawsuit, Cheney issued the instructions, citing potential liability for both the workers and the county. When Norman returned with a handful of Black citizens to vote later in the day, an altercation ensued between Norman and a few poll workers. He demanded the poll workers' names and exclaimed, "We will vote, by God!"

There is no consensus on what happened next, with accounts varying. Hoffman again notes that there are claims that Norman was armed when he faced the poll workers. According to other accounts, white Ocoee citizens searched Norman's car and may have located a firearm. In any case, Norman's voting rights were again denied, and he may have been struck with the stock of his own firearm. He then proceeded to the residence of his friend, July Perry, who was another prosperous Black man in Ocoee. Perry was born in 1870 in South Carolina and arrived in the township of Ocoee around 1888.

He married Estella Betsy in the 1880s and they had four children. In addition to being a businessman, Perry also helped broker land deals, was a church deacon, registered Black residents of Ocoee to vote, and arranged work for people in his community. People seeking to hire black workers were told they had to go through him first. People admired him for his bravery, rationality, and intellect. Before the Civil Rights Movement, he acted as a civil rights leader, urging Black youth to pursue education and assert their full citizenship. A large estate, complete with a house, barns, and outbuildings, served as the home for Perry, his wife Estelle, their three sons, and their daughter Coretha Perry Caldwell. People in need were always welcome and knew they could find solace on the premises.

Since Norman was in trouble, it was instinct for him to flee to Perry's house for refuge. Meanwhile, Colonel Sam Salisbury, a former Orlando police chief and a KKK member, led a white mob of over 200. The mob determined they'd find Norman and inform him his polling place conduct was unacceptable. They decided to prosecute him to warn other Black people against challenging white Democrats' power. Their investigation led them to be tipped off so that Norman went to Perry's house. Expecting trouble, the people inside Perry's home had already armed themselves by the time the men arrived. A shootout occurred at the residence; however, it remains uncertain who fired the initial shot, with conflicting reports suggesting Perry's daughter was responsible. Two white men were killed, and Perry was seriously hurt in the aftermath of the confrontation. He was subsequently taken by the sheriff to Orange County jail.

Following his escape from the scene, Norman vanished from the area. As the mob of over 250 white people, including many Klan members, swelled in Ocoee that night, word of the fight spread, culminating in the burning of the Baptist Quarters. The fire destroyed twenty-two homes, two churches, the Masonic lodge, school, and the wall of the Ocoee African Methodist Episcopal Church in the Methodist quarters. Sheriff Frank Gordon opened Perry's cell for a lynch mob at the Orange County jail just before dawn the next day. Immediately, they grabbed him and whipped him. They tied his neck to the back of a car and drove to Judge Cheney's house close to the entrance of the Orlando Country Club by Lake Concord. By the highway, the crowd bound Perry, at the point of death, to a telephone pole. The corpse, suspended in the air, showed multiple bullet wounds, which are suspected to have caused the final death blow. The horrifying sight was deliberately left there as a warning for both Cheney and the Black community in the vicinity, along with a note that read, "This is what we do to niggers who try to vote."

Many Black residents found refuge in Ocoee's swamps and groves, evading death, but almost none ever returned. While the exact figure is uncertain, it is believed that between thirty and sixty people perished that night. Although the Baptist Quarters' houses survived the November 3rd event largely unscathed, historical documents indicate that its church was completely burned down. The community's residents faced a stark choice: abandon their homes or face identical consequences. The carnage their friends and relatives in the north suffered made the decision clear. Following the incident, a KKK-enforced blockade surrounded the town for almost a week. Entry and exit required their authorization, underscoring their dominance. Their specific objective was to prevent the homeless Black residents of Ocoee from reaching Orlando or Winter Garden and forming alliances with other Black communities. There could have been a full-on race war had the people of Ocoee been successful in traveling to those areas.

Imprisoned in Tampa after the massacre, Perry's wife and daughter were eventually cleared of all charges. Judge Frank Smith appointed Captain Bluford Marion Sims to administer the Perry estate, rejecting the widow's claim. A forged signature of Mrs. Perry's was on the application to manage the family property. However, while the order Appointing Administrator was dated November 13, 1920, Mrs. Perry and her daughter's imprisonment lasted until about November 30th. The Perry family sought court intervention three years later to reclaim his estate, citing uncompensated losses. However, when Bluford Sims was deemed insane and his daughter, Eva, became Bluford's court-appointed guardian, she defied a court order to account for the estate's assets. When the February 1924 deadline passed, the case became inactive. A subsequent amendment to the deed restricted the property's sale or transfer to Black individuals. The amendment stated, "It is further agreed that the herein named property cannot be sold to or otherwise conveyed to a negro." Perry's family lost their property and were barred from ever buying it back. Perry's death entitled his wife, Estelle, to his property. In the documentary *Stolen Land: Ocoee Massacre*, Perry's great-grandson, Stephen Nunn, said his grandmother's name was falsified on documents, allowing local officials to sell off Perry's estate after his death. "It was actually stolen. It's still stolen land to this day. It's still land that belongs to not only July Perry, but other descendants of Ocoee. That land has blood on it."

Besides seizing the Perry estate, Sims also advertised stolen land from other Black Ocoee residents. The sale of the stolen Ocoee groves and land was advertised in both Orlando and Miami within two weeks after the election day violence. "Special Bargains, several Beautiful Little Groves Belonging to The Negroes that have just left Ocoee. Must be Sold—See B. M. Sims, Ocoee, Fla."

Just weeks after the massacre, only two Black people were left in town. By 1930, they had all disappeared from the census. It wasn't until 1978 that any African Americans lived in Ocoee. White supremacy in Orange County was strengthened politically, economically, and culturally by the complete

ADVERTISEMENT IN THE DECEMBER 20, 1920, EDITION OF THE *ORLANDO SENTINEL*, ORLANDO, FLORIDA.

lack of Black votes for eighteen years following the 1920 massacre. For years, Black people steered clear of Ocoee. A sign stating, "Dogs and Negroes Not Welcome," stood at the town boundary until at least 1959. The city of Ocoee didn't hire a Black person until 1986, and, well into the 1990s, Black families were warned to avoid the city after dark.

Violence from white people intimidated Black people, preventing them from going to Ocoee or openly discussing it. A July 23, 1921, report in the *Orlando Sentinel* detailed how fifteen men freed George Betsy, a Black resident of Ocoee before the massacre, from police custody after his prohibition law violation arrest. His lengthy talk about the Ocoee incident from the prior November resulted in his discovery the following morning, hurt and bound to a utility pole. Consider, also, Valentine Hightower, one of the original Black settlers of Ocoee mentioned earlier. He received only $10 for the family's 37-acre Clarcona-Ocoee Road pineland, destined for turpentine manufacturing.

The injustice of the Ocoee massacre is compounded by the fact that, more than a century later, white corporations now control property formerly owned by Black residents, with a current value exceeding $10 million.

Unfortunately, the Ocoee Massacre was not the last racially motivated mass killing to happen in Florida in that decade. The Ku Klux Klan in the 1920s continued making waves in Florida, inflicting violence and promoting white supremacy. In 1922, the Klan achieved a near-total victory in the June primaries of Volusia County, securing wins in Daytona, Ormond, and DeLand for all its judicial, municipal, and legislative candidates. The Klan continued to meet, initiate, march, and rally throughout the state to assert their political dominance.

The marching and demonstration throughout the state eventually made its way to Gainesville, home of the University of Florida. A Ku Klux Klan rally was held on the steps of the Alachua County Courthouse in Gainesville on December 31, 1922, and became a catalyst for renewed racial violence. The violence against Blacks in Ocoee had implications for land ownership and foreshadowed the destruction of Rosewood.

Seven homesteads lined the dirt trail to Cedar Keys by 1855, following initial settlement in 1847. Construction of a road linking Levyville and Cedar Keys through Rosewood was ordered by the Levy County Commission in 1857, with a school being requested near the area referred to as Roseville in 1861. The rise of the Rosewood Settlement spurred the establishment of a voting precinct, designated Outside Cedar Key, by 1870.[44]

Rosewood was never officially incorporated and did not amount to more than a settlement before 1870. Its significant expansion in the 1870s was linked to Cedar Key's success as Florida's biggest Gulf port for a short time. Taking advantage of the large cedar trees in the area, the Faber and Eagle pencil mills, based in Cedar Key, employed many local residents. Rosewood whites founded a Methodist church in 1878, while Rosewood's Black residents established their own African Methodist Episcopal Church in 1883. In 1886, Pleasant Hill saw the founding of a second AME church. By 1890, the red cedar forests were gone, and the pencil mills of Cedar Key were forced to close.

By 1900, white families moved from Rosewood and sold or leased their lands to Blacks. Despite this, the post office and school shut down and relocated three miles west to Sumner's new Cypress mill. Most of Rosewood's males worked at the large Sumner sawmill, while a small number of its Black females worked as house servants for white Sumner families. Also, a significant number of men were employed at a turpentine distillery situated one mile east in Wylly, another small village.

Other Rosewood Black residents were employed by M. Goins & Brothers Naval Stores, owned by an African American family. The company's success was due to its proximity to pine forests, a source of turpentine and rosin for its distillation processes. The Goins brothers' enterprise, which at its peak encompassed thousands of acres, included "Goins Quarters" as housing for many laborers. Other Rosewood African Americans, located ten miles southeast in the wide Gulf Hammock wetlands, lived off small farms and trapping. While some white residents relocated, others stayed, making them important figures in the ensuing massacre. Despite some whites remaining, the village's largest total population was 700 in 1915, consisting mostly of Blacks.

The two most powerful families in Rosewood were the Goinses and the Carriers. The Goinses were enriched by their turpentine factory but were also the second largest landowners—white or Black—in Levy County. To avoid legal action from competing white-owned businesses over land, the Goins family had mostly ended their Rosewood operations and moved to Gainesville by 1916.

Despite a minor decrease in the Black population by 1920 from its 1915 high, a strong sense of community persisted, with several small, Black-owned businesses such as a general store and sugar mill, remaining active. In Rosewood, residents valued their three churches, schoolhouse, Masonic lodge, and, as Lizzie Jenkins, a Rosewood descendant, noted, baseball team, the Rosewood Sluggers. A dozen or so two-story wooden plank houses, several smaller two-room houses, and a few empty plank structures for farm/storage purposes comprised the village. Middle-class African Americans in Rosewood often owned pianos, organs, and other status symbols. This demonstrated the community's journey from humble origins to progress, even with the challenges of the early 1920s. It also indicated Black nationalism in practice economically, politically, and culturally within its own territory. Wilson Hall, who grew up in Rosewood, recounted at the age of seventy-eight,

> *Well, Rosewood to me was a good time and place for the black people because each person had their own whatever they needed. Whether it was church, whether it was a large school, whatever it was, we had everything we needed right then. We had our own farm, we had our own sugar mill, we had our own grit mill, cane mill, so we didn't need nothing ... everybody would help everybody else. All we needed was God and God was all around us.*

A 1994 Florida House of Representatives report by a special master concluded that, before 1923, Rosewood had no history of overt racial conflict and that Black and white residents had generally positive relations. The Ku Klux Klan's large New Year's Day rally in Gainesville on January 1, 1923, forever changed the course of events.

In Sumner, Florida, a Black man's assault on a twenty-two-year-old white woman, Mrs. Frances Taylor, was reported to authorities. A visibly bruised Mrs. Taylor informed her neighbors that she'd been assaulted and robbed by an unidentified Black man while her husband, James, was at the sawmill. While the record doesn't detail the assault, the white community believed a sexual assault occurred, despite Mrs. Taylor never seeing a doctor.

After repeating her accusations, Mrs. Taylor collapsed and was transported to a neighbor's house. There were conflicting narratives about this event within the Black community. Mrs. Taylor received a visit from a white man before making her allegations on January 1, 1923, as recounted by Mrs. Sarah Carrier, a Black laundrywoman from Rosewood, and her granddaughter, Philomena Goins, who were present. In the Black community, the belief was that a fight with an unidentified white man, with whom Mrs. Taylor had a romantic relationship, led to her injuries. Responding to Mrs. Taylor's report of a Black assailant, a search party was formed by Sumner locals and workers from James Taylor's Cummer sawmill. James Taylor also sought assistance from Levy County and neighboring Alachua County, as a Ku Klux Klan event concluded in downtown Gainesville's courthouse square.

The Ku Klux Klan members had been marching in opposition of justice for Black people on December 31, 1922. News of Fannie Taylor's claims, telegraphed to Gainesville, prompted four to five hundred Klansmen to ride to Sumner to aid James Taylor. They started the search by looking for a Black suspect in the woods behind Taylor's house. Sheriff Robert Elias Walker of Levy County contacted Sumner at about that time to report the escape of Jesse Hunter, a Black convict, from a road construction crew near Otter Creek. Despite the lack of evidence of an escape, Jesse Hunter remained the primary target of the investigation. Sheriff Walker later that day initiated a bloodhound pursuit of the fugitive, beginning behind the Taylor house in Sumner and heading toward Rosewood. Before nightfall, Rosewood residents were terrified by the white supremacists' return.

Aaron Carrier, a Black man from Rosewood, was the first person the group encountered. He was interrogated, then forcibly dragged from his bed, tied behind a car, and hauled to Sumner, subjected to a furious tirade throughout the journey. He was freed, only to be subjected to a brutal beating and public degradation. Lizzie Jenkins, a descendant of the victims of the massacre, recounts that one perpetrator said, "He's damn near dead, let's finish the nigger off!" Sheriff Walker yelled, "No! I'll finish the nigger off!" Instead, the sheriff put Carrier in his car and drove 55 miles to Gainesville, where he begged his friend, Sheriff J. P. Ramsey, to put Carrier in his jail and not tell anyone he was being held there. Sam Carter's house was the dogs' trail's end, convincing the search party that he'd aided the fugitive's escape by hiding him in his wagon. The bloodthirsty men took Carter prisoner, hung him from a tree branch, and questioned him about where Hunter was. Unable to locate Hunter, the posse intensified their aggression and shot him repeatedly. His hanging from a tree was a public spectacle meant to terrorize Rosewood's Black community.

The white mob heard Sylvester Carrier[45] say that Fannie Taylor was "an example of what negroes could do without interference." Enraged by this lie, the white supremacist mob further advanced into Rosewood where they stopped at Sarah Carrier's house. There were estimates of fifteen to thirty Black people, including children, seeking refuge in the Carrier residence. The refugees were added to the extended Carrier family, including Sarah's grandchildren, who were visiting over the Christmas and New Year holidays. An armed Sylvester Carrier and the other men at the home provided protection for those within. Carrier had a reputation in the area as an independent man who hunted in addition to teaching music. White people considered him "uppity" and disrespectful. Varying reports suggest that when two members of the white supremacist mob attempted to advance into the Carrier house, two shots were fired. Sarah Carrier was struck in the head and killed. Having witnessed Aaron Carrier's abduction from his home a few days earlier, her nine-year-old niece, Minnie Lee Langley, went downstairs to see what the commotion was about. Decades later, Minnie Lee recalled Sylvester pressing a gun to her shoulder in the wood bin while the shooting continued. Several shots were exchanged, leaving the house riddled with bullets. However, the white supremacists' mob failed to capture it.

The bodies of Poly Wilkerson, Henry Andrews, Sarah Carrier, an unnamed Black child, and Sylvester Carrier (possibly) were discovered in the house on January 5, 1923. The question of Sylvester Carrier's death at Rosewood is still unresolved. Years after the Rosewood massacre, his family received Christmas cards from him, supporting their belief that he'd escaped. Despite this, Minnie Lee Langley and the other children fled through the Carrier house's back door and ran into the woods late at night. They crossed dirt roads, they hid under the heavy brush, and they navigated a murky, alligator-infested swamp to escape the roving band of killers.

After the violence at the Carrier house, the entire village was destroyed. White supremacists, both local and from out of state, invaded Rosewood to murder Black people and vandalize their property. Over several days, every Black home was incinerated, forcing Black residents to seek refuge in the woods. Rosewood was where Lexie Gordon, a woman of mixed race, remained due to a typhoid fever. While escaping her burning house through the back door,

PHOTO TAKEN ON JANUARY 4, 1923, IN THE JANUARY 20, 1923, ISSUE OF *LITERARY DIGEST* MAGAZINE WITH THE CAPTION, "DELIBERATE BURNING OF CABINS AND A CHURCH WIPED OUT THE NEGRO QUARTER OF ROSEWOOD AS THE INHABITANTS TOOK TO THE WOODS." (STATE ARCHIVES OF FLORIDA, FLORIDA MEMORY.)

she was shot and killed. A gang of men seized James Carrier, a member of the extended Carrier family, interrogated him, and then brought him to a cemetery, ordering him to dig his own grave, but he was unable to because of paralysis in at least one arm from two strokes. A few days after his brother and mother were killed, he was shot while standing over their graves. The men left his body splayed over the graves of his family members for all to see. Eight people died in the destruction of Rosewood—six Black residents and two white—leaving the town in ashes. The Rosewood family descendants, however, assert that the casualties, including the dead and missing, numbered as many as thirty-seven.

In the years following the massacre, the Cummer sawmill in Sumner was destroyed by fire. The opening of a new mill in Lacoochee, Pasco County, Florida, led to many Rosewood families relocating there. Jacksonville and Miami became new homes for some, with others moving to different states. Many Rosewood residents lost their properties due to unpaid taxes. However, there are records that indicate that a great deal of property was sold later for far less than its value. Attention was not drawn to the massacre for decades. The Ocoee massacre served as a stark reminder of the danger of discussing such matters openly, prompting family members to keep their conversations within their own circle. There was hardly any reference to the violence in Rosewood in official Florida state records because of the implications for property taxes, insurance, and deed assessments. There was also evidence that state officials directly participated in the events under the direction of the Ku Klux Klan and blatantly falsified public records afterward.

Fortunately, Arnett Doctor, the great-grandson of Sarah Carrier, learned of the Rosewood massacre growing up in Lacoochee. He eventually did further research on the massacre with family members and then turned over his findings to Gary Moore. Moore published these findings in the *St. Petersburg Times* in 1982, which then prompted an exposé by Ed Bradley on *60 Minutes* in 1983, featuring the testimonies of Minnie Lee Langley and other survivors. Descendants of the survivors would continue to talk about the massacre across the country. In 1992, the Florida representatives Al Lawson and Miguel de Grundy proposed a bill seeking direct compensation for the descendants of Rosewood's Black residents, acknowledging the emotional and financial hardship caused by the brutal persecution they endured.

Because it never reached the floor of the Florida House for a vote, the bill failed. Following this setback, a 1993 legislative commission was formed to examine what happened in Rosewood. This commission was composed of five academics: Maxine Jones, Larry Rivers, David Colburn, Thomas Dye, and William Rogers. Their report was submitted later in 1993 and was followed by Florida House bill HR 591, which called for direct payments to compensate for the state's failure to protect the property of the victims. Even with the commission's report, the bill still faced opposition in the state legislature. The *Tampa Bay Times* reported that the state House's Black caucus threatened to leave to symbolize their displeasure unless the Rosewood bill was considered. House Bill 591 initially requested over $7 million for those affected by the incident. The 1994 settlement reduced the compensation amount to $1.5 million, including $500,000 for property damage from the attack, and a $100,000 scholarship fund for survivors and descendants.

The stories of Rosewood, Ocoee, Black Wall Street, Mound Bayou, Africatown, Seneca Village, the Maroon and Black Seminole communities, and Fort Mosé represent the struggles and successes of Black Americans building their own communities. The creation of these communities was born out of the necessity for Black people to not only survive but thrive and enabled their members to lift themselves out of second-class citizenship. Unfortunately, these collectives were destroyed either by the brute violence of white supremacists, as in Greenwood, Ocoee, and Rosewood, or by eminent domain for the growing highway systems that eradicated Black communities by design or systemic housing practices rooted in redlining, redistricting, and gentrification, as happened in Seneca Village, Africatown, and the second iteration of Black Wall

Street. In the Reconstruction and post-Reconstruction era, white supremacist organizations such as the Ku Klux Klan helped confine African Americans to small subsections of city centers or to rural areas as a mechanism of control and retribution, for it was easier to rain down terror on an entire neighborhood if a few of the townspeople "step out of line."

The Federal Housing Authority, part of Franklin D. Roosevelt's 1934 New Deal, supported segregation by subsidizing mass-produced housing developments that excluded African Americans from homeownership. The FHA reasoned that Black homebuyers in or near these suburbs would lower the value of the white-owned homes they insured and, consequently, their loans would be jeopardized. There was not a shred of evidence to support this.

"IN SILENT PROTEST AGAINST THE RECENT KILLING OF NEGROES IN RACE RIOTS IN WACO, MEMPHIS AND EAST ST. LOUIS, 15,000 NEGROES MARCHED HERE YESTERDAY AFTERNOON. THE PARADE FORMED IN FIFTH AVENUE AND MARCHED FROM FIFTY-SEVENTH STREET TO MADISON SQUARE." *NEW YORK AMERICAN*, JULY 28, 1917. (C.T. ADAMS, LIBRARY OF CONGRESS.)

Industrial globalization that shifted manufacturing jobs from urban areas to suburban areas also contributed to the relegation of African Americans to an urban underclass. America became the hegemonic power of the world starting with its involvement in World War I because of the manufacturing capacity that ramped up to help rebuild the "Triple Entente" powers. African Americans both as laborers in the factories and as infantrymen were instrumental in this process and accelerated the calls for equal rights. White politicians recognized that Blacks who had fought in World War I had experienced a level of freedom in Europe that they did not have in the United States.

In a speech on the Senate floor in 1917, Senator James K. Vardaman of Mississippi predicted that Black veterans returning to the South would "inevitably lead to disaster. Once you impress the negro with the fact that he is defending the flag and inflate his untutored soul with military airs, his political rights must be respected."

By labeling the potential for Black men, empowered by wartime experiences and urban opportunities, to challenge white supremacy as a "disaster," Vardaman revealed his own belief in white supremacy and illustrated a white fear of Black men more generally. White supremacist groups such as the second iteration of the KKK used terror and unfair laws to dominate Black Americans, fueled by the false idea that Black men threatened white American values and ideals. Again, this violence manifested itself in the burning down of Black enclaves and the intimidation that ensured Black victims never spoke of it to conceal their significance in American history.

In the *60 Minutes* special on Rosewood, the survivor Minnie Lee Langley stated, "Don't never stay in a place where white folks can surround you. Because if anything happens somewhere else, they will run you out of your town just like they did us." Here, Langley emphasized key tenets of Black nationalism such as pride in the race, self-sufficiency, and the very real need for Black enclaves that incubate Black businesses and incentivize Black homeownership with efficient local economic and political institutions. Black enclaves that are effective in developing the aforementioned components to support this alignment of residents, businesses, and government institutions will undoubtedly serve as a model for replication and eventual return of Black Nationalist ideals and principles to the consciousness of the African American community in the twenty-first century and beyond. The first tangible step in achieving this ideal is the development and implementation of education that serves the interest of Black people and ends the hegemonic domination of Blacks by whites in America.

97

CHAPTER THREE

EDUCATION FOR DOMINATION

The one constant for Black people in the United States since the first Africans were imported in the sixteenth century up until the present is that Black people in all areas of society remain in servitude to white people and white-owned institutions. Education has been an important tool used by whites in power to ensure that Black people are programmed to serve their interests and that white people remain dominant.

The Supreme Court's 1954 *Brown v. Board of Education* decision, which overturned discriminatory state laws, gave Black Americans hope for improved socio-economic conditions. Up to that point, African Americans in public schools across the country were allocated substandard educational resources compared to whites. Although the Supreme Court deemed segregation in schools unconstitutional, the segregation of students along racial and class lines continued as usual. Later, in the 1950s to early 1970s, several major events compelled the federal government to enforce the *Brown v. Board of Education* ruling, culminating in the Supreme Court ruling in *Milliken v. Bradley* in 1974.

These events included the Supreme Court ordering the University of Florida to admit Virgil Hawkins into their law school; the admission of the "Little Rock Nine" in 1957;

the 1959 action by Prince Edward County, Virginia, in closing down its public schools rather than complying with integration; the Civil Rights Act of 1964 allowing the U.S. Department of Education to file lawsuits in cases of willful dismissal of school desegregation laws; the start of school busing in 1971; and the Supreme Court decision in *Swann v. Charlotte-Mecklenburg Board of Education* (1971) that allowed compensatory education and magnet schools to address segregation in school districts.

In 1964, Bayard Rustin, a civil-rights organizer and leader who favored school integration, remarked to the novelist Robert Penn Warren that

> *I think we have to say what kind of school system do we need—number one, to prepare youngsters for the nature of Twentieth Century life, which again includes automation, technological change. And how do we prepare people, not only to make a living, but to live creatively in a democracy? Now, out of these two things I come to the conclusion that we need quality schools, and we need integrated schools, because I don't believe it's possible for people to live together in a society, in a democratic society and be separated in going to school. School is not preparation for life—it is life, and it ought to be democracy.*

FOUR AFRICAN AMERICAN SCHOOLBOYS READING AT THEIR DESKS IN A CLASSROOM NEAR SOUTHEAST MISSOURI FARMS, NEW MADRID COUNTY, MISSOURI, AUGUST 1938. (RUSSELL LEE, NEW YORK PUBLIC LIBRARY, SCHOMBURG CENTER FOR RESEARCH IN BLACK CULTURE.)

To organize a walkout of Black parents and students in the New York City public school system in support of school integration, Rustin stated "the movement to integrate the schools will create far-reaching benefits." At the March on Washington for Jobs and Freedom in 1963, he read off ten demands of the "Big Six" leaders who organized the event. Two of those demands were for "Adequate and integrated education" and "Desegregation of all school districts."

The blatant resistance to school integration by the likes of Alabama's governor, George Wallace, was a predictable reaction to demands by the civil-rights leadership to change the socio-economic and political balance of power throughout the United States. However, Rustin and the "Big Six" civil rights coalition could not foresee that white America would subvert their efforts to integrate with a variety of schemes endorsed by white politicians. Many communities experienced a variation of these tactics: school district secession, also known as "splinter districts," parents enrolling their children in private or parochial schools, or parents simply moving from cities to majority-white suburbs. In the late 1960s, Rustin supported the largely-white United Federation of Teachers (UFT) against Black activists' and parents' calls for community control of schools in the City of New York.

This idea of community control arose from the Freedom Schools created by the Student Nonviolent Coordinating Committee (SNCC) (which Rustin advised) in Mississippi in 1964. The Freedom Schools' curriculum was designed to explore the personal experiences of students as they pertained to racism while also emphasizing books by Black authors and pan-African history. This was a radical undertaking, especially in a Deep South state like Mississippi during the civil rights era. Nevertheless, the impact of the Freedom Schools would be felt all over the country throughout the 1960s as Black power and Black nationalism became more mainstream.

A bitter power struggle over New York City's schools in 1968 pitted the UFT against Black activists. The call from Black communities for community control came after a lengthy, well-planned, and ultimately fruitless push for school integration in New York, a campaign largely unsupported by white liberal organizations such as the UFT. Because white resistance thwarted Black efforts to integrate education and fully participate in American life, Black parents and activists sought control over segregated schools. While Black activists sought community control to democratize schools, fight racism, and create school jobs for African Americans, teachers' unions saw these goals as undermining due process, job security, and their influence. New York thus became the focal point in the debate over racial disparities in public education. Black activists created a list of demands that they delivered to the school district:

> 1 *The right to hire and fire all principals, assistant principals, and teachers. Those who work hard to teach our children are welcome to stay. Those who won't cooperate—must and will go!*
>
> 2 *Right to control all our own money, in our own bank.*
>
> 3 *That every child in our district gets the same amount of money* [as] *children in white neighborhoods.*
>
> 4 *Right to buy our own books and supplies by direct purchase.*
>
> 5 *Right to build and rehabilitate our schools using Black and Puerto Rican companies and workers from our own communities.*[46]

In response to these demands, New York's mayor, John Lindsay, with funding from the Ford Foundation in 1968, created three community-controlled demonstration districts. These districts included areas such as Harlem, Chinatown, and Ocean Hill–Brownsville. This last area was of particular interest to the UFT because in the early part of the century it had been majority-Jewish but became majority African American and Latino in the 1950s. Despite this, almost every teacher and administrator in the Ocean Hill–Brownsville school district was Jewish. The Ocean Hill–Brownsville experimental school district was headed by Dr. Rhody McCoy, who had been an administrator of Ocean Hill–Brownsville when it was under central board control. McCoy, a Black man, was influenced by Black nationalism and committed to the success of the majority Black and Latino students. Charles Isaac, a Black teacher in the district, stated that "Rhody came with a vision of bringing black nationalism into the classroom, and he stuck with it as long as it was possible." Guided by his Black nationalist ideology, McCoy convened a locally elected board of parents and residents to determine the staffing of schools in the experimental district.

As a result, fifty teachers and administrators who were a part of the UFT were transferred, nineteen of them Jewish. This raised racial tensions, since the community board was mostly Black and because of McCoy's giant personality and unapologetically Black nationalist stance. An arbitration officer determined that the teachers should be reinstated. However, McCoy ignored this order, prompting a thirty-six-day teacher's strike at the beginning of the 1968 fall school term. Although the strike was in progress throughout New York City, with almost a million students affected, the experimental districts in Ocean Hill–Brownsville and in Harlem continued as usual. These districts hired their own teachers and developed their own curricula. According to Marc Pessin, who was a teacher in New York in the late 1960s and a member of the UFT,

> *The curriculum in the community-controlled districts was influenced by Black nationalism, emphasizing Black history, Black struggles and educating people to become activists and to fight for their rights. The local community board developed a curriculum that emphasized Black pride and a restoration of Black history that had not been told in the white-controlled schools. At that time, there were no Black people in the history books except Booker T. Washington and a few abolitionist leaders. The*

curriculum that was developed in these schools gave light to the contributions of Africans and African Americans throughout history. The idea was to give kids pride in themselves, and there was a reawakening around Black pride, Black history, and Black identity.

The influence of Black nationalist ideas and ideals among African Americans nationally was reflected and amplified by the actions of McCoy and the Ocean Hill–Brownsville community control board. In 1968, Rustin, despite his prominent role in the Black civil rights movement, made a conscious effort not to associate with Ocean Hill–Brownsville's Black nationalist activists. He stated that Black people could achieve greater progress through union alignment, with the UFT for example, than with protests focused solely on racial identity. Rustin's dedication to economic equality and integration during the school conflict caused him to distance himself from former allies such as the SNCC, which at that time had evolved into a Black nationalist organization led by H. Rap Brown, and in turn caused Rustin to become a rare prominent Black supporter of the UFT. The union eventually reached a deal with New York City government leaders to once again reinstate the teachers that were transferred and end the strike. The New York legislature ended the experimental districts and replaced them in 1969 with a central school board that once again controlled each of the thirty-two school districts in New York City. For his efforts and support, Rustin won the UFT's Dewey Award in 1968, which many saw as an endorsement of his opposition to Black nationalism and community control. In the 1960s and early '70s, debates over integration, busing, and magnet schools forced Rustin and major civil rights organizations to choose between majority-white labor organizations and Black nationalist ideals. The integration of public schools became the crossroads between respectability politics (civil rights) and Black Nationalism.

Take for example the historically-Black Blake and Middleton high schools in Tampa, Florida. Middleton was founded in 1934 and served majority-Black neighborhoods in East Tampa. Blake High School was founded in 1956 and served the Black neighborhoods of West Tampa. A study called "Schools as Imagined Communities" assessed the damage that was done to both schools and other majority-Black high schools when the Hillsborough County School District (which includes greater Tampa) implemented plans to integrate. In 1971, the Hillsborough County School Board closed Middleton and Blake as a way of meeting the court-ordered a Black–white ratio of 20:80 in each school, without alienating white parents who publicly resisted sending their children to schools in Black neighborhoods. This approach, like others across the nation, placed a disproportionate burden on Black students and parents to desegregate the school system, while greatly limiting busing of white children.

Blake and Middleton high schools, along with many others in predominantly-Black areas, were converted into sixth- or seventh-grade centers. In those communities, many Black first-through-fifth- and eighth-through-twelfth-grade students were transported to the suburbs to attend formerly all-white schools. In turn, white suburban children would be bused to sixth- and seventh-grade centers in the city that were formerly predominantly-Black schools. In the early 2000s, Blake and Middleton were both rebuilt as high schools thanks to community activists and alumni, with majority-Black student bodies and magnet programs. However, since the COVID-19 pandemic and the rise in "school choice" vouchers, their Black populations have decreased and are barely hovering over 50% as Latinos, Asians, and whites increase in number. Also, over the years, East and West Tampa have been a target for redevelopment and gentrification, which has significantly reduced the influence of the Black population in those areas. The establishment of charter schools, including high schools, in those areas, combined with the introduction of "school choice" vouchers and the growth of home schooling, has contributed to Black students leaving the district system.

These realities have greatly affected not only the enrollment at these high schools, but also the vital connection with the community before they closed as high schools in

1971. The story of Middleton and Blake High Schools—established for Black students, closed because of integration, reopened as middle schools, and eventually returned to high schools—is common in Florida and the nation.

The history of Black school closures as a result of integration in the early 1970s shows the schools were always reliant on white-controlled institutions like district school boards and state education departments. The renovation of Black high schools to accommodate white students only happened after they were converted to middle schools in the late '60s and '70s. Additionally, the busing of elementary and high school students from primarily-Black neighborhoods to all-white schools contrasted with the busing of white suburban children only to middle schools in predominantly-Black areas. This is a situation in which institutions ensure that whites continue to maintain an advantage in society. It is a disadvantage for Black students in these situations because they are assigned to schools in distant neighborhoods, mainly suburban, so they have to either ride the school bus or make other arrangements. The distance also prevents the forming of relationships with the new school, and the new school cannot serve as a resource outside of operating hours. It also means waking up a few hours before school starts to catch the school bus. That means less time for sleep, which can harm school performance. The busing of elementary and high school students also caused stress for parents who could not check on their children as easily.

Lavern Hill Brown, a school and public housing activist involved with the movement to "Save Blake," when asked why she and other parents wanted Blake to remain a high school, explained,

> *It was centrally located. Our children would just leave our public housing and go right across the street to school. It was easier for the parent, knowing your child is right across the street. I walked over to the school. I'm going to see about my child, you don't have to worry about bus fare, about getting a ride because*

> *we didn't have cars back then in those times. We were welcome when we would go over there to check on our child. But when we went, when the integration comes about, we could feel it, we could see it. You were not wanted there, they say "What do you want?" "Why are you here, you people?" We're always "you people."*

Black high schools before integration were cultural hubs where students, teachers, and administrators lived in the same neighborhoods and engaged in weekly activities like sports and dances, promoting community pride. The schools also provided services like GED courses for adults after school hours. Integration and busing ended the symbiotic relationship between the school and the community. The schools that did happen to revert to high schools decades after integration had to confront a new set of challenges that could not have been predicted by the alumni who advocated for their return.

Reactivated Black high schools in the early 2000s faced the challenge of adapting to shifting Black culture, alongside broader integration issues like white flight, private schools, and fragmented districts. In the '50s and '60s, Black culture was clearly defined by pride with distinct countercultural styles of appearance (Afros) and ideology (civil rights, Black power). When these schools were reopened, the magnet programs housed in these schools attracted a fair number of students who were not from the neighborhood.

This caused a natural rift with students who were from the neighborhood and those who were not, since the graduating classes had two different valedictorians, two different sets of administrators, different teachers, and different guidance counselors. The school was split into two. Students would also be relegated to different spaces for classes, with the magnet classes at one end of the school and classes for the traditional programs at the other end. In addition, different sections of the neighborhood devolved into cliques which would sometimes clash at the schools. For example, at Middleton High School in 2019, a series of fights culminated in a brawl which caused the police to be called. Several students were taken to the hospital.

In 2017 it was reported that students at Blake High School engaged in fights and brought guns and knives to campus. This violence was not innate in the students but, rather, symptomatic of the stress and disruption caused by integration.

A Black nationalist approach to education, by contrast, would emphasize parental and community control and a curriculum focused on the African American experience. The Black nationalist ideas of self-determination and self-reliance of the race outside of the system of oppression, as opposed to the mainstream civil rights ideology and its respectability politics rooted in working within the system to achieve "equality." Rustin and the "Big Six" civil rights organizations advanced the belief that Black kids sitting next to white kids and being taught by white teachers would "prepare youngsters for the nature of twentieth century life, which again includes automation, technological change."[47] As has been evident since the movement for integration, mainstream Black leadership was ready for integration to equalize the educational opportunities between Blacks and whites. However, whites in power on the school boards, in teacher's unions, and at state departments of education determined the parameters of what would be palpable and advantageous to white students and parents first.

To that end, although the "Big Six" did not recognize it during the 1960s, integration of public schools would go on to become a useful tool for whites to further their programming of servitude of Blacks to whites. This was cemented even further with the integration of majority-Black public high schools which for decades had become cornerstones in Black communities. Those who advocated integration did not take the rich history of these historically-Black high schools into account. What was needed was not forced integration, but the delivery of equitable financial resources to these schools, on par with white schools in suburban districts.

Not everyone within the "Big Six" agreed with the respectability-politics approach, as evidenced by the schism within the SNCC that led to the election of the more radically-minded Stokely Carmichael and H. Rap Brown

STOKELY CARMICHAEL, 1967. (DUKE UNIVERSITY ARCHIVES, DURHAM, NORTH CAROLINA.)

as chairmen in the late 1960s. Since the 1960s, individuals and organizations who propagate Black nationalist ideals in education have opposed educational policies, programs, and norms that are used by whites to dominate Blacks.

The purpose of most formal education in America in the twenty-first century and beyond is to attain the necessary credentials for a particular job. Dr. Amos Wilson argues that African American education would be different if the community prioritized job creation through formal education. He points out that job creation through formal education in the Black community would inspire them to build their own economic and political systems as well as recognizing themselves as key job creators. The act of Black people protesting for jobs and pushing to be employed causes him to ponder an important question: do African Americans know how many jobs they create for other people? Wilson then laments that Black Americans are a job-creating people and they do not realize it because they don't think in terms of nation. He finalizes his point by stating that if Black people saw themselves as a nation, they could see that they create jobs like any other nation.

In other words, if the point of attaining formal educational credentials is to secure jobs, yet Black Americans continue to lag not only in employment but also in salary and wealth, wouldn't the best way forward be for them to use their educational credentials and industry experiences to create their own employment opportunities? This is the question that activists in different spectrums of Black nationalist and

Black Empowerment thought ponder. This is especially true for Black women, who are increasingly earning college degrees yet earning stagnant wages below those of their white counterparts. Data show that public education does not equally prepare Black students compared to white students. On top of everything else, Black students must contend with structural issues such as health disparities, racial discrimination, family instability, and economic inequality that directly affect their education.

For example, the number of Black children under the age of eighteen living in poverty rose from 30% to 37% from 2000 to 2014. In that same period, white children living in poverty remained virtually the same at 12%. National Assessment of Educational Progress (NAEP) results reveal a growing gap in educational achievement, with a higher proportion of Black children living in poverty than white children. The NAEP is measured on a scale from 0 to 500, and in each measurable category Black students lag behind white students. For example, according to the National Center for Education Statistics (NCES), in 1992 white children in the twelfth grade in public schools read at a level of 297 and decreased slightly to 295 by 2015. However, Black children in the twelfth grade read at a level of 273 in 1992 and decreased significantly to 266. Asian students in 2015 read on a scale of 297, while Latinos read on a scale of 276.

In mathematics competency, according to NCES statistics, twelfth-grade white students in public education in 2005 performed at a level of 157 and increased slightly to 160 in 2015. Black students in the twelfth grade performed at 127 in 2005 and increased slightly to 130 in 2015. Asian students in the twelfth grade in 2015 performed at 171, while twelfth-grade Latinos scored at 139. As has been demonstrated in each quantifiable category of meaningful subjects in public education, racial integration has failed to even the playing field between Black and white students. Meanwhile, other minority students such as Asian and Latino students continue to improve compared to Black students.

Compounding the situation, in the 2015-2016 school year, 80% of teachers in the public education system were white while only 7% were Black, alongside 8% Latino and 2% Asian. Also, 77% of teachers during this time were women. The result is that the overwhelming majority of children in the United States are taught by white women. What makes this worse for Black students is that, according to NCES, Black children are raised in the highest percentage of "mother only" households, at 53% (compared to 36% for whites and 28% for Asians), resulting in white women becoming "parents" for Black children because of the amount of time teachers spend with students. This creates a dynamic of Black children during the most critical period of development in their lives not receiving formal educational instruction from someone that not only looks like them but also may share their colloquialisms and culture. This dynamic also plays a part in why integration has failed to equalize educational outcomes between Blacks and whites. Studies have shown that a two-parent home is more stable and beneficial for children to develop the ability to focus and have better educational outcomes in the classroom and consistent adult influences that reinforce a child's culture.

The destabilization of the Black family is not new and has its roots in the transatlantic slave trade. Thousands of African families were forcibly transported to multiple countries and regions in the western hemisphere in the slave trade up until the 1860s. From the point of capture to the perilous travel as cargo across the Atlantic Ocean to the Caribbean islands, to the final act of separating blood relations, each action was designed to fulfill the capitalistic ambition of the colonial powers.

This dehumanization did not stop on the Caribbean islands, however. When those Africans who were captured from Africa completed the seasoning and acclimation process of indoctrination in the Caribbean, they were shipped to mainland America and, again, further separated from their family and kinfolk and all that was familiar before they were sold to another white planter or corporation. The separation did not stop there either. Once on American soil, slaves were frequently sold or even killed for whatever reason that the white master deemed necessary, effectively eradicating the knowledge of lineage, family, and community.

SCREENSHOT OF 2011 "DECOLONIZING OUR UNIVERSITIES" CONFERENCE. (TV MULTIVERSITY, CREATIVE COMMONS LICENSE.)

Nor did the destabilization of Black families stop with the end of slavery, when Blacks were further separated during the Reconstruction and post-Reconstruction era through imprisonment or death by lynching. The reality of the destabilized Black family was established long before the modern era. And now, through laws and social norms, the field of education has become another obstacle for Blacks to establish a base to kill the domination by whites of its community. Molefi Kete Asante, a professor in the Department of Africology at Temple University, has developed a powerful educational framework called Afrocentricity. Asante defines Afrocentricity as "a frame of reference wherein phenomena are viewed from the perspective of the African person. The Afrocentric approach seeks in every situation the appropriate centrality of the African person. In education this means that teachers provide students the opportunity to study the world and its people, concepts, and history from an African world view."

Asante is careful to point out that Afrocentricity is not a Black version of a Eurocentric framework. Eurocentricity is based on white supremacist notions whose purposes are to protect white privilege and advantage in education, economics, politics, and the social order. Unlike Eurocentricity, Afrocentricity does not condone ethnocentric valorization by denigrating other groups' perspectives. Moreover, Eurocentricity presents the historical reality of Europeans as the sum of human experience.[48]

Afrocentricity as an educational tool to train those of African descent with the necessary rigor to kill the white supremacist domination of general education has been around for years. For example, the first iteration of the Nation of Islam created the University of Islam in the 1930s as an elementary school. However, after being reformed by the current Nation of Islam leader, Warith Deen Muhammad, in the 1990s, the University of Islam was re-conceptualized as the "Mohammed Schools," and it eventually progressed to serve primary and secondary grade level students. "Libera-tion Schools" and the Intercommunal Youth Institute, forerunners to Oakland Community School, were established by the Black Panther Party for Self-Defense. Both the Liberation and Mohammed Schools were based in predominantly-Black neighborhoods. Beyond basic subjects like arithmetic, English, and science, their curricula focused on tackling issues affecting Black communities.

The election of George W. Bush in 2000 brought in several educational policies and initiatives, such as the No Child Left Behind Act, passed in 2002, and implementation of standardized testing nationwide to track adequate yearly progress of students. The educational objectives of the Bush administration focused on college-preparatory and vocational curricula, which are the two main structured pathways of course-sequencing in secondary education (sixth through twelfth grade). A college-preparatory curriculum is designed to prepare students for college by requiring them to take standard liberal-arts courses. High school curricula emphasizing vocational education prepare students for immediate employment in technical or skilled fields, such as mechanics or nursing. With the Elementary and Secondary Education Act of 1965 and the Every Student Succeeds Act of 2015, which replaced it, the federal Department of Education has put more emphasis on college-preparatory curricula. Since the federal government is heavily involved in this sphere, in recent years it has strongly encouraged states to measure student success with several metrics, the most controversial being standardized testing.

There have been numerous studies of the negative effects of standardized testing on Black students in secondary education. These mostly involve the orientation of all teaching to desired test outcomes. The testing results revealed serious issues in low-income, inner-city schools with primarily Black and Latino students, leading assessors to conclude that the rigid curriculum and teaching methods yielded rote memorization instead of genuine learning experiences.[49]

Standardized testing has also become a business-industrial complex for state governments and outside vendors as hundreds of millions of tax dollars are spent on contractors to create and administer these tests. However, Florida began the process to become the first state in the nation to eliminate high-stakes, end-of-year standardized testing. Common Core's trademarked curricula formed the basis of Florida's standardized tests before the COVID-19 pandemic. An updated Florida assessment plan, F.A.S.T., is predicted to replace the Common Core–based standardized test. The state claims it will better monitor student progress and foster individual learning more effectively. The possibility of high-stakes standardized testing being eliminated in Florida provides an opportunity for private, charter, and parochial schools to become much more powerful in the state as these schools would no longer have state-mandated assessment requirements but would be free to develop their own. The danger lies in what an individual school or district decides are critical knowledge areas. According to critics, public education suffers due to the use of school vouchers or "choice vouchers," public money used by parents to send their children to private schools.

Voucher programs are controversial in many states because they take away funding from the public-school coffers as those allocations are calculated per student on school enrollment. Fewer students, less money. In 2021, Florida's governor, Ron DeSantis, enacted a $200-million school-choice program projected to expand voucher eligibility to roughly 61,000 new students, funded by taxpayers. DeSantis argued that these vouchers help families pay for private education and other educational costs and put parents in charge of their children's education. A long-standing push to increase school choice options continues with this legislation, drawing Republican support but Democratic opposition due to worries about private school accountability. A key factor in the heated school-voucher discussion is the varied student demographics of private versus public schools. Private schools have largely white student bodies, while public schools have a greater representation of African American and minority students. Private school attendance for African American students, frequently from public schools due to socioeconomic factors, could be increased with vouchers. Many African Americans, according to various surveys, back government-funded initiatives that use taxpayer funds for educational alternatives outside of regular public schools, such as educational savings accounts, charter schools, and vouchers. [50]

In 2020, a key Democrats for Education Reform survey published by *EdHat* revealed that 81% of voters—which includes 81% of Democratic primary voters and 89% of Black Democratic primary voters—favored increased public school choice options, such as magnet schools, career academies, and charter schools. A survey conducted by *EdChoice* in 2019 found that 78% of Democrats, 78% of Republicans, and 77% of independents were in favor of Education Savings Accounts (ESAs), which let families access money usually funneled to school districts to spend on education-related expenses for their children. Current school parents were 85% in favor of ESAs, including 78% of African Americans and 79% of Hispanic respondents.

What this shows is that African American parents are becoming aware of the alternatives to improve their children's prospects. Kayla Svedin, an African American mother in Arizona, advocates for Black parents to explore their options contrary to traditional public schools using school-choice programs:

> *Am I, a Black woman, who makes the conscious decision to utilize a school choice program that benefits my children, choosing to be "anti-Black"? Should*

Black children not have access to educational opportunities that meet their needs simply because of their socioeconomic status or the neighborhood in which they live? Should Black parents not be afforded the respect and deference they deserve when they want to exercise their agency in demanding other options for their children? It is the residentially assigned system of public schooling that has plagued the Black community for far too long, not the options for leaving that system. School choice programs give Black families an alternative to subpar schools, which is why Black "school choice moms" protect those choices with their votes. If anyone is "promoting racism," it is those who are still standing in the schoolhouse door trying to block Black families from entering, or leaving, the schools they wish to. If we really want to reform America's racist system of public education, we should start by empowering Black families with the freedom and resources to choose.

Svedin's pleas for Black parents to seek alternatives to the traditional public schools that are dominated and controlled by whites highlights the abysmal educational outcomes of Black students at traditional public schools. This has been the situation for decades, since the federal government has tracked results by race post-integration. The public education system as currently constructed is ill-equipped to prepare African American students to meet standard educational benchmarks as set forth by the federal government.

Given the racist history of school districts intentionally impeding the success of Black students with biased policies and Eurocentric curricula, Black parents must explore alternative measures. There must be more Black-owned schools, and they must exist where African Americans are concentrated, whether in the inner city, the suburbs, or rural areas. Ideally, African-American-owned schools would attract students of all colors, but their primary mission would be to serve African American students, especially those who had previously been in public schools but for whatever reason were not meeting

YOUNG STUDENTS AT SISTER CLARA MUHAMMAD SCHOOL IN CHICAGO, ILLINOIS, C. 1950S–60S. (CLARA MUHAMMAD FOUNDATION.)

standardized state and federal educational requirements.

These students may also have emotional needs that are not being met at home and are impeding their ability to master the Eurocentric curriculum mandated by school boards and state education departments. Given the predominantly white and female makeup of the teaching staff in public schools, these institutions should prioritize recruiting Black teachers from various ethnicities, genders, and educational backgrounds to promote a diverse range of teaching styles and approaches, but, until white supremacy is defeated in education, Black communities must create their own schools and pedagogy.

These new Afrocentric schools must develop an accountability apparatus where an independent yet powerful board exists to ensure that the goals of the school as well as the state metrics for achievement are met. This board ideally would be composed of parents, teachers, and community members with vested interests in the school. The community members should include activists, elected representatives, and business owners from the local community. This vibrant mix of individuals would give the school a diversity of voices and experiences to address a range of complex issues that may arise. The governing board and school administrators should meet on a consistent basis to ensure that they are keeping up with the latest in compliance and the general day-to-day affairs of the school.

The school should also hold monthly meetings with students, parents, administrators, members of the governing board, and the public to update all stakeholders on the progress of students, current events, and programs that may be available at the institution as well as in the community. In line with Black nationalist principles, the school must also develop initiatives that serve to elevate the community. These initiatives should include health screenings, voter registration, voting polls, after-hours tutoring, clothing drives, community gardening, and adult education programs. Each of these initiatives should encompass programs that are readily available not only to the students but to the public. These programs should be funded independently from the public school district, ideally primarily from private donations and secondarily through government grants. After these conditions are met, a curriculum that centers the experience of African Americans will be ripe for execution.

White students are at an advantage in most classrooms, irrespective of subject, but an Afrocentric curriculum supports African American children's self-esteem by incorporating their history and culture, fostering a sense of belonging and pride. When African American students view themselves as active participants in their education, they shift from passive knowledge-seekers to active contributors. For example, an Afrocentric model of teaching biology could focus on the Black biologist Ernest Just's or another Black biologist's research over a white theorist or researcher.

Since the Trump administration invested billions of dollars in the creation of charter schools during his first administration, creating schools with African-centered curricula would not be as financially challenging as it was in previous administrations. For the 2019 fiscal year, the U.S. Department of Education approved $440 billion dollars for the creation and advancement of charter school programs. In the first few years of the Trump administration, a few Afrocentric schools were created and received additional support from local school districts.

In 2019 the *New York Times* reported on six or so Afrocentric schools in central Brooklyn with roughly 2,300 students. These included private, charter (application-only), and non-zoned public high schools. Black and other minority staff made up most of these schools, which consistently showed high graduation rates and test scores, often at or above the city's public school averages. If these charter schools meet state standards, any principal can create a Black-focused curriculum with Black teachers and Black-culture-focused classes in literature, history, and art, with city approval.[51]

Opponents of Afrocentric schools contend that they harken back to segregation. Andre Perry, a Black researcher at the Brookings Institution, argues that "Segregation leads to inequality. You can't just do that. If you're going to ignore this issue, it will come back to haunt you." Other critics, such as Martell Teasley, dean of the University of Utah College of Social Work, contend that

> *there is need for reflective dialogue around curriculum alignment, instructional strategies, and assessment to make strides on standardized tests which is a major metric for Afrocentric charter schools. It is important that efforts toward school reform ensure that students are exposed to curriculum and instructional strategies that evoke high level academic skills that translate to passing scores on standardized test.*

African-centered education offers advantages beyond standardized test scores, which reflect Eurocentric standards. For years, Rashad Meade, principal of Brooklyn's Eagle Academy for Young Men II, has dedicated himself to finding innovative ways to educate Black boys in Brownsville. After a few years of running the school, Meade recognized the importance of cultivating Black pride for future success in largely white communities. He suggested some of his younger students were grappling with their identities and self-awareness. Jordan Pierre, an Eagle Academy senior who had just completed a Malcolm X biography, noted that such books address young men's societal struggles and portray self-advocacy as revolutionary.

The award-winning Marcus Garvey School in Los Angeles, which ranges from pre-kindergarten to ninth grade, exceeded educational norms for Black students. For example, algebra, trigonometry, and calculus were taught in the fourth grade. Third-graders scored higher than predominantly-white sixth-grade gifted students in reading and math. Amos Wilson suggests that the remarkable achievements of Black students at the Marcus Garvey School stem from its Afrocentric approach, its school culture, and the integration of Black history into all subjects. Nurturing Black identity, instilling pride through Black history, individualized attention, and adaptable pacing also contributed to the development of these students.[52]

In an Afrocentric math model called the Imhotep Program, implemented at Auburn Drive High School, a public school in Nova Scotia, Canada, teachers incorporate discussions about students' cultural backgrounds, history, and lived experiences while teaching them about everything from measurements to surface area to linear equations through an Afrocentric lens. The aim was to encourage tenth-grade Black students to take advanced math and to consider careers in science, technology, engineering, and math. Imhotep's program uses Egyptian pyramids to teach trigonometry, showcasing African culture in math.

Ember Charter School, an Afrocentric lower middle school in Brooklyn's Bedford-Stuyvesant neighborhood, uses an Afrocentric model to empower its students in all subjects and build mental resilience. While children of every race can apply to Ember, the school's enrollment (523 students) is mainly composed of Black and Latino students (516). Ember's educational model is built around Black leadership and the experiences of at-risk and underserved students. The curriculum emphasizes that the world existed before 1492 and the European conquest and colonization of the Americas, through focusing on Black culture and history.

Those who are interested in establishing African-centered schools should aim to effectively educate Black children not just in a liberal-arts curriculum, but also to help them become job-creators and entrepreneurs with the desire and practical knowledge to solve the problems of Black people. However, there are a growing number of parents who are seeking to home-school their children, either partially or full-time. The rise of online delivery fueled by the COVID-19 pandemic presents new possibilities, not only for traditional home-schooling centered on Afrocentric curricula but also for a modernized version that embraces online modular learning.

For instance, in Florida, online learning from kindergarten to twelfth grade is primarily served by Florida Virtual Schools, which supplies course materials to schools and families throughout the country. Reputable accrediting bodies for judging the quality of educational standards such as Cognia and the Southern Association of Colleges and Schools

Commission on Colleges (SACSCOC) have accredited Florida Virtual Schools, its district, and schools since 1997, offering online learning to students nationwide.

In addition to offering full-time online curricula, it also offers courses for students who are home-schooled and students who attend brick-and-mortar institutions part-time. The platform has been growing in demand for several years and since the COVID-19 pandemic has seen a spike in enrollment, going from 5,788 enrolled full-time students for the 2019-2020 pre-pandemic school year to 12,600 students in 2020-2021. Although there are studies that both criticize and promote online and hybrid learning, online delivery of education will probably continue to expand.

As Amos Wilson wrote in the early 1990s,

> *Since Afrocentrism and the Afrocentric movement encompasses Black Nationalism, advocate an economic and social philosophy contrary to that of the ruling white establishment, are avowedly committed to the overthrow of white supremacy and to the development of Pan-Africanist solidarity and independence, all such orientations which are viewed with alarm by the white powers-that-be, it is obvious that the Black media as currently constituted will be of little direct value for achieving true Black liberation. In fact, they may retard its progress in this regard. Consequently, the Afrocentric movement and the movement to develop authentic Black power at home and abroad must continue to develop alternative means of its own to reach the Black masses.*

The act of Black people creating primary and secondary educational institutions to address and solve the problems of the community is itself a display of liberation, power, and nationalism because, without the community having the sacred spaces to educate itself on these issues, solutions that are centered on liberation, power, and nationalism could not be created. To that end, space, no matter whether it is physical or virtual, is necessary if an Afrocentric movement of education is to begin and continue. In addition to the many African-centered brick-and-mortar schools that exist to define the problem and disseminate solutions, a growing number of African-centered curricula and schools that have online platforms have become more visible.

One example of an online Afrocentric school is the Education for Life Academy, which offers live online lectures, an online curriculum, and a certificate program. According to its website, the institution covers Black history from the origins of human life 200,000 years ago in Africa to the contemporary period. By engaging students through an exploration of primary source documents including maps, timelines, newspaper and journal articles, hundreds of photographs, slideshows, documentaries, videos, e-books, and more, Education for Life Academy's "Standing on the Shoulders of Giants" curriculum brings Black history to life.

Kamali Online also offers an online curriculum that is Afrocentric from preschool to eighth grade (ages 6–16). Kamali Online is unapologetic in offering an African-centered curriculum as it specifically state on its website that it was founded on those principles. "Kamali Academy Virtual provides a Live Online Community with Afrikan-Centered Guides who help warrior scholars develop Critical Consciousness through Our story, Character Building, Core Skills, Project and Game-Based Learning, Writer's Workshop sessions, and more. Live Online Sessions for 2+ hours a day for the younger warriors and 3+ hours a day for the older warriors."

The school labels traditional subjects of reading, writing, and math as "core skills" that are taught using "adaptive online systems and educational gaming." Warrior scholars develop crucial real-world skills alongside traditional subjects such as science, social studies, and history through carefully designed projects.

For what would be guided discussions and lectures in public schools, the Kamali Academy again takes an African-centered approach in ensuring that the student is centered in the discussions and activities. At Kamali, instead of lecturing like experts or using leading questions, Guides facilitate discussions in a manner reminiscent of elders sharing wisdom under a baobab tree. A Kamali guide uses scenarios and questions to encourage African-centered critical thinking via discussion and questioning. Pertaining to writing, Kamali Academy emphasizes freedom as well as creative constraints in guiding the student toward writing goals.

Kamali's Writer's Workshop aims to cultivate a lifelong love of writing, reading, and storytelling in young people, empowering them through clear communication. Each session of the Writers' Workshop is based on a different genre. For every session, the guides create a new writing quest, giving students free rein over their topics. As the appetite for alternatives to brick-and-mortar education continues to grow, it is imperative for African-centered educational options to be available for online as well as hybrid delivery. The online platform aligns with the concept of "Education for Liberation" and aims to promote it further.

The ability to move freely while receiving an African-centered education via online at the K-12 level will offer limitless opportunities for children who choose to partake in this form of delivery and instruction. It will also allow parents to monitor their children's learning in real time and further create the symbiotic relationship, albeit virtually, between parent, teacher, and child which is the key ingredient of reinforcement of the material.

Amos Wilson argues that it is incumbent on predominantly-Black colleges and universities and the Black and African-American Studies programs in these and the predominantly-white institutions to develop teaching, training, and research departments in all areas vital to Black people's interest. Majority-Black institutions should require all students to attend courses taught from an African-centered perspective and designed to achieve African-centered ends. This includes business, economics, and the social and physical sciences. Wilson says these schools should be training the community to solve its problems. One would assume that, because they are labeled historically-Black colleges and universities (HBCUs) and that most administrators and faculty at that these institutions are Black, they would create curricula and

ENTRANCE SIGN TO FORT MOSÉ STATE PARK, FLORIDA. (JUSTIN WATERS, CREATIVE COMMON LICENSE.)

provide services that would elevate the standing of Black people in America. However, the purpose of HBCUs is to ensure that its students graduate with a degree that lands them employment with a company or institution most often owned and controlled by white people. Education for this purpose directly conflicts with an education designed to confront and solve the problems of Black people.

Wilson charges that HBCUs exist to do the exact opposite of African-centered education because they are beholden to the white philanthropists that fund their operations. In the early twentieth century, major philanthropists, including John D. Rockefeller via the General Education Board, the American financier George Peabody, the benefactor Caroline Phelp-Stokes, and the businessman Julius Rosenwald, supported the idea of developing a very small number of educational institutions to serve African Americans. They founded two top-tier universities and three mixed-model colleges; these institutions aimed to cultivate leaders who would instill white American values in the Black community. The goal of top-tier Black education was to support and enhance American and Southern industrial productivity. Black intellectuals were still expected to accept the South's and America's racial hierarchy without complaint.

Despite significant funding gaps compared to predominantly-white institutions, HBCUs have received billions in private donations from white philanthropists and corporations since the COVID-19 pandemic. For the 2020-2021 fiscal year, twenty-three HBCUs received a $560-million donation from Mackenzie Scott, the ex-wife of Amazon's executive chairman Jeff Bezos. A $100-million donation to Meharry, Howard, Morehouse, and Charles R. Drew medical schools was made by Michael Bloomberg, the former New York mayor and former chief executive officer of Bloomberg L.P. Before the pandemic, the Charles Koch Foundation and Koch Industries (headed by the brothers Charles and David Koch) donated $26 million dollars to the Thurgood Marshall Scholarship Fund, which supports forty-seven HBCUs. They also donated $25 million dollars to the United Negro College Fund. The Koch brothers are infamous for supporting right-wing conservative causes that leftist critics deem anti-Black. An example of the Koch brothers' problematic stance on race was their inclusion of the controversial political scientist Charles Murray as a keynote dinner speaker at a 2016 summit. Murray co-wrote the 1994 book *The Bell Curve*, which argued Black people have lower IQs than whites and Asians, which contributes to their below-average life outcomes compared to other ethnic groups. Hardly an advocate for Black excellence.

Whether from liberal or conservative sources, one must question the intent of the donations as well as the leverage that white donors gain with the school from their donations. Wilson theorizes that white philanthropists and white-owned corporations that donate to HBCUs acquire the power to dictate not only the curricula at these institutions but also speakers, social activities, and political lobbying.[53] And, because most Blacks who attend these institutions lag in wages and assets yet at the same time have higher amounts of student loan debt compared to their white counterparts, leaving far less discretionary income, it is a challenge for alumni to donate to the HBCUs that they attended. This then puts these institutions in the precarious position of procuring funds from non-Black and, in many cases, anti-Black sources. Wilson highlights how this recurring cycle involving HBCUs and funding prevents liberation curricula from reaching the broader Black population and actively works against the interests of students enrolled at HBCUs which is the lifeblood of those institutions.

The relationship between white funding sources and curriculum development impedes Black nationalist goals. If this is not addressed, HBCU graduates, like graduates from white institutions with sizable Black populations, will be mis-educated on the problems of the Black community. These graduates ultimately will work against their best interests and become effective and unwitting accomplices to white supremacy as individuals and in organizations and corporations. If the insidious relationship between HBCUs and their benefactors is disrupted and HBCUs recommit themselves to Black values and concerns, the African-centered education model can be implemented in higher education. Then, Black students at these institutions can take or demand African-centered courses and earn degrees that prepare them to solve the problems that they will face once graduated, as well as problems that are endemic to the African American community. Once a reorientation to African-centered education is achieved, the community will then be able to enact Black nationalist principles and solve problems associated with the lack of capital, knowledge, and leverage in political, economic, and social spheres. This will then begin the process of killing the psychological effects of white supremacy that have long plagued Black people in America. This will also ready the African American to take on the challenge of recapturing the spaces where they exist, whether it be small neighborhoods or entire city centers, and dominate them fully economically, politically, and culturally to uplift the African Americans in those spaces. African Americans will have to develop a centralized political agenda that addresses the past, solves the problems of the present, and sets itself up for future success. That political program starts with the politics of reparations.

127

CHAPTER FOUR

POLITICAL REPAIR

Since the election of Barack Obama, reparations for African Americans have become the dominant anthem of Black politics. Ta-Nehisi Coates in his 2014 *New Yorker* essay "The Case for Reparations" argued, "Perhaps no statistic better illustrates the enduring legacy of our country's shameful history of treating black people as sub-citizens, sub-Americans, and sub-humans than the wealth gap. Reparations would seek to close this chasm. But as surely as the creation of the wealth gap required the cooperation of every aspect of the society, bridging it will require the same." In the aftermath of COVID-19, two organizations emerged as leading advocates for reparations: the National Coalition of Blacks for Reparations, formed in 1987, and the National African American Reparations Commission, founded in 2015. These organizations have spearheaded national campaigns on the subject and have participated in political hearings about reparations at the local and national level.

Representative John Conyers initially introduced H.R. 3745, a bill proposing a study on reparations for African Americans, in 1989 at the request of the N'COBRA member Ray Jenkins; this later became H.R. 40. From then on, Conyers reintroduced the bill at the start of each congressional session until his 2017 retirement, at which point Representative Sheila Jackson Lee became the main sponsor. Lee organized a House panel hearing on February 17, 2017, to call witnesses in support of and opposition to the bill. Kamm Howard, the co-chair of N'COBRA, testified in favor, arguing that

> *.... during the 32 years in which the bill has languished in Congress, many years have been wasted, many lives lost, and untold sorrows of African descendants have continued and abounded. Even the financial loss to this nation in delaying redress since HR 40's first introduction, is calculated to be near $25 trillion dollars, about two or three times the cost of any minimally viable reparation plan. This means America would have gotten a 100% to 200% return on a reparations program if it had taken the steps to do so. America would in fact be greater today if it had acted correctly at any time in its past. Even still, the opportunity for true greatness can begin with the rightful action of this 117th Congress. HR 40 purports to establish a Commission to do a comprehensive investigation into the wide scope of harms committed and the range of injuries still being suffered by 44 million Black people in America.*

Others who testified at that landmark hearing included Kathy Masaoka, co-chair of Nikkei for Civil Rights & Redress; Dreisen Heath, an assistant researcher and advocate with Human Rights Watch; E. Tendayi Achiume, a professor of law at the UCLA School of Law and a United Nations Special Rapporteur on Contemporary Forms of Racism, Racial Discrimination, Xenophobia, and Related Intolerance; and Hilary O. Shelton, the director of the NAACP's Washington bureau. As of 2025, the bill to explore reparations for African Americans remains stalled in committee.

Nonetheless, there has been movement in the direction of support for reparations by both Black and white Americans.

A 2014 poll conducted by YouGov suggested that 79% of white Americans opposed cash payments as a form of reparations (6% supported; 15% were unsure). In contrast, only 19% of Black Americans were opposed (59% supported and 22% were unsure).[54] In the 2021 poll, 72% of white Americans opposed this form of reparation (28% supported), while only 14% of Black Americans did (86% supported).[55] This positive trend is the result of decades of political efforts by various organizations.

A pioneering group of twenty Black Baptist and Methodist Episcopal preachers, ministers, and elders from Savannah, Georgia, in 1865 formed the first coalition advocating for reparations for African Americans. Edwin Stanton, the U.S. secretary of war, Major General William Tecumseh Sherman of the U.S. Army both consulted with this coalition at a merchant's home to determine the best post-war course for newly freed Black people. The leading figure in the conclave was the sixty-seven-year-old retired minister Garrison Frazier, who spoke for the coalition. A native of Granville County, North Carolina, Frazier was enslaved until he and his wife used $1,000 in gold and silver to buy their freedom in 1857. Although he was a Baptist minister for thirty-five years, Frazier retired because of his declining health.

The purpose of the meeting was to find out what exactly the new freedmen want from the federal government in the form of reparations. What follows are notes of this meeting that were published in February 1865 by the *New York Daily Tribune*, which was considered favorable to the radical Republicans who supported abolition of slavery.

> Sherman: *State in what manner you think you can take care of yourselves, and how can you best assist the Government in maintaining your freedom.*
>
> Frazier: *The way we can best take care of ourselves is to have land, and turn it and till it by our own labor—that is, by the labor of the women and children and old men; and we can soon maintain ourselves and have something to spare. And to assist*

the Government, the young men should enlist in the service of the Government, and serve in such manner as they may be wanted. (The Rebels told us that they piled them up and made batteries of them, and sold them to Cuba; but we don't believe that.) We want to be placed on land until we are able to buy it and make it our own.

Sherman: *State in what manner you would rather live—whether scattered among the whites or in colonies by yourselves.*

Frazier: *I would prefer to live by ourselves, for there is a prejudice against us in the South that will take years to get over; but I do not know that I can answer for my brethren.*

[Mr. Lynch says he thinks they should not be separated, but live together. All the other persons present, being questioned one by one, answer that they agree with Brother Frazier.] [56]

After the meeting, General Sherman issued Special Order 15 four days later, on January 16, 1865. As it pertains to reparations, the order specifically states:

I *The islands from Charleston, South Carolina, the abandoned rice fields along the rivers for thirty miles back from the sea, and the country bordering the St. Johns River, Florida, are reserved and set apart for the settlement of the negroes now made free by the acts of war and the proclamation of the President of the United States.*

II *At Beaufort, Hilton Head, Savannah, Fernandina, St. Augustine and Jacksonville, the blacks may remain in their chosen or accustomed vocations—but on the islands, and in the settlements hereafter to be established, no white person whatever, unless military officers and soldiers detailed for duty, will be permitted to reside; and the sole and exclusive management of affairs will be left to the freed people themselves, subject only to the United States military authority and the acts of Congress. By the laws of war, and orders of the President of the United States, the negro is free and must be dealt with as such.*

III *Whenever three respectable negroes, heads of families, shall desire to settle on land, and shall have selected for that purpose an island or a locality clearly defined, within the limits above designated, the Inspector of Settlements and Plantations will himself, or by such subordinate officer as he may appoint, give them a license to settle such island or district, and afford them such assistance as he can to enable them to establish a peaceable agricultural settlement. The three parties named will subdivide the land, under the supervision of the Inspector, among themselves and such others as may choose to settle near them, so that each family shall have a plot of not more than (40) forty acres of tillable ground, and when it borders on some water channel, with no more than 800 feet water front, in the possession of which land the military authorities will afford them protection, until such time as they can protect themselves, or until Congress shall regulate their title.*[57]

From the exchange between Sherman and Frazier and subsequent field order by Sherman, it can be concluded that a sizable contingent of Southern African Americans after the Civil War not only desired their own land to govern themselves but also preferred to live separately from whites. This amounts to a nationalist position, in Martin Delany's terms. The prejudice which Frazier said "will take years to get over" has unfortunately never subsided. In fact, one could argue that the prejudice of white people in general and the government in particular intensified not long after the Sherman order was submitted to President Lincoln.

The historian Henry Louis Gates writes that the reaction to the order was instantaneous. A February 1865 *Christian Recorder* printing of the meeting's transcript included an editorial comment suggesting that Southern Black people were more intelligent than many believed, highlighting ongoing North–South and class tensions within the Black community that persisted into the modern civil rights era. Gates states that the South was electrified by the effect, and freedmen quickly used the order to their advantage. The Baptist minister Ulysses L. Houston, a member of the group of leaders that had met with Sherman, led 1,000 blacks to Skidaway Island, Georgia, where they established a self-governing community with Houston as the "'Black governor." By June, Gates indicates that "Sherman Land" had provided homes for 40,000 freedmen across 400,000 acres. The phrase "forty acres and a mule" was coined when Sherman directed his army to give the new settlers their mules. Established in March 1865, the Freedmen's Bureau assisted former slaves in their transition to citizenship, and it facilitated land redistribution following Sherman's directives. Weeks after the settlements commenced, Lincoln was assassinated, on April 15, 1865. After Lincoln's death, President Andrew Johnson overturned Sherman's order, returning the land to its former Confederate owners, with a proclamation on May 29, 1865, pardoning all former slaves who fought for the Confederates and any whites who swore an oath to never enslave a person.

The Oath read as follows:

> *I, [Name], declaring that I do, freely and forever, disclaim, and that I will never assert, right or title to slaves, and that I will never hereafter own a slave, or any interest therein, pursuant to the President's proclamation of date — day of —, 1865, do solemnly swear (or affirm) in the presence of Almighty God that I will henceforth faithfully protect and defend the Constitution of the United States, and the union of the States thereunder.*

Johnson's pardons coupled with the Freedman's Bureau's restoration of settled lands to planters set the stage for thousands of Black families to be evicted from the so called "Sherman Land." On September 12, 1865, Commissioner Oliver Otis Howard (for whom Howard University is named) issued Circular No. 15. This document specifically states:

> *Abandoned Lands held by this Bureau may be restored to owners pardoned by the President, by the Asst Commissioners to whom applications for such a restoration should be forwarded, so far as practicable through the Superintendents of the Districts in which the lands are situated. Each application must be accompanied by—1st: Evidence of especial pardon by the President, or a copy of the oath of amnesty prescribed in the President's Proclamation of May 29, 1865, when the applicants is not included in any of the classes therein exempted from the benefits of said oath. 2nd: Proof of title.*

After Howard's decree, former planters regained their land and reestablished their plantations. With nowhere to go, millions of freedmen who did not have legal titles to the land continued to till those same lands but now as sharecroppers for former slave-masters. Since the rescinding of Special Order No. 15, African American groups and companion organizations have attempted to argue for reparations based on the original 1865 proposition.

The first of these organizations founded in the post-Reconstruction era was the Ex-Slave Pension Club, founded by the former Confederate captain Walter Vaughn. Vaughan, who was white, increasingly argued that the federal government owed a debt to the former slaves. Between 1890 and 1903, Vaughan persuaded congressmen from Nebraska, Illinois, Kansas, Alabama, North Carolina, and Ohio to sponsor bills in the U.S. Congress, all containing essentially identical language, proposing an ex-slave pension. To promote his cause, Vaughan formed the fraternal organization Vaughan's Ex-Slave Pension Club, with membership open to any African American over

FORMERLY ENSLAVED MOTHER CALLIE HOUSE BEGAN LEADING THE NATIONAL EX-SLAVE MUTUAL RELIEF, BOUNTY AND PENSION ASSOCIATION IN THE 1890S. (RECORDS OF THE DEPARTMENT OF VETERANS AFFAIRS.)

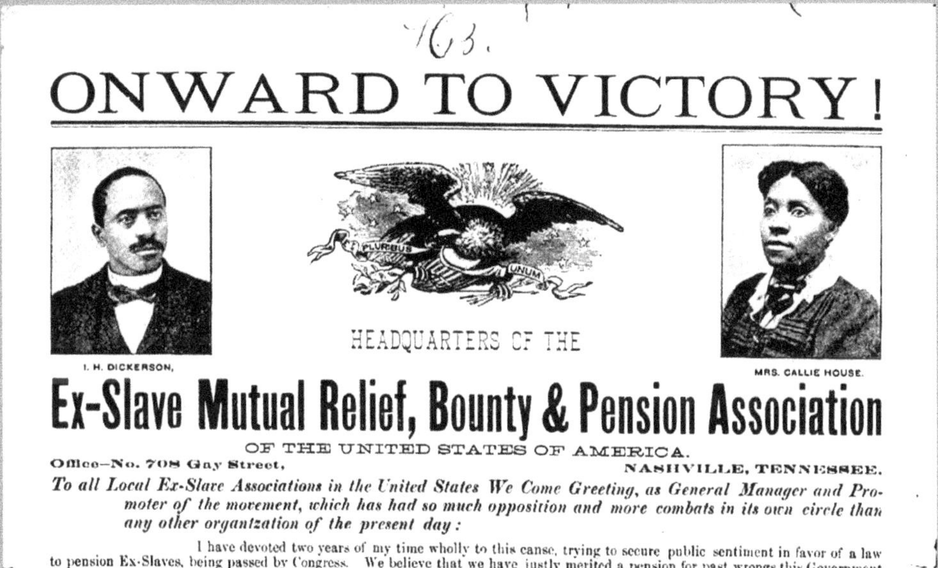
163.

ONWARD TO VICTORY!

I. H. DICKERSON,

HEADQUARTERS OF THE

MRS. CALLIE HOUSE.

Ex-Slave Mutual Relief, Bounty & Pension Association

OF THE UNITED STATES OF AMERICA.

Office—No. 708 Gay Street, NASHVILLE, TENNESSEE.

To all Local Ex-Slave Associations in the United States We Come Greeting, as General Manager and Promoter of the movement, which has had so much opposition and more combats in its own circle than any other organtzation of the present day:

I have devoted two years of my time wholly to this canse, trying to secure public sentiment in favor of a law to pension Ex-Slaves, being passed by Congress. We believe that we have justly merited a pension for past wrongs this Government sixteen years of age. Each member paid an initial fee of 25¢ and 10¢ monthly thereafter, with the funds used for lobbying Congress for passage of the legislation. The continued lobbying resulted in the first ex-slave pension bill, H.R. 11119, which was introduced by Rep. William Connell of Nebraska in 1890.[58]

Frederick Douglass also directly influenced Vaughn. In a letter to Vaughn, Douglass wrote:

> *The Egyptian bondsmen went out with the spoils of his master, and the Russian serf was provided with farming tools and three acres of land upon which to begin life, but the Negro had neither spoils, implements nor lands, and today he is practically a slave on the very plantation where formerly he was driven to toil under the lash.*

Another organization that advocated for reparations was the National Ex-Slave Mutual Relief, Bounty and Pension Association. The Reverend I. H. Dickerson, who was Black, organized the association in 1897 in Nashville, Tennessee.[59] He stated the objective of the group was

> *to unite all the ex-slaves and their friends in petitioning Congress to pass the Mason Bill, first introduced into the lower House of Congress by W. J. Cornell, of Nebraska, on June 24, 1890, as H.B. 1119, by W.R. Vaughan's request; and in the Senate on February 6, 1896, by Senator Thurston of Nebraska, and also for mutual assistance of all its members in good standing.*

Following Dickerson's death, Callie D. House became s ecretary and took control of the association. Throughout the South, the Mutual Relief, Bounty and Pension Association sponsored numerous groups and agents, convening annually. Resolutions and petitions advocating for the pension bill's passage were created during the meetings.

The organization backed a pension plan based on beneficiary age, a feature of every post-1899 ex-slave bill.

The plan stipulated that ex-slaves seventy and over at payout time would get a $500 start-up payment and $15 per month afterward. Those sixty to sixty-nine would get a $300 payment plus $12 monthly, while those aged fifty to fifty-nine would receive $100 and $8 monthly. Lastly, a $4 monthly pension would go to those under fifty. Compensation was to be provided for caretakers of former slaves who were elderly or unable to care for themselves. A higher pension became available to former slaves after reaching a particular age.

Other organizations from that period which advocated for reparations included the Ex-Slave Petitioner's Assembly, the Western Division Association, the Ex-Slave Pension Association of Texas, the Great National Ex-Slave Union, Congressional Legislative, and Pension Association of U.S.A., and the Ex-Slave Pension Association of Kansas. Although none of these organizations gained traction with legislators in getting reparations bills signed into law, they did lay a foundation for Black politics.

Black leaders who advocated for political nationalism throughout the centuries included Robert F. Williams, Assata Shakur, Richard Wright, Wilson Jeremiah Moses, W. E. B. Du Bois, and Kwame Nkrumah. These leaders advocated for policies centered on specific benefits for African Americans, whether it be reparations in the form of land, cash payments, or tax deductions based on their lineage that is traceable to the plantations in the United States. They also implored African Americans to become more self-reliant by relying less on the white power structure that oppresses them. The sociologist J. Herman Blake argues that Black nationalism has been expanded to include an emphasis upon land and on self-determination for Black communities and accountability of Black leaders. [60]

Although physical separation may not be realistic for the majority of African Americans, Black nationalist ideology will remain relevant as long as America's political and economic institutions function to directly and indirectly undermine the advancement of African Americans. Remnants of political nationalism throughout the 1960s and into the 1970s continued to influence those who aligned with civil-rights advocacy or Black power groups. The two most prominent leaders associated with civil rights and Black power in the modern era were and continue to be Martin Luther King, Jr., and Malcolm X, though they had different approaches to the question of Black nationalism.

Malcolm X believed that self-defense by "any means necessary" was essential for African Americans to maintain and fight for their human rights, while King believed in nonviolent confrontation to attain civil rights. In King's and Malcolm X's leadership roles in the Southern Christian Leadership Conference (SCLC) and in the Nation of Islam and Organization of Afro-American Unity (OAAU), respectively, they both fought for equal access to resources for Black Americans during their lifetime and, after their deaths, their work continued.

Malcolm X was born Malcolm Little on May 19, 1925, in Omaha, Nebraska. During his childhood, Jim Crow laws and the influence of the Ku Klux Klan were at their zenith in the South and Midwest. The KKK used lynching to maintain white supremacy over African Americans. Malcolm personally witnessed the inequalities in America as his family was targeted by KKK members and was forced to move from Omaha to Lansing, Michigan, because of threats from them. There, a militant extremist sub-group of the KKK called the Black Legionnaires burned down the Little family home in 1931.

Malcolm's mother thought the Black Legion had killed his father for his ties to Marcus Garvey's UNIA. Malcolm's ideas about systemic racism were formed by his mother's beliefs. He recalled his father's belligerence toward his siblings, but not him, and believed his lighter skin was the reason for his father's favoritism, despite his anti-white views. Malcolm's childhood experiences were described by him in his autobiography as being desolate after the death of his father beginning with four of his uncles being murdered shortly after his father's death. His mother was placed in an institution because of a mental breakdown, and his siblings were sent to multiple foster homes. Unlike his brothers and sisters, Malcolm, due to his lighter skin color, was placed in a white home, in a neighborhood that would be considered middle- to high-class. As the only Black student at an otherwise all-white school, he learned to fit in and gain acceptance from white people. Although his environment changed, Malcolm had repeated experiences that reminded him of the challenges of a racist environment. One example of thousands of incidents is when one of his white teachers explained that his dream of having a career in law was not a reality for "a nigger."

Although he was at the top of his class, Malcolm dropped out of high school at age fifteen. He reached a low point in his life during which he got caught up in dealing drugs, robberies, and prostitution, which landed him in jail in 1946. His brother introduced him to Elijah Muhammad's teachings during his imprisonment. Once his sentence had ended, after his conversion, he rapidly ascended within the Nation of Islam. Malcolm, aligned with Nation practices of the time, changed his last name from Little to X because the Nation held that the surnames given to American Blacks were considered "slave names." The X represented the unknown name of African ancestors and the culture that had been lost during slavery. This is also around the time Malcolm became the spokesperson for the Nation of Islam. In his later role as Minister, he eloquently conveyed Black nationalist solutions to the problems that African Americans faced.

In contrast to King, Malcolm X believed that nonviolence was not necessary for African Americans to gain respect for their humanity. His departure from the Nation of Islam in 1964 and subsequent founding of the OAAU and Muslim Mosque, Inc., broadened his perspective on race in America. In the last year of his life, he was challenged by a participant at one of his meetings to "tell us where you're at with them white folks." His response was, "I haven't changed. I just see things on a broader scale." He said in a speech on March 18, 1964,

> *Already we have begun to get responses from so-called Negro students from coast to coast, who aren't actually religiously inclined, but who are*

> *nonetheless strongly sympathetic to the approach used by Black Nationalism, whether it be social, economic, or political. And with this new approach and with these new ideas we think that we may open up a new era here in this country. As that era begins to spread, people in this country—instead of sticking under your nose or crying for civil rights—will begin to expand their civil rights plea to a plea for human rights. And once the so-called Negro in this country forgets the whole civil rights issue and begins to realize that human rights are far more important and broad than civil rights, he won't be going to Washington, D.C., anymore, to beg Uncle Sam for civil rights. He will take his plea for human rights to the United Nations. There won't be a violation of civil rights anymore. It will be a violation of human rights. Now at this moment, the governments that are in the United Nations can't step in, can't involve themselves with America's domestic policy. But the day the black man turns from civil rights to human rights, he will take his case into the halls of the United Nations in the same manner as the people in Angola, whose human rights have been violated by the Portuguese in South Africa.*

Malcolm X's activism, including his promotion of Black nationalism and his appeal to the United Nations to investigate U.S. human rights abuses, led the FBI and other government agencies to initiate public smear campaigns against him and the Nation of Islam. The FBI referred to Malcolm X in classified files as "a militant figure in the civil rights field."

Born in Atlanta, Georgia, on January 15, 1929, Martin Luther King, Jr., was raised with Christian values in the Black Baptist tradition. His family wasn't wealthy at all, but his upbringing was stable due to his mother's position as a teacher and his father's as a pastor. King's childhood neighborhood, during the Great Depression, was middle-class, had very low crime, and was strongly Christian. His first experience with racial segregation came at the age of five when a white friend's father prohibited his son from playing with him because of his skin color. During childhood, King was heavily influenced by his traditional religious upbringing and by W. E. B. Du Bois's philosophy focused on attaining education. His time at Morehouse College, Crozer Theological Seminary, and Boston University's School of Theology greatly expanded his worldview. At Morehouse he read Henry David Thoreau's influential essay "Civil Disobedience," and in graduate school Mahatma Gandhi's works shaped his views on nonviolent demonstrations.

During the Montgomery bus boycott in 1955, King was a staunch advocate for civil disobedience. It proved to be extremely effective in Montgomery, resulting in the lifting of racial restrictions in the public transportation system. He maintained that nonviolent resistance was a highly effective method for achieving justice, benefiting not only Black people but all oppressed groups. The aftermath of the bus boycotts saw King and his family subjected to harassment, a bombing of their home, and an overwhelming amount of hate mail from white supremacists. Armed Black volunteers were eventually assigned to guard his home.

Despite these circumstances, King continued to promote the ideals of civil disobedience and nonviolence. In a 1957 speech, "Birth of a New Nation," King said, "The aftermath of nonviolence is the creation of the beloved community. The aftermath of nonviolence is redemption. The aftermath of nonviolence is reconciliation. The aftermath of violence is emptiness and bitterness." King argued against violence as a means for racial justice, deeming it both ineffective and unethical. He believed Malcolm X's tactics only incited further violence, resulting in an endless cycle of aggression by both whites and Blacks. King's integrationist beliefs were in direct opposition to Malcolm X's advocacy for separatism and Black nationalism. Compared to Malcolm X's philosophies, King's advocacy for integrationist policies, once considered radical by white America, now seemed moderate. A contingent of Blacks, including Malcolm X, thought that King's methods amounted to nothing more than accommodating white supremacy in its domination of Black Americans.

The King Institute today notes that King always stressed the active parts of his nonviolent method and that the refusal to physically hurt others was the only dimension that was passive. King's unwavering commitment to nonviolence was evident from the Montgomery bus boycott of 1955 to the Selma march of 1965. The success of the 1960 student sit-ins, the 1961 Freedom Rides, the 1963 Birmingham demonstrations, and the 1963 March on Washington for Jobs and Freedom also proved his philosophies to be effective in influencing sweeping change.[61] The media coverage was dramatized by the stark contrast between the nonviolent movement and the violent actions of white radicals. The 1964 Civil Rights Act and the 1965 Voting Rights Act gained momentum due to his commitment to nonviolence. However, the Watts riots in 1965 and the rise of the Black power movement in 1966 caused many young Black activists to question King's nonviolent approach.

THE REV. MARTIN LUTHER KING, JR. AND MALCOLM X MEET AT THE U.S. SENATE ON MARCH 26, 1964, AFTER A HEARING ON THE 1964 CIVIL RIGHTS ACT. (LIBRARY OF CONGRESS.)

In contrast to King, Malcolm X advocated Black nationalist philosophy, but many of King's critics, including Malcolm X, still admired his dedication to Black rights. Many white people lauded King's commitment to nonviolence but later rejected him for his public anti-war stance. From 1966 to 1968, the fragmentation of the Big Six Council for United Civil Rights Leadership weakened the overall movement. King's "Beyond Vietnam" speech, which labeled America the "greatest purveyor of violence," damaged his standing with both white and Black Americans.

King's antiwar sentiment during the Vietnam War also created tension between him and President Lyndon B. Johnson. A sizeable portion of the country viewed King as a civil rights activist that did not have the credibility to comment on foreign affairs. King initiated the Poor People's Campaign in response to the Vietnam War, demanding an end to the war and a stronger commitment to poverty reduction. On December 4, 1967, King detailed the Poor People's Campaign's objectives:

> *The Southern Christian Leadership Conference will lead waves of the nation's poor and disinherited to Washington, D.C., next spring to demand redress of their grievances by the United States government and to secure at least jobs or income for all. We will go there; we will demand to be heard and we will stay until America responds. If this means forcible repression of our movement, we will confront it, for we have done this before. If this means scorn or ridicule, we embrace it, for that is what America's poor now receive. If it means jail, we accept it willingly, for the millions of poor already are imprisoned by exploitation and discrimination. In short, we will be petitioning our government for specific reforms and we intend to build militant, nonviolent actions until that government moves against poverty.*

King also advocated for reparations to African Americans, arguing in a speech in 1967,

> *Our government was giving away millions of acres of land... not only did they give the land they built land grant colleges with government money to teach them how to farm, not only that, they provided county agents to further their expertise in farming, not only that, they provided low interest rates in order to mechanize their farms not only that, today these people are receiving millions of dollars not to farm and they are the very people telling the Black man that he needs to lift himself up by his own boot straps... this is what we are faced with! this is the reality! Now when we come to Washington in this campaign we are coming: to get our check!*

King's expansion of the civil rights movement for Blacks to a class movement for poor people—most of whom were Black—was akin to Malcolm X's move to being an advocate for human rights. The FBI also noted that King "had been influenced by Communist advisers." (In addition to King and Malcolm X, hundreds of lesser-known civil rights and Black nationalist leaders were targeted for surveillance and "covert ops" by the United States government.) In that sense, toward the ends of their lives, the objectives of both Malcolm X and King converged. Both ended up taking general Black nationalist approaches by advocating for the self-determination and unity of Black people and by resisting the oppression of white supremacy.

While their goals were alike, the difference was how and why they pursued them. Both sought to address the problem of inequality between Blacks and whites in America. Malcolm X's goal was for Blacks to control their own resources by way of political and economic nationalism. King's aspirations were for full integration and specific benefits for people based on race and class. Malcolm X's pursuit of his goals might involve violence, unlike King's strictly peaceful approach. Though unlikely allies during their prime, they eventually came to appreciate each other's viewpoints and goals in their later years. The men converged in their views on the necessity of powerful Black institutions, the effective use of nonviolent resistance in Black activism with a focus on human rights, and the significance of positive Black identity, all principles that are essential to Black nationalism.

In a speech in 1963, Malcolm X argued that the Kennedy administration "is only using civil rights as a political football to gain more legislation and power for itself. Our people are being used as pawns in the game of power politics by political hypocrites." During the question-and-answer session, he was asked why African Americans can't infiltrate the political machine and use power politics for themselves. He responded,

> *If he studies the science of politics, he probably would. Most Negroes don't. They become involved politically from an emotional point of view rather than a scientific point of view. You show me a Negro politician, and I'll show you one who's controlled by the white political machine. And if you show me one who isn't controlled by the white political machine, I'll show you one whom the white political machine has labeled as a racist, an extremist.*
>
> *Adam Powell is one of the best examples of it. Anyone that they endorse, who will do what they want him to do, he's all right. But when you become politically independent in this country, the white media, they label you as a racist. The reason for this is, the only way you can become politically independent of the white political machine is to have the support of the Black masses. The only way you can get the support of the Black masses is to say how they think and how they feel. And when you begin to speak to the Black masses, how they feel and think, then the whites call you a racist. Because you have to talk in the context of the intense degree of dissatisfaction that exists in the Negro community. Whites don't want to hear this. They want to be told that the problem is being solved. You're not solving the problem for anybody but a few handpicked, Uncle Tom Negroes who benefit from your token integration.*

CIVIL RIGHTS LEADERS ROY WILKINS, JAMES FARMER, MARTIN LUTHER KING, JR., AND WHITNEY YOUNG MEET WITH PRESIDENT JOHNSON AT THE WHITE HOUSE ON JANUARY 18, 1963. (YOICHI OKAMOTO, LYNDON BAINES JOHNSON LIBRARY AND MUSEUM.)

In this response, Malcolm X outlines several Black nationalist points that remain relevant. African Americans evaluating politics from an emotional perspective instead of scientifically has led them to vote for one party overwhelmingly in national elections since 1964. The motivating emotions were based on President John F. Kennedy, a Democrat, arguing for civil rights in June 1963 on public radio and then introducing a civil rights bill to Congress later that summer. After Kennedy was assassinated, Johnson took up the mantle of the civil rights bill and was able to get it through Congress with the help of Representative Adam Clayton Powell, Jr., ultimately signing it in July 1964. During the signing, Johnson shook hands with King, solidifying the practical yet emotional relationship that African Americans would have with the Democratic Party for generations.

In saying that the Black politician is controlled by the political machine, Malcolm X alludes to the number of interests that Black politicians must appease as they climb up the political ladder. Aside from the desires of their constituents, who may be majority white depending on the district, Black politicians, like all politicians, must contend with political action committees, lobbying organizations, consumer advocacy groups, and the platform of their own party. Political action committees are often fronts for corporations and the extremely wealthy to influence politicians and political parties with campaign financing. Lobbying organizations use public opinion and leverage the use of affiliated political action committees to influence politicians.

The *Congressional Quarterly Almanac* published in 1961 reported that the 1960 presidential and congressional election campaigns cost $28,326,322, encompassing 189 political committees and sixty-seven Senate and 825 House candidates. Of the $28.3 million total, $23.5 million was reported by national-level committees and $4.8 by candidates and committees in individual Congressional campaigns. Republicans reported $14.7 million, Democrats $10.2 million, and combined labor groups $2.5 million, with the remaining $0.92 million recorded by minor parties and unaffiliated political groups.[62] Estimates of the total cost of the 1960 primary elections have reached as much as $175 million. An indicator of how hard it was to track campaign contributions under the regulations of that time is the fact that not one member of the Kennedy family appears in the long list of contributors of $500 or more compiled from the reports to the House and Senate. As the Kennedys were very wealthy and had considerable interest in the 1960 campaign, it is inconceivable that none of them made such contributions. Similar situations among both Republicans and Democrats explain why the reported contributions are considered much lower than the actual total.

Black politicians with national aspirations must support agendas that they may not agree with or that may not benefit Black people because of the political action committees that donate to their campaigns. During the 1960s, the main issues for African Americans were integrating public institutions and private businesses and fighting anti-Black discrimination. Legislative wins for the Big Six included the 1964 Civil Rights Act and the 1965 Voting Rights Act, but the process for attaining these victories by the Big Six was arduous and led to disagreements over funding, which eventually led to its demise as a civil rights cooperative.

The Big Six—the Southern Christian Leadership Council (SCLC), the Congress of Racial Equality (CORE), the Student Nonviolent Coordinating Committee (SNCC), the National Urban League, the National Council of Negro Women, and the National Association for the Advancement of Colored People (NAACP)—were the face of Black politics during the civil rights era. On the morning of June 19, 1963, a group of Big Six leaders—A. Philip Randolph, Bayard Rustin, John Lewis, Martin Luther King Jr., James Farmer, Roy Wilkins, Whitney Young, and Dorothy Height—appealed to wealthy individuals gathered inside the Carlyle Hotel. No journalists reported from inside the meeting, and no records exist of who attended. Wilkins spoke first, then left to attend Medgar Evers's burial at Arlington National Cemetery. Height spoke about police abuse toward Black women in the South. The historian Evan Faulkenbury noted that Height stated, "At the end of the discussion, Whitney Young made it plain that all of us knew more about what needed to be

THE CARLYLE HOTEL, NEW YORK CITY.
(NEW YORK TIMES ARCHIVES.)

done and how to do it than our resources would allow. We are all hurting."[63] Stephen Currier, who was white, picked up the total bill of $1,062.85 for renting the meeting space. The 1963 breakfast motivated the ninety-six attendees to pledge $1,500,000 to the newly formed but still nameless collective by the end of 1964. Because funds were arriving and more were expected, Currier and the civil rights leaders agreed that the new umbrella organization should allocate funds and comply with federal tax laws. The organization received its official name, the Council for United Civil Rights Leadership (CUCRL), a few days following the breakfast meeting. In its early stages, the CUCRL was both a financial clearinghouse and a continuation of the Assessment Project's monthly meetings, distributing funds to members and establishing a framework for consistent communication, with financial backing from the Ford and Rockefeller Foundations as well as Currier's Taconic Foundation. By mid-July of 1963, $565,000 had been raised, and by the end of August the group had collected $800,000 from several sources. Although the CUCRL as an organization did not officially form a political action committee, it funded the lobbying activities of the Big Six at its founding since, up until that time, none of the six was registered as a 501(c)3 charity organization and they operated on small budgets and relied on volunteers.[64]

Malcolm X criticized this meeting and the subsequent CUCRL in his "Message to the Grassroots" speech delivered on November 10, 1963:

> *And Negroes was out there in the streets. They was talking about [how] we was going to march on Washington. By the way, right at that time Birmingham had exploded, and the Negroes in Birmingham—remember, they also exploded. They began to stab the crackers in the back and bust them up 'side their head—yes, they did. That's when Kennedy sent in the troops, down in Birmingham. So, and right after that, Kennedy got on the television and said "this is a moral issue." That's when he said he was going to put out a civil-rights bill. And when he mentioned civil-rights bill and the Southern crackers started talking about [how] they were going to boycott or filibuster it, then the Negroes started talking—about what? We're going to march on Washington, march on the Senate, march on the White House, march on the Congress, and tie it up, bring it to a halt; don't let the government proceed. They even said they was going out to the airport and lay down on the runway and don't let no airplanes land. I'm telling you what they said. That was revolution. That was revolution. That was the Black revolution. It was the grass roots out there in the street. [It] scared the white man to death, scared the white power structure in Washington, D.C., to death; I was there. When they found out that this Black steamroller was going to come down on the capital, they called in Wilkins; they called in Randolph; they called in these national Negro leaders that you respect and told them, "Call it off." Kennedy said, "Look, you all letting this thing go too far." And Old Tom said, "Boss, I can't stop it, because I didn't start it." I'm telling you what they said. They said,*

"I'm not even in it, much less at the head of it." They said, "These Negroes are doing things on their own. They're running ahead of us." And that old shrewd fox, he said, "Well if you all aren't in it, I'll put you in it. I'll put you at the head of it. I'll endorse it. I'll welcome it. I'll help it. I'll join it." A matter of hours went by. They had a meeting at the Carlyle Hotel in New York City. The Carlyle Hotel is owned by the Kennedy family; that's the hotel Kennedy spent the night at, two nights ago; [it] belongs to his family. A philanthropic society headed by a white man named Stephen Currier called all the top civil-rights leaders together at the Carlyle Hotel. And he told them that, "By you all fighting each other, you are destroying the civil-rights movement. And since you're fighting over money from white liberals, let us set up what is known as the Council for United Civil Rights Leadership. Let's form this council, and all the civil-rights organizations will belong to it, and we'll use it for fund-raising purposes." Let me show you how tricky the white man is. And as soon as they got it formed, they elected Whitney Young as the chairman, and who [do] you think became the co-chairman? Stephen Currier, the white man, a millionaire. Powell was talking about it down at the Cobo [Hall] today. This is what he was talking about. Powell knows it happened. Randolph knows it happened. Wilkins knows it happened. King knows it happened. Every one of that so-called Big Six—they know what happened. Once they formed it, with the white man over it, he promised them and gave them $800,000 to split up between the Big Six; and told them that after the march was over, they'd give them $700,000 more. A million and a half dollars—split up between leaders that you've been following, going to jail for, crying crocodile tears for. And they're nothing but Frank James and Jesse James and the what-do-you-call-'em brothers. [As] soon as they got the setup organized, the white man

made available to them top public relations experts; opened the news media across the country at their disposal; and then they begin to project these Big Six as the leaders of the march. Originally, they weren't even in the march. You was talking this march talk on Hastings Street—Is Hastings Street still here?—on Hastings Street. You was talking the march talk on Lenox Avenue, and out on—What you call it?—Fillmore Street, and Central Avenue, and 32nd Street and 63rd Street. That's where the march talk was being talked. But the white man put the Big Six [at the] head of it; made them the march. They became the march. They took it over. And the first move they made after they took it over, they invited Walter Reuther, a white man; they invited a priest, a rabbi, and an old white preacher. Yes, an old white preacher. The same white element that put Kennedy in power—labor, the Catholics, the Jews, and liberal Protestants; [the] same clique that put Kennedy in power, joined the march on Washington ... I know you don't like what I'm saying, but I'm going to tell you anyway. 'Cause I can prove what I'm saying. If you think I'm telling you wrong, you bring me Martin Luther King and A. Philip Randolph and James Farmer and those other three, and see if they'll deny it over a microphone. No, it was a sellout. It was a takeover. When James Baldwin came in from Paris, they wouldn't let him talk [at the March on Washington], 'cause they couldn't make him go by the script. Burt Lancaster read the speech that Baldwin was supposed to make; they wouldn't let Baldwin get up there, 'cause they know Baldwin's liable to say anything. They controlled it so tight they told those Negroes what time to hit town, how to come, where to stop, what signs to carry, what song to sing, what speech they could make, and what speech they couldn't make; and then told them to get out town by sundown. And everyone of those Toms was out of town by sundown. Now I know you don't like

> *my saying this. But I can back it up. It was a circus, a performance that beat anything Hollywood could ever do, the performance of the year. Reuther and those other three devils should get a Academy Award for the best actors 'cause they acted like they really loved Negroes and fooled a whole lot of Negroes. And the six Negro leaders should get an award too, for the best supporting cast.*

The Big Six organizations continued to advocate integration, with the CUCRL serving as the funding arm of these endeavors. Although Stephen Currier's death in 1967 was a contributing factor in the disbanding of the CUCRL that year, so were long-standing disagreements among the organizations that received funding from it. Points of contention ranged from disbursement to ideology to strategies. When CORE and the SNCC started to embrace Black nationalism after the death of Malcolm X in 1965, this compounded some of the differences.

However, the CUCRL's impact cannot be denied. It contributed to the passage of the Civil Rights Act of 1964, the Voting Rights Act of 1965, and, ultimately, the Fair Housing Act of 1968. By this point the constituent organizations appeared, on the surface, to be achieving their goals of social progress.

However, what these organizations and leaders failed to anticipate was that forced integration alone wouldn't improve the status of Black Americans or alter white perceptions of Black people, as H. Rap Brown pointed out in his autobiography *Die Nigger Die* in 1969:

> *White people got hung up on integration. Segregation was the problem and the elimination of segregation was the solution, not integration. It was the unequal nature of segregation that Black people protested against in the South, not segregation itself. Separate but equal is cool with me. What's the big kick about going to school with white folks? Them that want to do that should have the chance. But that ain't no solution.*

H. RAP BROWN (JAMIL ABDULLAH AL-AMIN) AT A WASHINGTON, D.C., PRESS CONFERENCE, JULY 27, 1967. THE BANDAGE ON HIS FOREHEAD IS WHERE BROWN WAS STRUCK BY A SHOTGUN PELLET THE NIGHT OF HIS SPEECH. (U.S. NEWS & WORLD REPORT COLLECTION, LIBRARY OF CONGRESS.)

During the civil rights and Black power eras, white-collar jobs were replacing many manufacturing jobs. This shift hurt Black Americans who were more likely than whites to lack the education needed for these higher-salaried jobs. Starting in the 1960s, many corporations began moving manufacturing plants to other countries. Many jobs in manufacturing disappeared in urban areas where most Black people lived by the late 1970s. This resulted in whites fleeing to suburban areas where the best of the white-collar jobs were located and a significant decline in the Black working and middle classes.

Black leaders started winning mayoral elections in major cities during this transformative era, tackling issues relevant to the African American community. Floyd J. McCree was elected mayor of Flint, Michigan, in 1966. Carl Stokes became the first Black mayor of Cleveland in 1967. Howard Nathaniel Lee became the first Black mayor of a predominantly-white city in the South in 1969: Chapel Hill, North Carolina. James R. Ford was elected mayor of Tallahassee, Florida, in 1972, making him the first Black mayor of a state capital. The year 1973 marked a significant rise in Black political power, as Coleman Young, Maynard Jackson, Tom Bradley, and Leila Foley achieved mayoral victories in Detroit, Atlanta, Los Angeles, and Taft, Oklahoma, respectively. Foley was the first African American woman to be elected mayor of an American city. These and other Black mayors attempted to implement policies to elevate the conditions of their constituents.

Jackson pushed through the expansion of Atlanta's airport in the late 1970s. As a political newcomer, his persistent effort to win airport contracts for minorities occasionally brought him into conflict with Atlanta's powerful, mainly white business community. Those contracts allocated to African Americans increased to 35% percent from less than 1%, for a project initially valued at $450 million.[65] During his time as mayor of Detroit from 1974 to 1994, Young integrated the police force and enhanced its professionalism. Despite shrinking tax revenue and reduced funding from the federal and state governments, Young balanced the city's budget. Under his leadership, city contracts to Black- and women-owned businesses increased.

Despite these successes in the 1970s and '80s, African Americans over all were still locked into a permanent financial underclass compared to whites. This disparity, which had existed since the Civil War, was exacerbated in the 1980s with tough-on-crime policies and the Iran-Contra Affair.

Joe Biden, while a senator, was the father of the federal crime policies enacted in the early 1980s that contributed to the mass incarceration of Black people, particularly Black men, throughout that decade and into the next. This was a revival of Lyndon Johnson's 1965 "War on Crime" and 1968 Omnibus Crime Control and Safe Streets Act, which created the Law Enforcement Assistance Administration.[66] After Johnson left office in 1968, tough-on-crime rhetoric shifted to Richard Nixon's "War on Drugs" and the creation of the Drug Enforcement Administration. Biden borrowed from this legislation to shape his policy agendas on crime and drugs in the 1980s.

The 1982 Violent Crime and Drug Enforcement Improvements Act, co-sponsored as a bill by Biden and Strom Thurmond, increased penalties for narcotics charges, including increasing the removal of assets, the elimination of parole for federal offenses, and mandatory minimum sentencing requirements. The bill also limited access to bail—a provision denounced by the American Civil Liberties Union for "reversing the presumption of innocence."

After the bill, with mitigating bail and parole elements removed by the House of Representatives, passed by wide margins in Congress, President Ronald Reagan vetoed the bill because of "costs, a belief that parts of the measure are unconstitutional, and a concern that it would create another layer in the drug enforcement bureaucracy." However, the bill's punitive priorities reappeared in later legislation. The 1984 Comprehensive Crime Control Act, another bill influenced by Biden, also aimed to limit bail, increase removal of assets, abolish parole, create a commission for sentencing guidelines, and raise finances for criminal justice programs and departments at the state level. The Anti-Drug Abuse Act of 1986, a bill that Biden spearheaded, imposed harsher penalties for various crimes and implemented the iconic and

SENATOR JOE BIDEN AND SENATOR STROM THURMOND (SC) DURING THE 1993 CRIME BILL HEARINGS. (ROLL CALL ARCHIVES.)

controversial 100:1 sentencing imbalance between crack and cocaine offenses. The 1988 Anti-Drug Abuse Act created Biden's longed-for post of drug czar and increased federal prison sentences, leading to a massive surge in the federal inmate population—from 24,000 in 1980 to nearly 216,000 by 2013. A 2020 U.S. Sentencing Commission report revealed that Blacks accounted for 77.1% of crack convictions.

While these tough-on-crime policies were being implemented, the Iran-Contra affair was beginning to take shape. This was really two distinct covert foreign-policy operations, each addressing a separate issue in a different country and handled differently, a set of overlapping strategies employed by high-ranking officials like Lieutenant-Colonel Oliver North and John Poindexter under Reagan in dealings with Iran and the Contras. The first operation was the continuation of support for the Contras, a rightist rebel group fighting the Sandinista government in Nicaragua, following the termination of its congressional funding. Illegally providing arms to Iran to secure the release of American hostages held in Lebanon by Iranian-backed entities was the second clandestine foreign policy action. When the conspirators channeled Iran arms sale profits through third parties and private funding to aid the Nicaraguan Contras, the two policies overlapped.

Senator John Kerry's Drugs, Law Enforcement and Foreign Policy Committee report, published on December 1, 1988, found that the aid to the Contras used an extensive criminal and clandestine governmental agency network to traffic not only arms but drugs:

> *Individuals who provided support for the Contras were involved in drug trafficking, the supply network of the Contras was used by drug trafficking organizations, and elements of the Contras themselves knowingly received financial and material assistance from drug traffickers. In each case, one or another agency of the U.S. government had information regarding the involvement either while it was occurring, or immediately thereafter. The Subcommittee found that the Contra drug links included: Payments to drug traffickers by the U.S. State Department of funds authorized by the Congress for humanitarian assistance to the Contras, in some cases after the traffickers had been indicted by federal law enforcement agencies on drug charges, in others while traffickers were under active investigation by these same agencies. These activities were carried out in connection with Contra activities in both Costa Rica and Honduras.*

The U.S. Department of Justice's Office of Inspector General reported that Oscar Danilo Blandon, a Contra, provided drugs to U.S. dealers, including the notorious "Freeway" Rick Ross. An African American from South Central Los Angeles, Ross had begun selling marijuana in the 1970s. He moved on to selling crack cocaine in the 1980s and soon established a vast distribution network across the United States, primarily in African American neighborhoods, that would net him millions of dollars daily at the pinnacle of his operation. The controversial investigative reporter Gary Webb of the *San Jose Mercury News* alleged that Ross bought his cocaine at extraordinarily marked down prices from Blandon, who would then funnel the sale of the proceeds back to the Contras. Blandon informed the Office of the Inspector General that he independently started acquiring and distributing cocaine. Blandon admitted to a significant role in drug trafficking, sourcing cocaine from Colombia, Mexico, and Nicaragua and distributing large quantities to Ross and other buyers.[67] With the Iran-Contra supply network being supported by members in Reagan's administration, one may arrive at the conclusion that he and his administration may have had nefarious motives in targeting the African American population by pushing crack cocaine in their community with the proceeds being used as a launch pad to fund the Contras.

Nevertheless, what is certain is that Biden's tough-on-crime proposals and policies that he spearheaded in that era as well as the Iran-Contra supply network helped usher in mass incarceration, especially of Black men beginning in the 1980s. As the sociologist Bruce Western points out,

> *at the dawn of the prison boom, in 1980, the incarceration rate for young Black men was 5.7 percent, more than twice as high as that for "low-education whites." By 2004, 13.5 percent of Black men in their twenties were in prison or jail. The combination of high incarceration rates with a large proportion of fathers among inmates means many children at that time had incarcerated fathers.*

From 1980 to 2000, the number of children with imprisoned fathers jumped sixfold, from approximately 350,000 to 2.1 million. This rise affected about 3% of all children nationally in the year 2000. Among whites, the fraction of children with a father imprisoned is relatively small, at about 1.2% in 2000. The figure is about three times higher (3.5%) for Hispanics. More than a million African American children, or one in eleven, had an incarcerated father in 2000.[68]

With mass incarceration of Black men increasing in the 1990s, Biden, with the support of President Bill Clinton, once again sponsored another crime bill that would affect Black families. In 1991, the United States experienced its peak in violent crime, with a rate of 758 incidents per 100,000 individuals. The Violent Crime Control and Law Enforcement Act, which Clinton signed in 1994, was enacted to confront this crisis.

The act called for the creation of 100,000 police positions, $9.7 billion for prisons, and $6.1 billion for crime prevention initiatives. Proponents predicted it would increase the government's capacity to address issues stemming from criminal aliens, allocating $2.6 billion to agencies like the FBI, DEA, INS, and Department of Justice to boost prosecutions and support the Treasury Department. This 1994 act shaped how politicians and academics approached the relationship between crime and African Americans. The results? Between 1995 and 1999, Black Americans became convicted felons and served more time in jails and prisons than whites convicted of similar crimes, at, depending on the state, from 13 to 36 times that of whites according to a 2000 Human Rights Watch study. During this same period, Black families' wealth decreased while white wealth increased. These trends, of mass incarceration and growing racial disparities in wealth, continued through the 1990s and into the new millennium.

It has been argued that America in the twenty-first century is still in the Reagan era. In the decades since Reagan left office, the political and economic benchmarks that civil rights proponents set for measuring the conditions of Black Americans have not been met. This is due to Black Americans remaining the political and economic footstool of American society, forced to anchor itself to the confines and norms of a country built for white American survival.

During the mid-1990s, America was at another crossroads between Black nationalist ideas and the integrationist civil rights tradition of the established African American leadership class. Culturally, Black communities felt the impact of punitive drug laws, loss of jobs, and how drugs themselves destroyed families. Disconnected from the 1960s civil rights movement, subsequent generations of young Black people explored more radical methods for expressing political and social opposition through culture. A new, grittier musical style needing specific skills and talents, rap was adopted by these young Black men in the early 1980s as a form of oppositional culture. The growth of rap into the late 1980s and into the '90s overlapped with a small yet burgeoning political awakening that was occurring in the community. One of the most charismatic and politically conscious rappers at that time was Tupac Shakur, who released several chart-topping songs and albums and acted in movies which catapulted him into being a premier Black cultural icon. His story is rooted in Black nationalism. He was the son of a Black Panther member, Afeni Shakur, while his stepfather Mutulu Shakur was a part of the Revolutionary Action Movement and the Republic of New Afrika. Afeni Shakur had gained notoriety as part of the "Panther 21." That celebrated case involved New York city police arresting a group of twenty-one Black Panther Party members in April 1969 on charges of plotting to bomb department stores and a police station. In May 1971, all twenty-one members that were arrested were acquitted. Afeni Shakur represented herself at trial while pregnant with Tupac, who was born a couple months after her acquittal in June of 1971.

Tupac Shakur's life was significantly shaped by his father, Billy Garland, as well as his stepfather and mother, all three of whom were involved in pro-Black movements. He became a de facto spokesman on social and political issues for millions of African American teens maturing during the late-'80s and early-'90s crack epidemic. In a 1994 interview Shakur exclaimed,

> *I feel like I'm doing God's work, because these ghetto kids are God's children, and I don't see any missionaries coming through there. So I'm doing God's work while Reverend Jackson does his [thing] up in the middle class, and while he goes to the White House to have dinner and pray over the president, I'm up in the hood doing my work with my folks.*

At the time, Jesse Jackson was a highly effective Black civil rights leader and an avid supporter of President Clinton. Despite Jackson's support, Shakur vehemently disagreed with Clinton's approach to crime and African Americans. Shakur's

TUPAC SHAKUR AT THE CLUB AMAZON,
NEW YORK CITY, JULY 28, 1993.
(AL PEREIRA, MICHAEL OCHS ARCHIVE/GETTY IMAGES.)

reference to Jackson and other Black politicians who attended an event at the White House to honor Aretha Franklin highlighted the frustration that he felt with the Black leadership class of his day, especially regarding "three strikes" laws, lack of housing, and wealth and educational inequality between whites and Blacks. Shakur had seen the effects of such issues firsthand both as a child and as an adult.

"Three strikes" laws compelled judges and juries to impose harsh sentences on those who were convicted of a third felony. California in 1994 passed "three strikes" laws that imposed prison sentences of twenty-five years to life for a third felony. Shakur, himself a convicted felon, criticized such laws because they disproportionately increased the imprisonment of African Americans, particularly men. He felt that Black leaders were more concerned with cozying up to the white political establishment than finding alternative solutions for the root causes of the increase in violent crime in the African American community. Unlike Clinton and Biden, Shakur believed that tackling foundational causes of violence such as poverty, family structure, and education would be more effective than simply addressing violent crime itself.

Despite Shakur leading the counterculture in opposing tough-on-crime policies through his interviews and music, lawmakers went ahead and ensured the expansion of prisons, the increase in police officers, and the expansion of mandatory minimum sentences. The 1994 law also allowed juveniles as young as thirteen years old to be charged as adults for crimes involving handguns. Many Black leaders, including Representative Kweisi Mfume, chairman of the Congressional Black Caucus (CBC), and the former Baltimore mayor Kurt Schmoke, supported and voted for the bill, in part because Clinton marketed it as the solution to violent crimes like rape and murder portrayed by the media as endemic in the African American community. Schmoke publicly advocated the bill in 1994 in congressional hearings on Capitol Hill as part of a delegation of mayors from around the country. While Mfume originally opposed the bill, he, like most of the CBC representatives, ended up voting for it. But other African American leaders were more aligned with Shakur's opposition

U.S. CONGRESSWOMAN MAXINE WATERS AT THE 2019 CALIFORNIA DEMOCRATIC PARTY STATE CONVENTION IN SAN FRANCISCO, CALIFORNIA. (GAGE SKIDMORE, CREATIVE COMMONS LICENSE.)

to the bill, including Maxine Waters of California, Bobby Scott of Virgina, and Charlie Rangel of New York. Waters and Scott objected to the bill's reliance on extreme, prison-focused measures, but Rangel's position was more complex.

In 1971, Rangel had just won the House seat representing Harlem, New York. With other CBC members, he visited President Nixon and urged him to ramp up what would soon become his War on Drugs. He voted for the crime bills sponsored by Biden in the 1980s. Nonetheless, Rangel voted against the 1994 crime bill. The conflicting feelings that Black political leaders had about violent crime in the African American community were echoed by grassroots organizations. Although Shakur was irked by Jackson's support of Clinton, Jackson and his National Rainbow Coalition opposed the 1994 crime bill and made alternative proposals to stress crime prevention. These included job training (mirroring Waters's program that helped 5,000 youth obtain jobs in the Los Angeles area) and a March on Washington of Black youth from all over the country to encourage the Clinton administration to create a jobs bill. Other grassroots groups, such as local NAACP chapters, backed the 1994 crime bill due to its funding of youth and safe-neighborhood initiatives.

Two years after Clinton won the presidency, the Democrats lost control of Congress through the efforts of Georgia's Representative Newt Gingrich and his "Contract for America," which ginned up crime statistics and renewed the culture wars with thinly-veiled racist attacks. Republicans used Clinton's impeachment trial and the reach of expanding media to promote their agenda, diverting focus from crucial civil rights legislation. The fiercely contested 2000 election, awarded to George W. Bush over Al Gore by the Supreme Court, set a contentious tone for his presidency, which was dramatically altered by the September 11th attacks.

The economic recession caused by the attacks and the dot-com bubble disproportionately affected working and middle-class families. The Bush administration answered the terrorist attack by attacking Afghanistan in late 2001 and then Iraq in 2003. The so-called War on Terror marked the end of the recession but the beginning of decades-long military actions in the Middle East, with Black people making up 15% of military enlistees while being only 14% of the adult population of the United States.[69]

Later events compelled African Americans to become more involved in national politics in the mid-2000s, both domestically and in foreign policy. The most iconic was Hurricane Katrina, a category-five storm that devastated the Gulf coast. Louisiana and Mississippi were the hardest hit. Of the over 1,800 people that died from hurricane-related illness and injury, 93% were black. The United States government slowed or withheld aid to the majority-Black city of New Orleans, setting the conditions for armed gangs of white supremacists and even the police to inflict further mayhem on Black residents.

The recession in 2007, triggered by the housing crisis, was particularly hard on African Americans, who were already facing other economic challenges. We see the evidence of a loss of African American wealth and lack of recovery when comparing home ownership and foreclosure statistics among ethnic groups. First, death caused by law enforcement is grossly under-reported, with wild variation by state. Second, police have killed 38% more Black people since 1980. The data show slight fluctuations by year, but the overall trend over the past four decades confirms what Black people know: any interaction with police is dangerous. Self-appointed "law enforcers," in effect vigilantes, have been emboldened by changes in gun and property laws that have led to white people killing Black people without consequence. Martin Lee Anderson was murdered in Florida. Sean Bell was murdered in New York. Timothy Thomas was murdered in Cincinnati. Oscar Grant was murdered in Oakland. However, those named above represent only a small portion of the thousands of Black individuals killed by law enforcement.

Loss of jobs. Loss of wealth. Loss of homes. Loss of life. African Americans had (and have) lost so much material wealth and political power during the 1980s and '90s that by the time the full scope of the racialized treatment of New Orleans by the Bush administration had become apparent, the socio-economic foundations were in place for the historic election of President Barack Obama in 2008.

Obama was relatively unknown to the African American community before his keynote speech at the 2004 Democratic National Convention. His political career, however, had begun in the mid-1980s in Chicago, where he was hired by Chicago's first Black mayor, Harold Washington, as a community organizer. He worked on Chicago's predominantly poor and Black South Side from 1985 to 1988 on public housing and civil rights. It was then that he joined the Reverend Jeremiah Wright Jr.'s Trinity United Church of Christ, also located on the South Side. Wright was a student of the theologian James Cone, a proponent of Black Liberation Theology, a Christian derivative of Black nationalism. Wright's sermons emphasized Black power, social activism, and community organizing. His sermons greatly influenced Obama, as noted in his 1995 memoir *Dreams from My Father*.

Obama used these themes as he began his political career,

first by becoming director of Project Vote's Illinois chapter. Under his leadership, voter registration of African Americans in Chicago alone increased by 150,000. There was also an increase in voter participation of African Americans in Illinois more generally. This is credited with electing the first African American woman, Carol Moseley-Braun, to the Senate in 1992. She was a native Chicagoan and had been a classmate of the infamous Black panther Fred Hampton, who was the chair of the Illinois chapter. Obama's work with Project Vote eventually led to his election to the Illinois Senate, where he served from 1997 to 2004, then a successful campaign for the U.S. Senate in 2004, followed by his announcement of his run for the presidency in 2007. The only political loss that he suffered along the way was in 2000 against the former SNCC and Black Panther Party member Bobby Rush for the U.S. House of Representatives' 1st District seat.

Obama's 2007 presidential-run announcement at the Old State Capitol in Springfield, Illinois, where Lincoln gave his "House Divided" speech, was no coincidence. Obama would continually use subtle yet effective symbolism to appeal to the African American community, from his 2007 book *The Audacity of Hope: Thoughts on Reclaiming the American Dream* to the one he published before the election in 2008, *Change We Can Believe In: Barack Obama's Plan to Renew America's Promise* and right down to his signature campaign "Hope" poster. He ran a nearly flawless campaign that reinvigorated especially the African American community about the possibility of reparations due to him identifying as African American and being a serious candidate for the presidency.

Despite rhetoric about empowerment and reparations from the African American grassroots in their support of him, there were clues during his campaign that Obama was more interested in appeasing and not offending his multicultural supporters than having serious policy discussions on economic inequality, much less reparations. As the campaign was hitting its stride in early 2008, Obama's membership at Wright's church came under scrutiny. Major media networks uncovered some of Wright's sermons aggressively criticizing U.S. domestic and foreign policy. In the aftermath of the September 11, 2001, attacks, Wright had railed,

> *We bombed Hiroshima, we bombed Nagasaki, and we nuked far more than the thousands in New York and the Pentagon, and we never batted an eye. We have supported state terrorism against the Palestinians and black South Africans, and now we are indignant because the stuff we have done overseas is now brought right back to our own front yards. America's chickens are coming home to roost.*

And in a fiery sermon in 2003, Wright had exclaimed,

> *The government gives them the drugs, builds bigger prisons, passes a three-strike law and then wants us to sing "God Bless America." No, no, no, God damn America, that's in the Bible for killing innocent people ... God damn America for treating our citizens as less than human. God damn America for as long as she acts like she is God, and she is supreme.*

The sermons received nonstop media coverage and almost derailed his campaign. To put an end to the controversy and reassert his image as a uniter of all races, Obama gave a speech in March of 2008 titled "A More Perfect Union," in which he disavowed Wright's remarks. He left the Trinity United Church of Christ later that month. In June, Obama rejected the notion of reparations to African Americans outright, stating, "I have said in the past—and I'll repeat again—that the best reparations we can provide are good schools in the inner city and jobs for people who are unemployed." However, while Obama was disavowing Black nationalism and reparations, academics and activists were amplifying the issue to national audiences. The economist William Darity in 2008 envisioned reparations as a portfolio rather than a fund to be used in a single way. He argued that a total of $1 to 6 trillion could materialize into direct payout to eligible recipients: "The payout need not take place in one lump sum but could be allocated over time."

The human-rights lawyer and activist Randall M. Robinson, on the other hand, in *The Debt: What America Owes Blacks*, argued that reparations shouldn't be direct payments. Instead, they should be funds distributed to Black-owned businesses, education programs, and training centers. In line with political nationalism, reparations would ideally include land grants dedicated to African Americans, which would add to African American wealth, since land ownership is the pathway to wealth creation and ultimately autonomy. With the attainment of property, African Americans would have more autonomy in determining their political destiny and would be able to set the parameters of their advancement because of their economic stability.

As illustrated throughout this chapter, many of the challenges African Americans face involve the criminal justice system, where racism is constantly in action. A political nationalist approach to land ownership and cash payments directly to descendants of slaves, plus building wealth as separately as possible from mainstream America, would further the return of Black nationalism to the collective consciousness of African Americans and the death of white supremacy. Then, African Americans could address not only mass incarceration, but also family dynamics and educational and economic disparities. These problems are contextualized in an American institutional and economic perspective in the next chapter.

171

CHAPTER FIVE

INSTITUTIONAL REPAIR

As shown in previous chapters, American institutions, whether political, cultural, or economic, were all built on a system of white supremacy. Their purpose is to ensure that whites dominate while Blacks remain indebted and in service to those institutions. Every so often the system itself experiences major shocks that, on the surface, appear to herald great changes. The Great Depression, John F. Kennedy's assassination, the Vietnam War, the Iran-Contra Affair, the 9/11 attacks, Hurricane Katrina, and the great recession of 2007 all triggered national soul-searching to reevaluate the treatment of African Americans. Yet, despite the media's predictions, the position of Black Americans has not changed. There was a glimmer of hope that change would finally come with the election of Barack Obama. Yet after eight years, Obama's presidency ended with a vengeful pushback by white supremacists and their allies.

Few, if any, experts predicted Donald Trump's rise to the presidency. He was a long shot to win the Republican nomination in 2016, as the field was ripe with more seasoned politicians such as Jeb Bush, Chris Christie, Ben Carson, John Kasich, and Carly Fiorina. These were Republican Party veterans and were given more favorable odds to become the nominee. However, using crude and politically unorthodox tactics, Trump eliminated each Republican candidate in the primary one by one to win the nomination. One of these tactics was devising nicknames for his opponents like "Lyin' Ted" for Ted Cruz, "Little Marco" for Marco Rubio, and "Pocahontas" for Elizabeth Warren. The nickname that had the most devastating effect was "Low Energy" Jeb Bush. During a primary debate in South Carolina, Trump repeatedly referred to Bush as being "low energy" and took jabs at his brother, the former President George W. Bush, regarding the United States involvement in Iraq. It was a risky move for Trump since South Carolina had a large pro-military, Republican electorate. Trump's strategy worked, and Bush dropped out of the race shortly after the debate and his poor primary results in South Carolina. Trump went on to receive the bulk of the news media coverage that would eventually carry him to be the official nominee to run against the Democratic nominee, Hillary Clinton. Trump deployed the same strategy against Clinton, using his social media accounts, mainstream media interviews, and tough-guy- who-is-a-political-outsider persona to brand her as "Crooked Hillary," which ultimately helped propel him to defeat her for the presidency.

After Trump took office, African American wealth continued to decline. In 2007, the average net worth of a white family was $802,520 while that of a Black family was $156,285. By 2016, the gap widened, with the average wealth of Black families declining to $139,523 and that of white families increasing to $919,336. Data from 2018 to 2019 showed that African Americans experienced higher unemployment rates than white Americans regardless of their educational background. There was a 2.8% unemployment rate for Blacks with a college degree from November 2018 to October 2019, compared to a 2% unemployment rate for whites with a degree. Also, the average weekly earnings for full-time Black workers in 2019 was $727, compared to $943 for full-time white workers. And finally, an African American worker was 55.4% likely to receive health insurance through their employer, compared to 74.8% for white workers in 2018. Overall, historical evidence has shown that Blacks are at a higher risk of being hurt by an economic recession since Blacks face unemployment first and the longest. This was also exemplified during the coronavirus pandemic with white unemployment in June 2020 at 12.4%, compared to 16.8% for Black workers. What these economic data confirm is that African Americans do not own or control enough businesses or enterprises to establish self-sufficient political organizations that influence government institutions to address the at-this-point everlasting wealth gap between whites and African Americans. While Trump continuously touted low unemployment numbers for African Americans, the data from 2009 to 2019 show that Black Americans were paid less than whites.

The median yearly income for whites increased from $43,940 to $53,872 from 2009 to 2019. For African Americans it increased from $32,292 only to $39,988 in the same period. An increase of only $7,500 within ten years proves that the socio-economic conditions during this decade were not suitable for African Americans to build generational wealth, which also made it difficult to set the foundations needed to destroy white supremacy. This is a favorable reality for politicians that especially target Black voters because they can tout raw employment numbers as a measure of "doing something" for Black people, all the while continuing policies that are anti-wealth-building for the Black community and ultimately maintain the wealth and wage gaps between whites and Blacks.

There are people who have the misconception that, because all African Americans have legally defined equal rights, they therefore receive equal treatment. It's inaccurate to conclude that constitutional amendments guaranteeing citizenship and voting rights to Black Americans have eliminated anti-Black practices like redlining and gentrification, which continue to impede equality. Redlining began with the Federal Housing Administration (FHA) in the 1930s literally using red ink to mark where African Americans lived on maps of major city centers to signal to appraisers that the area was not suitable for the insurance of mortgages. The FHA encoded this into regulation in their underwriting manual published in 1934, which stated, "incompatible racial groups should not be permitted to live in the same communities." Redlining led to a lack of investment in infrastructure in Black neighborhoods, which then led to poor housing conditions and ultimately less economic opportunity than whites—a situation which persists today.

Interestingly, the African American neighborhoods that were redlined the longest have now grown as much as tenfold or more. Parramore, in Orlando, the oldest African American neighborhood in central Florida, has been 80% Black or more since the 1930s and for much of its existence was a victim of redlining. Close to the downtown business district, Parramore has gentrified since 2020, with updated infrastructure such as a new soccer stadium. Although this has pleased politicians and business leaders, higher rents have forced African Americans who were there for generations to look for affordable housing elsewhere, since these developments did not come with community benefit agreements to guarantee that the developers also build affordable housing complexes.

African Americans have been the victims of gentrification throughout American history, being forced from neighborhoods that have increased in value from heightened interest and development. Other factors include the nullification of federally subsidized housing loans or vouchers and construction of highways near their communities to intentionally separate them from affluent white neighborhoods.

Additionally, discriminatory practices like misleading contracts result in Black borrowers facing higher interest rates and harsher eviction terms from private financial institutions. The District of Columbia's U.S. District Court alleged that Wells Fargo discriminated against approximately 4,000 Black borrowers from 2004 to 2008, pushing them toward subprime loans even when they met the bank's prime loan criteria. However, white borrowers with similar credit ratings received traditional prime mortgages. The government also noted that Wells Fargo charged about 30,000 African American wholesale borrowers higher fees and rates than white borrowers, based on their race or nationality rather than their creditworthiness. In the end, Wells Fargo settled with the Justice Department for more than $230 million to compensate borrowers. The discriminatory housing policies of private institutions like Wells Fargo, targeting Black people, have reduced their ability to purchase and maintain homes, particularly during economic downturns. It has also contributed to white consumers receiving favorable treatment from financial institutions to purchase their homes. This gives whites the ability to pass wealth to future generations and create barriers for African Americans to do the same, thus widening the wealth gap. In U.S. survey data from 1940 and 2017, only 41% of Blacks are likely own a house, compared to 73% of whites. They also found that whites on average have ten times more wealth than Blacks. In the second quarter of 2024, the Federal Reserve reported that the average wealth of white households was $1,320,000 while the average wealth of Black households was $307,000.[70]

SOCIAL MEDIA INFLUENCE

A distinctive feature of the Trump presidency has been his social media postings targeting the Black community. His controversial tweets receive round-the-clock media attention. For instance, the January 17, 2017, tweets directed at Congressmen John Lewis and Elijah Cummings generated a firestorm of reaction—many supportive and many more denouncing the statements from the public. Trump intimated that the two legislators' districts were "crime infested" and that no "human being" would want to live there. These racist tweets and the response to them exposed general white perceptions of Black neighborhoods. However, they also highlighted long-standing systemic issues in Black communities. On social media and talk shows, Black folk expressed outrage over Trump's provocative language. Ironically, Obama had also referred to citizens of Baltimore in disparaging racial terms in April 2015 when he described demonstrators in that city as "thugs" and "criminals."[71] Obama had made those comments after the widespread protests over the death of Freddie Gray, an unarmed Black man, in police custody. The focus of his comments was protests and police brutality, but other concerns such as poverty among Baltimore's Black population also emerged as a narrative in the mainstream American media circuit.

INTERNAL REFLECTION

Black politicians in Baltimore have failed to represent the city properly. Baltimore's decline, according to Prosperity Now, is partly due to a population decrease of one-third since the 1950s, mostly due to the closing of steel plants and shipyards at the end of World War II. Inner-city Baltimore's economy shifted to the service sector, including tourism, retail, and nursing homes. This shift brought low-wage jobs, high turnover, lack of job security, sparse benefits, and virtually no union representation. Baltimore also became more Black as whites migrated to the suburbs. Blockbusting—that is, real estate agents persuading whites to sell their homes at fire-sale prices based on the racist notion that Black people will bring down their property values—played a significant role in white flight to the suburbs from the 1950s to 1970s. Once a real estate agent was able to sell a good number of homes in the area, they would then turn around resell them to African Americans way over market value. The Morris Goldseker Company in the late 1960s acquired homes in inner-city Baltimore for, on average, $7,320. They then sold those same homes for an average $12,387 to African American buyers, a 70% markup. In 1950, Baltimore's suburban population was 387,656, but by 1997 it had jumped to 1.8 million. In contrast, in 1950 Baltimore's inner-city population was 950,000, but by 1997 it had declined to 657,000. By 2014, it had declined to 622,000. Jobs that Blacks were trained for in the manufacturing industry in the 1950s left Baltimore altogether while whites fled to the suburbs where access to high-paying jobs in the medical and technology fields were more abundant.

As a result, the inner city lost much of its tax base. Citizens that remained in the inner city were forced to rely on social services to make up for the low-paying jobs that remained as well as the increase in sales taxes on basic goods to maintain infrastructure. When a city loses its taxpaying residents, its tax revenue shrinks, leading to less money for essential services like education, road repairs, public transit, and utilities. This presents challenges for politicians, and especially Black politicians, to propose policies that elevate the condition of African Americans in that city.

Beginning in the 1960s, Baltimore became reliant on federal dollars to perform its basic services. In 1989, 55% of its expenditure came from federal or state aid. By 2023, only 38% of what Baltimore spent came from federal or state funding sources. Since the decline of federal and state sources of funding for public projects, Black politicians in Baltimore have been forced to acquiesce to the corporate demands of their campaign contributors by giving them heavy tax breaks for private investment in public infrastructure rather than putting forth policies and solutions to uplift the Black community. Nowhere are these misplaced agendas clearer than when the demographic makeup of Baltimore and other tangible factors are analyzed.

In 2023, Blacks accounted for 61% of Baltimore's inner-city population while whites accounted for 28% and Latinos 6%. The NAACP reported that the unemployment rate for Blacks in Baltimore is consistently at least at 13% (not accounting for those who stopped looking for work), while the unemployment rate of whites at that time was 3.6%. They also reported that only 22% of businesses in the inner city of Baltimore are Black-owned, compared to 70% that are white-owned. They also report that less than 5% of Black-owned businesses in Baltimore have employees. What these data show is that, although African Americans in Baltimore are the majority ethnic group, they are economically indigent compared to other ethnic groups in the city. The economic situation in Baltimore greatly handicaps any effort by African Americans to build wealth and control the resources within their community.

In 2015, Baltimore's homicide rate reached its all-time high. The death toll was 343, with Black people accounting for more than 90% of the victims. Baltimore's surge in violent crime disproportionately affected African Americans, who made up 85% of its incarcerated population; upon release, their wages grew 21% more slowly than those of white ex-inmates. The education outcomes in Baltimore also outline the stark contrast between Blacks and whites in the city. For example, 21.8% of African Americans in Baltimore did not possess a high school diploma while only 12% of whites in the city did not attain one. Only 13% of African Americans had at least a B.A. degree while 51% of whites did. Again, the crime and education disparities in Baltimore reduce the prospects of African Americans building wealth and controlling resources and also decrease the chances of practicing the economic nationalism described by Malcolm X and other Black nationalists.

How did Baltimore and similar cities get to a point where African Americans remain stagnant or regress socially and financially for forty years? Why? Asking that question would force Black politicians, mainstream media outlets, and the Black community itself to take a long hard look at the inherent racist policies that are in the very fabric of America, regardless of who occupies the White House.

The question then becomes, why should Black America have faith in the Black political class? Politicians have never shown the fortitude to close the racial gaps in economics, society, and education, especially in our cities. The lesson here for Black America is that it cannot rely upon political parties for its prosperity. Although the overall wealth of African Americans has increased incrementally in the 2020s, it only amounts to barely 10% of white wealth and has not kept up with the cost of living and inflation.

The only remedy is a reawakening of Black nationalism. The way to achieve that is for African Americans to rebuild financial institutions which they own and operate, create political institutions like political action committees and lobbying organizations that are funded by Black Americans and in turn fund candidates that are devoted to reparative policies, and propagate African-centered education in which Black people own education centers and are centered in academic curricula.

As Malcolm X said, "the Black man should control the politics and politicians in his community." As demonstrated by the Cuban community in south Florida, establishing a powerful economic base by pooling economic resources through business ownership, apprenticeship, and real estate investment as a collective is the surest way for a community to control its destiny. Black Americans who profit from deploying economic nationalism could then organize political action committees and lobbying organizations at a local grassroots level.

The majority of PACs advocate for business, labor, or ideological causes. PACs can give up to $5,000 to a candidate committee per election (primary, general, or special). They can also give up to $15,000 annually to any national party committee and $5,000 annually to any other PAC. PACs may receive up to $5,000 from any one individual, PAC, or party committee per calendar year. Prominent political action committees that are owned, operated, and funded by a specific demographic group and their fundraising and expenditures are listed below:

ETHNIC GROUP INTEREST	POLITICAL ACTION COMMITTEE	FUNDS RAISED	TOTAL SPENT FOR ELECTIONS IN 2018
LATINO	LATINO VICTORY FUND	$4,087,000	$3,678,618
JEWISH	J STREET PAC	$5,187,951	$5,123,978
LGBTQ	EQUALITY PAC	$3,260,713	$2,982,965
ARAB	ARAB AMERICAN PAC	$41,065	$30,353
ASIAN	80-20 NATIONAL ASIAN AMERICAN PAC	$91,593	$36,824
BLACK	THE COLLECTIVE PAC	$1,069,284	$998,042

Data derived from author's calculations from the Center for Responsive Politics

Lobbyists are defined as those who dedicate at least 20% of their time to lobbying a specific client, frequently engage with legislative staff and government officials, and receive over $5,000 in compensation from a client over a six-month period for their services.[72] Any organization using in-house lobbyists must register with the federal government if its lobbying expenses surpass $20,500 in a six-month period. Reporting mandates the inclusion of all lobbying expenses for legislative advancement, from preparation and research to coordination with other lobbyists. Below is a chart of interest groups and their most prominent lobbying organizations:

ETHNIC GROUP INTEREST	LOBBYING ORGANIZATION	YEAR	TOTAL SPENT FOR ELECTIONS IN 2018	TOP ISSUES LOBBIED
LATINO	UNIDOSUS	2018	$370,661	AGRICULTURE, FED. BUDGET & APPROPRIATIONS, BANKING, HOUSING, IMMIGRATION, TAXES
JEWISH	AMERICAN ISRAEL PUBLIC AFFAIRS COMMITTEE	2018	$3,518,028	FED. BUDGET & & APPROPRIATIONS, FOREIGN RELATIONS, HOMELAND SECURITY, TRADE
LGBTQ	NATIONAL GAY AND LESBIAN TASKFORCE	2008	$615,972	CIVIL RIGHTS & CIVIL LIBERTIES
ARAB	ARAB AMERICAN AND CHALDEAN COUNCIL	2018	$39,000	ECONOMICS & ECONOMIC DEVELOPMENT
ASIAN	ASIAN AMERICAN HOTEL OWNERS ASSN	2018	$130,000	LABOR, ANTITRUST & WORKPLACE, SMALL BUSINESS, TAXES, FOREIGN RELATIONS
BLACK	AFRICAN AMERICAN AGRICULTURALIST ASSN	2019	$20,000	AGRICULTURE, CIVIL RIGHTS & CIVIL LIBERTIES

The data shows that other groups spend more on political activities than Black Americans. Although there are Black-run political action committees, they do not coordinate effectively with lobbying organizations on issues pertinent to Black Americans. An example of an ethnic affinity group that uses PACs and lobbying organizations to influence government officials, whether elected or staff, is the Jewish lobby. For example, H.R. 1697, the Israel Anti-Boycott Act, introduced in the House of Representatives on March 23, 2017, declares that Congress (1) opposes the United Nations Human Rights Council resolution of March 24, 2016, which urges countries to pressure companies to divest from or break contracts with Israel and (2) encourages full implementation of the United States–Israel Strategic Partnership Act of 2014 through enhanced, governmentwide, coordinated U.S.–Israel scientific and technological cooperation in civilian areas. The bill also prohibits any U.S. person engaged in interstate or foreign commerce from supporting any request by a foreign country to impose any boycott against a country that is friendly to the U.S. and that is not itself the object of any form of boycott pursuant to a U.S. law or regulation, or any boycott fostered or imposed by any international governmental organization against Israel or any request by any international governmental organization to impose such a boycott. In other words, the U.S. opposes international pressure to divest from and boycott Israel and Israeli businesses and makes it illegal to call for or participate in any such boycott at the request of a foreign entity.

J Street, a pro-peace Jewish organization, opposed the bill, claiming that "this dangerous bill erases the distinction between Israel and the occupied territory it controls, blurring the Green Line under the guise of combating BDS [the "Boycott, Divest, Sanctions" movement]. Treating Israel and the settlements as the same under US law would make a two-state solution and peace in the Middle East harder to achieve."[73] J Street made at least four different attempts in 2017 and four more in 2018 to stop the bill from passing and contributed to the campaigns of members in the House of Representatives in 2018 whose votes they hoped could be influenced, including Sanford Bishop (D-GA), with $5,000, and Adam Smith (D-WA), with $4,500. Bishop chaired the Agriculture, Rural Development, Food and Drug Administration, and Related Agencies Appropriations Subcommittee, served on the Financial Services and General Government Subcommittee, and was vice-chair of the Military Construction, Veterans Affairs, and Related Agencies Subcommittee. Smith chaired the House Armed Services Committee and had earlier served on the House Foreign Affairs and Permanent Select Intelligence Committees. J Street targeted congressional members in powerful positions that dealt specifically with their cause and could threaten to withhold funds from lawmakers in the next cycle if they did not withdraw their support. Other Jewish organizations which contributed to congressional campaigns on either side of this issue included the American Israel Public Affairs Committee (AIPAC), the Israeli American Coalition for Action, and the American Jewish Committee. Asian, LGBTQ, Arab, and Hispanic and Latino interest organizations also facilitate cooperation between PACs and lobbying organizations. They contribute to the campaigns of politicians, lobby politicians and bureaucratic agencies, and coordinate with consumer advocacy groups to bring public awareness to policies that affect them. They also encourage engagement of policy via letter-writing, social media postings, phone banks and protests to advance their causes.

Organizations owned, funded, and operated by Black people do this less consistently. Typically, the Black community relies on white-influenced consumer advocacy groups that are concerned with the broader context of "civil rights" of all peoples while treating African American interest as a subsect of their larger goals. The most prominent of these organizations include the National Association for the Advancement of Colored People (NAACP), the Black Lives Matter Global Network, and the Urban League. These organizations do not focus on specific issues pertaining to Black Americans and do not contribute to the campaigns of influential politicians, nor are they officially registered as lobbying organizations. The political, economic, and social issues of African Americans cannot begin to be resolved without multiple political action committees, lobbying organizations, and consumer advocacy groups coordinating on issue-focused legislation. They must be owned, funded, and operated by African Americans, through either individual proprietorships, non-profits, or limited liability corporations. They also must coordinate efforts to fund and lobby politicians dedicated to the economic uplift of African Americans and encourage civic engagement on pertinent policies. This will allow African Americans to leverage policies that will benefit them and become a more powerful voting bloc that politicians cannot ignore. Then, issues pertaining to African Americans, such as the H.R. 40 bill to study a program for reparations, would not languish in committee.

After Trump's re-election, African Americans should be following economic nationalist principles to develop a robust economic power base, which can then use campaign contributions from political action committees to hold politicians who have an interest in the Black community accountable for their votes and form lobbying organizations to leverage for set-asides for the needs of African Americans. African American–centered organizations should play a significant role in selecting local candidates with proven records of advocating for policies that uplift Black people.

Black-owned businesses and financial institutions should support African-centered educational institutions and coordinate with consumer advocacy organizations. This kind of education would train students on the inner workings of local economic and political institutions that Black people control. This would allow African Americans to begin to undo wealth inequality, discriminatory homeownership practices, and discriminatory employment practices.

Black nationalist organizations that have attempted to educate the general population about hurdles faced by Black people include the Nation of Islam, the Universal Negro Improvement Association and African Communities

League, the Black Liberation Army, and US Organization. Unfortunately, the messages and missions of these Black nationalist organizations were either never received or severely misinterpreted by the dominant white hegemonic society and to a certain extent by the Black community itself. The Nation of Islam first appeared on a nationally televised documentary in 1959, *The Hate That Hate Produced*, narrated by the award-winning white male journalists Mike Wallace, who falsely described the Nation of Islam as "Black supremacists" teaching Muslim children "how to hate white people." Wallace played upon white people's fears of Black people and Black-centered organizations which dared to challenge the American political and economic system with Black nationalist ideology and practice. Although the Nation of Islam did receive a boost in membership following the airing of the documentary, they and other Black nationalist organizations were still seen as fringe groups without much influence.

As it stands today, an array of politicians and media personalities argue that reparations to African Americans may be the best way to relieve economic disparities. However, without Black leaders or Black-owned institutions or organizations to drive the issue, there is little reason to believe that reparations could be considered as a national program. So, why has the African American leadership class since the conclusion of the civil rights era been so ineffective? For one thing, their message since the election of Trump is less coherent than the coordinated efforts during the 1960s. Also, some African Americans mistakenly believed in 2008 that the election of Obama would automatically improve their socio-economic circumstances. But the progress of African Americans since the 2007 recession is questionable, with some arguing that, instead, there was significant economic regression with no end in sight. African Americans account for about 52% of homeless families with children, while whites account for about 35%, and Blacks have the lowest participation rate in the labor force of any racial group. African Americans continue to face predatory lending and disparities in access to healthcare and higher education. After Obama's election, such issues were not emphasized by any major news platform; still less did any political parties debates them in any election cycle after Obama left office. African Americans have been staunch supporters of the Democratic Party since the 1960s: in 2016, 88% of them voted for the Democratic candidate, Hillary Clinton, while Trump only received 8% of Black votes. In 2020, Joe Biden garnered 92% of the Black vote while Trump again received 8%. The CNN commentator Van Jones remarked after the January 2020 State of the Union address that Trump "is going after the Black vote." Trump was aware of African American faithfulness to the Democratic Party, but few policy proposals from Democratic or Republican lawmakers sought to remedy the socio-economic problems of African Americans in that election cycle. This chasm between promises and results again provides an opportunity for a fresh, non-partisan African American political leadership class that uses Black nationalism as its guide. The leaders should be Blacks from varying socio-economic and educational backgrounds who can organize a system of media, advocacy, lobbying, and political action committee organizations.

Since the passing of the 1994 crime bill, the political and social landscape of America has changed. The trend began under Obama and continued under Trump. Social media has changed the way politics is discussed, with platforms such as Facebook and X (formally Twitter) at the forefront. Obama and Trump both extensively used social media platforms to reach voters during their campaigns. Hashtag slogans like #MAGA and #Obama2012 helped shaped the narrative of their policy plans and helped their campaigns engage intimately with their supporters and opponents.

Since Obama's election, many politicians have bypassed traditional media and used social media to communicate directly with the public. A contingent of Black political and social commentators has arisen, boasting millions of followers across various social media platforms, including the Breakfast Club, Roland Martin, Yvette Carnell, and Dr. Boyce Watkins. The Breakfast Club cycle was a trio of radio personalities: Charlemagne the God, Angela Yee, and DJ Envy. Their daily radio show, which also streamed on social media platforms in 2020, appeared Monday through Friday on Power of 105.1 in New York City, the Revolt TV network, and X. It was the center of controversy when Biden declared to Charlemagne during the 2020 Democratic primaries that "if you have a problem figuring out whether you're for me or Trump, then you ain't black." The interview went viral, receiving millions of mentions and reposts.

Martin is known primarily for appearances on CNN and TV One as a political commentator. In 2020, he created a digital show that airs daily on YouTube. Carnell, a former Congressional staffer, launched a digital show on YouTube in 2020 and is the creator of the #ADOS hashtag, which stands for American Descendants of Slavery. CNN and Fox News have hosted Watkins, a prominent author, political commentator, and former Syracuse University professor, to comment on African American economic issues. He has written multiple books and articles on wealth creation and has a YouTube show on the subject. Each of these people focuses on reparations for African Americans.

Carnell and her co-host Antonio Moore pushed the issue forward with their #ADOS hashtag, with its narrative that African Americans deserve reparations for America's original sin of slavery. They suggested reparations should include either guaranteed jobs, bonds, or cash payments. Although these personalities agreed that reparations are owed to African Americans, they differed on what form it should take.

Carnell and Moore proposed a complete rewrite of H.R. 40 to benefit American Descendants of Slavery, including direct cash payments and other support. Martin took the position that the issue should be studied first. Social media saw sharp divisions on reparations in mid-2019, fueled by the House Judiciary Subcommittee hearing with Senator Cory Booker and Ta-Nehisi Coates.

After the murder of George Floyd in early 2020, the #Reparations and #ADOS hashtags on social media received millions of mentions and repostings. That and other media attention eventually spurred the House of Representatives to hold a second hearing on the issue, on February 17, 2021. Since then, however, a consensus on addressing the issue within the African American community remains elusive.

In recent years, conservative lawmakers have argued that the teaching of critical race theory—a form of anti-racist education related to African-centered education—in K-12 education is divisive. Critical race theory, developed by the legal scholar Derrick Bell and grounded in education, law, psychology, and sociology, is focused on the concepts of *racial realism* and *interest convergence*. Racial realism is the recognition that racism is forever entrenched in American society and that white and Black people in America will always be unequal. Bell states that there can be no justice for African Americans until their interests *converge* with those of whites. For Bell, the legislative achievements of the civil rights movement maintained the status quo of white supremacy rather than solving racial problems in America.

DERRICK BELL, 2007. (DAVID SHANKBONE, CREATIVE COMMONS LICENSE.)

The philosopher Nathan Luis Cartagena identifies several components of critical race theory: first-person narratives, storytelling, allegory, interdisciplinary legal treatment, and the embrace of creativity. Because its anti-racist orientation criticizes typical civil rights, integration, affirmative action, and neo-liberal strategies, critical race theory is often disruptive. But not all supporters of critical race theory reject neo-liberal ideology. The American theorist Gloria Ladson-Billings states that "Critical Race Theory in education, like its antecedent in legal scholarship, is a radical critique of both the status quo and the purported reforms." Critical race theorists, therefore, reject paradigms designed for universal appeal, viewing them as futile and supportive of the existing order. Instead, they echo Marcus Garvey's belief that the problem Black people face is universal racial oppression and requires race-based emancipation programs to solve it.

Although critical race theory can be taught at all levels, it is typically taught in graduate school, because most educators at the K-12 level lack the necessary credentials. There may be courses at the middle or high school level that discusses African American history, but usually not focusing on critical race theory. Thus, it was peculiar for conservatives during the 2020 election cycle to gin up controversy over critical race theory.

Much of Trump's and the media's alarm over critical race theory stemmed from the 1619 Project, an ongoing initiative from the *New York Times Magazine* starting in August 2019, the 400th anniversary of the beginning of American slavery, which aims to reframe the country's history by placing the consequences of slavery and the contributions of Black Americans at the center of our national narrative. The publication *Media Matters* notes that Fox News mentioned the term "Critical Race Theory" in disparaging headlines a total of 1,935 times from June 2020 to June 2021.

On September 17, 2020, Trump, speaking at the White House History Conference, further derided critical race theory:

> *Students in our universities are inundated with critical race theory. This is a Marxist doctrine holding that America is a wicked and racist nation, that even young children are complicit in oppression, and that our entire society must be radically transformed. Critical race theory is being forced into our children's schools, it's being imposed into workplace trainings, and it's being deployed to rip apart friends, neighbors, and families. A perfect example of critical race theory was recently published by the Smithsonian Institution. This document alleged that concepts such as hard work, rational thinking, the nuclear family, and belief in God were not values that unite all Americans but were instead aspects of "whiteness." This is offensive and outrageous to Americans of every ethnicity, and it is especially harmful to children of minority backgrounds who should be uplifted, not disparaged. Critical race theory, the* 1619 Project, *and the crusade against American history is toxic propaganda, ideological poison that, if not removed, will dissolve the civic bonds that tie us together. It will destroy our country.*

Five days later, he issued an executive order banning racial-sensitivity training of federal contractors and military service members:

> *The participation of contractors' employees in training that promotes race or sex stereotyping or scapegoating similarly undermines efficiency in Federal contracting. Such requirements promote divisiveness in the workplace and distract them from the pursuit of excellence and collaborative achievements in public administration. Therefore, it shall be the policy of the United States not to promote race or sex stereotyping or scapegoating in the Federal workforce or in the Uniformed Services, and not to allow grant funds to be used for these purposes. In addition, Federal contractors will not be permitted to inculcate such views in their employees. If a contractor provides a training for agency employees relating to diversity or inclusion that teaches, advocates, or promotes the divisive concepts set forth in section 2(a) of this order, and such action is in violation of the applicable contract, the agency that contracted for such training shall evaluate whether to pursue debarment of that contractor, consistent with applicable law and regulations, and in consultation with the Interagency Suspension and Debarment Committee.*

After losing the 2020 election to Biden, Trump wrote a scathing op-ed against critical race theory:

> *In classrooms across the nation, students are being subjected to a new curriculum designed to brainwash them with the ridiculous left-wing dogma known as "critical race theory." The key fact about this twisted doctrine is that it is completely antithetical to everything that normal Americans of any color would wish to teach their children. Instead of helping young people discover that America is the greatest, most tolerant, and most generous nation in history,*

> *it teaches them that America is systemically evil and that the hearts of our people are full of hatred and malice. Far from advancing the beautiful dream of the Rev. Martin Luther King Jr.—that our children should "not be judged by the color of their skin, but by the content of their character"—the left's vile new theory preaches that judging people by the color of their skin is actually a good idea. Teaching even one child these divisive messages would verge on psychological abuse. Indoctrinating generations of children with these extreme ideas is not just immoral—it is a program for national suicide. Yet that is exactly what the Biden administration endorsed recently in a rule published in the Federal Register aimed at inflicting a critical race theory-inspired curriculum on American schoolchildren.*

With Fox News and Trump leading the charge against critical race theory, which typically is only taught in post-secondary settings such as law schools, conservative governors and state legislatures across the country responded with legislation to ban the subject in K-12 curriculum. Eight states—Idaho, Oklahoma, Tennessee, Texas, Iowa, New Hampshire, Arizona, and South Carolina—banned "critical race theory," while twenty more are considering similar legislation. Texas House Bill 3979, which became law in September 2021, went so far as to ban any discourse involving slavery or racism in the classroom. The language in the law also attempts to expel slavery and racism from the founding of America: "slavery and racism are not with respect to their relationship to American values, slavery and racism are anything other than deviations from, betrayals of, or failures to live up to, the authentic founding principles of the United States, which include liberty and equality."

The hysteria over critical race theory hit a fever pitch in Texas when James Whitfield, principal at Colleyville Heritage High School, was placed on leave by the Grapevine-Colleyville, Texas, school district, accused of teaching critical race theory. Parental activists' complaints cited a letter

Whitfield sent to the district after the death of George Floyd, who was a native of Texas. "Education is the key to stomping out ignorance, hate, and systemic racism," Whitfield wrote. "It's a necessary conduit to get 'liberty and justice for all.'" The feedback to that letter was nothing short of spectacular, Whitfield said. He didn't hear a single negative comment. He felt there was a consensus in the community. But a little over a year later, his words backfired. At a school board meeting, Stetson Clark, a former school board candidate, used the letter to accuse Whitfield of teaching and promoting "critical race theory." At the podium, Clark named Whitfield four times, even though the board had asked him not to criticize employees. The first time, someone in the audience yelled out, "How about you fire him?" Clark continued to name Whitfield, completely ignoring the rules, and called for the board to fire him. "He is encouraging the disruption and destruction of our district," Clark said. When his time wrapped up, Clark walked away from the podium to cheers from the audience. In the ensuing days, Whitfield found himself at the center of the debate over how race is taught in Texas schools. He received a disciplinary letter from the district a few weeks later and was placed on administrative leave soon after that. On September 13, the school board decided not to renew Whitfield's contract. Whitfield, whose job was administrative and who didn't teach classes, maintains that he never taught critical race theory or mentioned it to teachers, students, or parents. Clark pinned his case on Whitfield's belief that "systemic racism exists."

This controversy is an example of whites exercising their supremacy. By using political rhetoric, media, executive orders, and educational policy fueled by their worldview to ban a phantom curriculum, whites assert their dominance and ensure that anything that challenges their views on race is silenced. This mentality harkens back to the education theorist Robin DiAngelo's concept of white fragility. As she puts it, "When ideologies such as colorblindness, meritocracy, and individualism are challenged, intense emotional reactions are common," including "the outward display of emotions such as anger, fear, and guilt, and behaviors such as argumentation, silence, and leaving the stress-inducing situation." These actions restore the racial balance favoring white people when there is pushback from nonwhites or especially Black people. This instance of pushback then creates racial stress to give white people an out to exit the situation, never taking accountability of what could have been a teachable moment.

For Black nationalist educational, political, or economic programs to be effective, Black Americans must start thinking of themselves as a "nation within a nation." This concept was promoted by Amos Wilson, who argued in *Blueprint for Black Power*,

> *The power of the concept of nation as an analytical instrument used to arrive at a practical understanding of problems faced by the African American community, can be demonstrated by applying it in the analysis of a broad range of social problems. For example, the basic cause of institutional under-performance and/or dysfunctionality [e.g., inadequate educational, recreational, socialization institutions; lack of employment opportunities; family instability and disruption; inadequate housing; antisocial, criminal behavior; individual distress and dysfunctionality] can in significant part, be traced back to the general state of African American community considered as a nation. For this litany of problems which afflicts the national Black community may in large measure be said to reflect the disorganization of the Black American economy. More specifically, if the African American community were perceived as a nation, it would become immediately apparent that its fundamental problem, like many other African nations which present similar problems, is its national debt.*

This requires Black people evaluating what family means internally to the community. The first step for the evaluation to be effective is for Black people to envision for themselves what the social institution of family entails and how that vision plays apart of their economic, political, and cultural uplift in America.

Family in American culture has shifted as various groups and leaders alike advocate for their vision of what is an ideal family. Some may argue that families are not only realms of choice but also realms of constraint. Feminists agree that the gender hierarchy in American society is unjust, although they differ on what creates the imbalance. Various feminist ideologies emphasize the family as the "linchpin" of gender injustice against women, while other feminists blame the structure of work and opportunity. The Institute for Women's Policy Research acknowledges that the Black family since the election of President Trump is deficient both in formation and economically. For example, most Black women who are mothers are taking care of their families on a single-income wage that is either below or near the poverty line. This forces them to procure higher debt percentages relative to income, further pushing the economic limits of their family.[74]

A key tenet of Black nationalism within the context of culture is self-determination, which stresses the importance of controlling one's destiny and not having to rely on the very institutions that work against the best interests of African Americans to have an equitable economic and social existence in America. In ideal circumstances, a Black family with children should have two parents not only visible but also taking on child-rearing duties equally to provide balance and understanding to the children when teachable moments that involve self-determination arise. Black parents often cannot instill principles of self-determination in their children because they are too focused on survival. In other words, parents cannot teach self-control and self-determination when they themselves do not have control over their own economic destiny.

From a Black nationalist conception, family would entail not only a stable nuclear family in which parents and children live together with the parents having equal voices as it pertains to finances and education, it would also entail the teaching of common values which in this case is fiscal responsibility and high self-esteem as a standard behavior that promotes the Black nationalist tenet of self-determination.

Common values that should be emphasized consistently in a family that centers itself on self-determination include spirituality, Afrocentric education, and the arts. The teaching of common values in a family environment would lead to reinforcement of Black identity and culture, which then promotes the ideals of self-determination for African Americans to free themselves from domination, whether by whites or nonwhites.

The passiveness that plagues African American culture was on full display when, as related above, Biden lectured the public on who is Black based on their political preferences. This was a form of voter intimidation, an insinuation that Black people who do not vote for him are not only doomed but also somehow not Black. Biden has a history of talking down to the Black community and painting them in a disparaging light to maintain white supremacy. For example, in advocating for the 1994 crime bill, Biden remarked,

> *Unless we do something about that cadre of young people, tens of thousands of them, born out of wedlock, without parents, without supervision, without any structure, without any conscience developing, because they literally have not been socialized, they literally have not had an opportunity . . . we should focus on them now. If we don't, they will—or a portion of them will—become the predators fifteen years from now, and Madam President [Acting President Pro Tempore of the Senate, Dianne Feinstein], we have predators on our streets that society has in fact in part because of [our] neglect created.*

Biden's 2020 comments to the National Association of Black Journalists and National Association of Hispanic Journalists, suggesting Latinos are more diverse than African Americans, are another example of him belittling the Black community:

> *By the way, what you all know but most people don't know, unlike the African American community*

> *with notable exceptions, the Latino community is an incredibly diverse community with incredibly different attitudes about different things. You go to Florida; you find a very different attitude about immigration in certain places than you do when you're in Arizona. So it's a very different, a very diverse community.*

Biden then followed up those comments on a Zoom call in December 2020 with "civil rights leaders" including Al Sharpton, the NAACP president Derrick Johnson, and Biden's vice-president-elect Kamala Harris, chiding them on police reform and working with Latinos:

> *If we cannot make significant progress on racial equity, this country is doomed. It is doomed, not just because of African Americans, but because by 2040 this country is going to be minority white European. Hear me? Minority white European. And you guys are going to have to start working more with Hispanics, who will make up a larger portion of the population than y'all do. I also don't think we should get too far ahead ourselves on dealing with police reform in that, because they've already labeled us as being "defund the police" anything we put forward in terms of the organizational structure to change policing—which, I promise you, will occur. Promise you. That's how they beat the living hell out of us across the country, saying that we're talking about defunding the police. We're not. We're talking about holding them accountable. We're talking about giving them money to do the right things.*

However, none of this prevented Biden from garnering African American support. His support among Black voters was first cemented during the Obama administration when he served as vice president. His presidential campaign started with visits to Black media outlets, churches, and HBCUs.

Criminal justice and wealth inequality took center stage in elections, largely due to the Black Lives Matter movement after the Ahmaud Arbery and Floyd killings. Wealth disparities between African Americans and whites were featured constantly in mainstream and social media platforms thanks to the persistent wealth and income gap between African Americans and all other demographics to further explain how not only race but class played a role in the executions of Arbery and Floyd. However, despite these issues, Biden's approval ratings among African Americans remained high in the first few months of his presidency, reaching 89% in March 2021. If Black America had viewed its politics from a Black nationalist perspective as a collective, it would have punished Biden at the polls, by, perhaps, voting for third-party candidates who had reparations as well as the abolition of law-enforcement institutions in their platforms or by leaving the presidential space on their ballots unmarked.

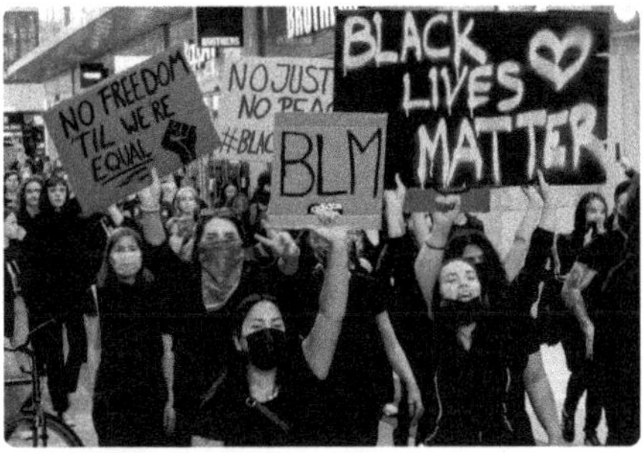

BLACK LIVES MATTER PROTEST IN STOCKHOLM, SWEDEN, SUMMER 2020. (FRANKIE FOUCANTHIN, CREATIVE COMMONS LICENSE.)

ABOUT 300 PEOPLE GATHERED OUTSIDE THE MINNESOTA CAPITOL BUILDING TO DEMAND REPARATIONS FROM THE UNITED STATES GOVERNMENT FOR YEARS OF SLAVERY, JIM CROW, SEGREGATION, REDLINING, AND VIOLENCE AGAINST BLACK PEOPLE FROM POLICE. ST. PAUL, MINNESOTA, JUNE 19, 2020. (FIBONACCI BLUE, CREATIVE COMMONS LICENSE.)

Many may feel that non-voting is counterproductive and say, "Your ancestors fought for you to exercise your vote." Yes, at face value that statement has validity. However, what would be more honest would be to say, "Your ancestors fought for you to have the choice to vote." To the political establishment, a vote or a non-vote conveys valuable information about the preferences of various voting groups. Du Bois said as much in his 1956 essay "Why I Won't Vote:"

> *We can make a sick man President and set him to a job which would strain a man in robust health. So he dies, and what do we get to lead us? With Stevenson and Nixon, with Eisenhower and Eastland, we remain in the same mess. I will be no party to it and that will make little difference. You will take large part and bravely march to the polls, and that also will make no difference. Stop running Russia and giving Chinese advice when we cannot rule ourselves decently. Stop yelling about a democracy we do not have. Democracy is dead in the United States.*

Amidst a growing awareness of Black issues and the racist policies of Trump, the Green Party aimed to attract African American voters in the 2020 general election, with a platform that included reparations are for the descendants of African Slaves in America:

> *The community of people of African ancestry whose family members were held in chattel slavery in what is now the United States of America have legitimate claims to reparations including monetary compensation for centuries of human rights violations, including the Transatlantic slave trade now recognized by the United Nations as a "crime against humanity." As our Nation has done in the past with respect to the Choctaw, the Lakota, the Lambuth, and more recently for Japanese Americans and the European Jewish community, reparations are now due to address the debt still owed to descendants of enslaved Africans.*

If African Americans had thought of themselves as a "nation" in the 2020 election, their leaders would have been more vocal in response to Biden's voter-intimidation language, by either demanding more of Biden or threatening to back other political parties like the Green Party, which had a platform that mentioned for the African American community. This would have forced candidates from the two main political parties to recognize the Black voting bloc as a force to be reckoned with and address their concerns with tangible policies.

All political parties study voting patterns and seek strategies for getting ahead in the next election. Voting blocs, in particular African American voters, may show their displeasure for a candidate or party that they supported in previous election cycles by not voting all together. This can motivate parties or candidates to offer more tangible policy proposals to gain back the bloc's support. This type of bargaining of the vote can create leverage for better policies and accountability of politicians who rely upon the African American vote.

Biden's remarks, detailed above, show that he never respected the Black community as a powerful voting bloc. Waiting for a political "savior" to solve problems exemplifies a kind of passivity that has been common since the civil rights bills of the 1960s. It is no wonder that in the Trump era the dominant society equates "civil rights" with "Black rights."

However, in modern politics, civil rights do not have anything to do with issues specific to Blacks. Civil rights encompass LGBTQIA issues, immigration, women, and class. The restriction of the term "civil rights" to Black concerns feeds into the white supremacist narrative that the issues that Black people face in America are not serious enough for redress on their own accord. President Biden alluded to this notion when he said Blacks will have to work with Latinos because they are also socially minorities that will cut into the economic resources like education scholarships and social services that have traditionally supported the subsistence of African Americans. Biden also intimated that white people may also cut more into these resources because they will be a minority by 2040.

American society continues to be built on the ideals of whites, and if by 2040 they are a minority, whites will still be the hegemonic power in the United States because the systems in place were built by them to maintain their dominance. Historically, white men in America have always done what was in their best interest, even as subjects of the British Empire. These men aggressively took freedom from the British when the opportunity presented itself. Empowered by a spurious interpretation of early Christian writing that believes God granted white people dominion over the planet, white men continue to exert control over others while claiming freedom for themselves. The founding father Patrick Henry may have shouted, "Give me liberty or give me death," while convincing Virginian leaders to send troops in support of the Revolutionary War, but the liberty Henry sought was for whites only.

With the growing trend of remote working and education at all levels, it is possible for Black people to attain all levels of degrees and credentials via virtual learning as well as using their education and the technology to build the type of wealth that can put them on an equal economic playing field at the very least with other ethnic minorities. By building economic equity with other ethnic groups, African Americans can achieve liberation in the era of Trump and beyond not only by building institutions amongst themselves, but also refocusing on family and creating political leverage to seriously influence elected officials and political institutions. One group in Florida that has striven to achieve many of these goals on a local level is the African People's Party, better known by the name of its affiliate, the International's People's Democratic Uhuru Movement, or simply Uhuru Movement.

201

CHAPTER SIX

LIBERATION

The International People's Democratic Uhuru Movement (InPDUM), spearheaded by the African People's Socialist Party (APSP), thrust Black nationalism into the Florida media spotlight in the mid-1990s after two white St. Petersburg police officers, James Knight and Sandra Minor, killed TyRon Lewis, an eighteen-year-old, in 1996. The officers stopped Lewis's car for speeding and, according to the police investigation, "Lewis locked his car doors and refused to get out. Knight drew his gun and stood in front of Lewis's car, which began rolling forward. Knight fired three shots through the windshield."[75] Witnesses said Lewis had done nothing to prompt the shooting and that his car was moving slowly. "The boy wasn't going fast enough to run them over. He wasn't even going two miles per hour," one said, adding that Knight fired five times. Lewis died before reaching the hospital.

What many at that time concluded was that Lewis was murdered by law enforcement because he was a Black male. This perception sparked riots in St. Petersburg that continued for days. Hundreds protested with rocks, bricks, bottles, and Molotov cocktails. A grand jury's failure to indict led to renewed violence two weeks later.

In 1996, St. Petersburg was a city of roughly 240,000

people and had a 20% Black population. However, nearly all the city's Black residents lived in South St. Petersburg, far from the glittery downtown high-rise office buildings and condominiums. The dividing line between white and Black neighborhoods is Central Avenue. During the Jim Crow era, St. Petersburg had "sundown laws" that forbade Blacks from crossing Central Avenue into white areas after dark. Poverty affected about 37% of Black residents in the neighborhood that experienced the 1996 riots. The median household income at that time was $14,000. Unemployment was above 10% at that point, high school graduation rates were 41%, and only 3% had college degrees. InPDUM became a galvanizing force after November 1996, when a grand jury decided that the officers were justified in shooting and killing Lewis. InPDUM called for the execution of police officers, which led to an increased police presence at the group's headquarters:

> *The trouble began shortly after 6 p.m., when a police officer was shot in the leg outside a house where members of a black separatist group, the National People's Democratic Uhuru Movement, meet. The group has called for the executions of the police officers involved in last month's shooting. The streets were immediately blocked off, and moments later dozens of gunshots were heard. There were shouts of "Get down, get down," and tear gas filled the area. "KILLER COP GOES FREE" read a flier the group handed out after the grand jury ruling while another read "GET ORGANIZED!" One leader of the group said, "We will not be shot down in the streets like dogs. Neither will we be pushed into jails for defending our community." Police arrested three leaders of the group to try to prevent violence and collected more than 6 tons of rocks and bottles stashed in trash bins and other spots in the neighborhood, Stephens said. Within half an hour after the officer was shot, groups of youths began crowding the streets, throwing rocks and bottles at passing cars in a scene that, while smaller and more contained, resembled previous nights of violence.*[76]

"It was really ill-advised to make those arrests. I think that incited people," said Bill Laubach of the Pinellas County Police Benevolent Association. In the hours after several arrests, St. Petersburg was hit by violent clashes that left two police officers with gunshot wounds, many more seriously hurt, and at least twenty-nine structures destroyed by fire. The police reaction to the violence reflected their frustration with the National People's Democratic Uhuru Movement. At one point during the uprising, the group held a "tribunal" that called for the executions of the mayor, the police chief, and the two officers involved in the fatal traffic stop. The state prosecutor, Bernie McCabe, angrily remarked, "I was incensed that they would hold a so-called tribunal and call for the execution of four people. They are nothing but a bunch of lawless thugs."[77] A raid on Uhuru headquarters followed the grand jury's decision and the enraging statements from law enforcement.

Residents were furious when police fired tear gas into a meeting attended by women and children. The former NAACP executive Marvin Davies said, "There are many ways to get to the same place, and we are beginning to see that." After Lewis was murdered, a diverse African American coalition, including local ministers and leaders from groups like the SCLC and NAACP, briefly rallied behind the Uhuru Movement. The local SCLC president at the time reflected, "We found common ground around the need to essentially stop the killing of young black males." The InPDUM believed that the police had made a calculated effort to intimidate them by arresting a few of their members and ransacking their homes. According to a memorandum sent by their members they explained that

> *Following the Tribunal, St. Petersburg police tried to frame the Uhuru Movement by planting cocaine near Uhuru House. In spite of this, the African community debunked it as a setup. Military maneuvers by police surrounded Uhuru House on November 13, 1996, preceding a planned Grand Jury acquittal announcement. Later, 3 Uhuru members became*

THE NATIONAL PEOPLE'S DEMOCRATIC UHURU MOVEMENT MARCHED FROM 18TH AVENUE SOUTH TO ST PETERSBURG CITY HALL IN 1997 TO PROTEST THE POLICE KILLING OF 18-YEAR-OLD TYRON LEWIS. (*TAMPA BAY TIMES.*)

> *targets under the false claim of preventing violence. Questionable charges led to the arrests of Keith Stewart and David Willard, while Chairman Omali Yeshitela and Kinara Zima were maced by the police. Authorities declared the NPDUM community meeting unlawful and ordered attendees to depart.*[78]

The consequences of the riots shaped race relations in St. Petersburg for a long time. To combat police brutality, the St. Petersburg National People's Democratic Uhuru Movement held an emergency conference in 1997. There, according to the *Tampa Bay Times,*

> *A panel of activists and women who have lost family members gathered at Uhuru headquarters to speak to a racially diverse audience about the exclusion of African Americans and other minorities from the democratic process. The event, held on Independence Day, aimed to shed light on this issue. Three women shared their stories of losing loved ones to police violence, including Dorothy Copp Elliott, Lorita Cooper-Geddie, and Akua Njeri whose husband, Fred Hampton, was a leader of the Black Panthers in Illinois.*

The St. Petersburg Citizen Review Committee, which reviewed St. Petersburg Police Department internal affairs decisions, appointed Chimurenga Waller in 1998; Waller later became president of the city's InPDUM chapter. Although the panel lacked decision-making authority, it made recommendations to police officials on how to deal with the Black community.

According to the *Burning Spear*, the once print and now online newspaper published by the InPDUM, the group opened the "Black Gym of Our Own" in 1994 in St. Petersburg to improve the individual and collective health of the "African" (meaning persons of African descent in America) community. To increase visibility and accessibility for a wider membership, the gym relocated in 2001 to a separate location on Martin Luther King Jr. Street, under the direction of the nonprofit African People's Education and Defense Fund (APEDF). They renamed the gym the All People's TyRon Lewis Community Gym, which, for the InPDUM, embodies the "African" community's self-determination, representing their own creation and use. The slogan "A Gym of Our Own!" echoes this. They also hire primarily African Americans to staff the gym.[79] On October 24, 2021, the InPDUM held a twenty-fifth-anniversary memorial event for Lewis on the street where he was killed. "Lewis's family and members of the community are still fighting for justice," as a local journalist put it. "The group is also pushing to rename 18th Avenue to TyRon Lewis Avenue." [80]

Although the TyRon Lewis tragedy played a signficant role in launching the InPDUM to a national audience in the 1990s, its umbrella organization the APSP had laid the important groundwork decades earlier. The APSP defines itself as an "African internationalist organization." It also engages in Black nationalist activity under the InPDUM brand by creating Black-owned institutions to serve St. Petersburg, including Burning Spear Productions, Black Star Industries, Uhuru Foods, the African People's Education and Defense Fund, the All-African Peoples Development and Empowerment Project, the African National Women's Organization, and Uhuru Furniture. The APSP uses the Swahili word *uhuru* to represent the quest for liberation by uniting African people for freedom, social justice, self-sufficiency, and economic progress—the foundation of Black nationalism. The APSP was founded in 1972 by its first chairman, Omali Yeshitela, who had been born Joseph Waller on October 9, 1941, in St. Petersburg. Like many small cities in the South, St. Petersburg in the 1940s had a sizeable Black population but was deeply segregated by strict municipality policy.

In 1920 St. Petersburg was 17% Black, according to census figures. But St. Petersburg's 1930 city directory understated the Black population; the census reported 18%, while the directory claimed only 9%. The Black population

JOE WALLER AND A GROUP OF MEN IN 1966, JUST BEFORE THEY WERE ARRESTED FOR RIPPING DOWN THE MURAL WHICH HUNG IN ST. PETERSBURG CITY HALL. (JESSE MOORE, *TAMPA BAY TIMES.*)

Moral Principles
Are Sold here
To "Boss"
Goldner

grew 61.6% percent from 1930 to 1940, climbing from 7,416 to 11,982. Over the same period, the white population grew only 48%. The rise of Black visibility and population led to white leaders calling for a more formalized, rigid system of housing segregation. But the St. Petersburg historian Olive McLin notes that, according to the updated municipal charter adopted in 1931, one of St. Petersburg's primary civic goals was "to establish and set apart in said city separate residential limits or districts for white and negro residents." The enforcement of residential segregation would no longer be through covenants or racial custom; instead, the city charter empowered city officials "to prohibit any white person from taking up or establishing a place of residence or business within the territorial limits of said city so set apart and established for the residence of negroes, and to prohibit any negro from taking up or establishing a place of residence or business within the territorial limits of said city so set apart and established for the residence of white persons."[81]

The segregationist policies in St. Petersburg that Yeshitela experienced as a child shaped his understanding of race relations. Joe Waller, as he was then known, was raised by his single mother and his grandmother Della Thomas. Beginning when he was two, Waller's grandmother introduced him to reading with the *St. Petersburg Times*. St. Petersburg during Waller's youth was known for tourism and retirement living but also limited job opportunities, low wages, and societal discrimination of African Americans. An example of this was in 1951 when Waller, at the age of ten, refused to dance for white customers at a shoeshine stand, leading to an argument with the owner and his subsequent departure.[82]

The text describes the experience of Waller, who joined the army in 1960 with the belief that whites and Blacks would work and fight together for the common purpose of protecting the United States. However, his ideals were challenged when a fellow white recruit expressed racist sentiments toward a Black recruit. Despite this, Waller completed his basic training and was deployed to Berlin in 1961. He was involved in a tense armed standoff at Checkpoint Charlie during the Berlin Crisis, when Soviet and U.S. troops faced off for sixteen hours.

According to the journalists Sue Landry and David Rogers of the *Tampa Bay Times,* at the height of the Cuban missile crisis in 1962, Waller's unit was sent to Patrick Air Force Base near Melbourne, Florida, and his convoy stopped in Palatka, a small town between Jacksonville and Orlando, for a meal. As he recalled years later, "We walk into this restaurant in our G.I. outfits. We were going to save Florida from the dirty Russians and Cubans, right? When we got in there, they said, 'We don't serve niggers.'"

Back in Georgia, a sergeant interrogated Waller about an allegation from a white woman. In giving money to Black soldiers, the woman made a point of maintaining distance. However, dealing with Waller, he ensured that their hands made contact. Waller said the conversation ended when he said he didn't like white women because they looked "like the underbellies of fish and frogs." Waller's superiors referred him to a psychiatrist due to his political writings distributed around the base; the psychiatrist concluded, "There's nothing wrong with you. You're just a Garveyite!"[83]

Waller then wrote a letter to President Kennedy requesting discharge from the army due to his belief that the nation was unjust. After finally receiving an honorable discharge in 1963, he returned to St. Petersburg where his anger against America intensified. Despite struggling to communicate with his family, he found work as a copy clerk. One night, he faced a police officer stop, jail time, and a vagrancy charge while walking home from work, but the charges were later dropped and the arrest ruled illegal by a judge. Landry and Rogers observe that Waller wrote of the incident in a 1969 column that "It's not just a matter of one big eye-opening experience, for Blacks anyway."

Waller went to Los Angeles in 1965 while on leave from the news organization, intending to attend college, but the Watts riots broke out. Though the violence horrified many, Waller was struck by the power and cooperation of the rioters. The author Anita Cutting conducted an interview with Waller in which he recalled his inspiration by the 1965 Watts riots: "I had never seen anything like that in my life. For just a moment, the African people had a real democratic situation going there." During and after the riot, he wrote correspondence pieces for the *Times*. With access to places and information inaccessible to white journalists, he kept the Sunshine City abreast of the turmoil, and for the first time in his life witnessed the "the power of the people."[84]

Waller returned to St. Petersburg as an inspired Black militant. His introduction to the NAACP, and thus his active involvement, came through the *St. Petersburg Times* award-winning journalist Peggy Peterman, who was Black. At one point, he participated in NAACP meetings and demonstrations to desegregate cinemas. He quickly concluded, though, that the NAACP's work was futile and unworthy of his attention. He focused his attention on Peggy's husband Frank Peterman, who was also Black, and his ambitious, though failed, bid for a state legislature seat, driven by a desire for meaningful reform. He was close to the Petermans, but their middle-class activist circle always made him uneasy. This feeling of unease was shared by Jim Sanderlin, Peterman's law partner, who always resented Waller's presence at their law firm.

After the campaign, Peterman sent Waller to South Carolina to work for CORE's Voter Education Project (VEP). The CORE attorney John Due assigned Waller to lead voter registration and antipoverty programs in north Florida using nonviolent civil-rights-style strategies. Waller, on the other hand, was not happy about this approach. Waller's advocacy of "Black Power" at a Gainesville rally ended his time with the VEP, much to the dismay of the director, Vernon Jordan. As racial tensions escalated in the mid-1960s, Waller set up Florida's chapter of the Student Nonviolent Coordinating Committee, which at the time was influenced more by H. Rap Brown and Stokely Carmichel. November 1966 saw a week-long strike by the city's sanitation workers, who were mostly Black and represented by Sanderlin and Peterman, fighting for better wages. Lynn Andrews, the city manager, publicly mocked the strikers and initially declined negotiations. Within forty-eight hours, tensions arose, with 70% of sanitation workers being laid off, replacements hired, and the police gearing up for riots. After days of mounting tension, Andrews finally relented and settled. Feeling the frustration of the turmoil that would embody the mid-1960s nationally as well as in St. Petersburg locally, Waller would later in 1966 take direct action against a mural created by world-renowned sculptor and artist George Snow Hill.

Hill, who was white and originally from Michigan, was a recipient of Civil Works Administration funds which he used to paint five large murals, each portraying a different historical era of Florida. He became a resident of St. Petersburg in 1933 after moving from Michigan for health reasons. He was commissioned to create two murals in the St. Petersburg City Hall thanks to an award that he won that was sponsored by the Federal Art Project in 1940.[85] His local government-approved idea was to illustrate the daily life of St. Petersburg's citizens. World War II and the subsequent loss of federal funding for public art did not discourage Hill. He declared he'd personally pay for the paintings' completion and in 1945 saw the framing and hanging of the seven-by-ten-foot canvases on the first-floor stairway landing's walls.

The painting *Fishing on the Pier* featured a family fishing on the north side's Million Dollar Pier, with a foreground pelican anticipating scraps. Men fishing in Tampa Bay can be seen in the background. *Picnicking at Pass-a-Grille* was bestowed upon the south wall. From behind, a leisure scene shows a white family seated beneath a thatched pavilion at Pass-a-Grille Beach. The musicians' portrayal, consistent with the era's racist pop culture, used stereotypical minstrel-show imagery of Black people, including wide white eyes and oversized white lips.

For nearly twenty years, this painting adorned the walls of St. Petersburg City Hall. In 1959, Ruth MacLellan, a St. Petersburg Council on Human Relations member, and her spouse voiced their concerns to the City Council regarding the mural, and Waller formally asked St. Petersburg officials to remove it. "It depicts Negroes in a most despicable, derogatory manner," he wrote and expressed confidence that

Mayor Herman Goldner, who proclaimed to be the mayor of "all the people" of St. Petersburg, would do the right thing and remove it. Goldner replied, "I find nothing offensive in the portrayal of strolling troubadours and picnickers at Pass-a-Grille Beach. . . . I think you know that I, personally, am not a racist. I think that all of our minority groups must mature to the point where self-consciousness is not a motivating factor for complaints."

A couple of weeks later, on December 29, 1966, Waller and other members of the SNCC marched on City Hall. They protested the $50-million federal grant for downtown beautification, noting the lack of funding for nearby Black neighborhoods. Waller denies being at City Hall initially doing anything against the painting but says he was triggered by the laughter of white reporters and police at an elderly woman's expense, resulting in his destruction of the artwork. A roar echoed through the silent space as the painted canvas was torn from the wall, the sound reverberating off the marble staircase. A woman standing on the staircase landing above screamed, "Black bastards!" With their adrenaline pumping, Waller and his associates left the premises and ran toward Central Avenue, where they were arrested.

CHAIRMAN OMALI YESHITELA, FOUNDER AND LEADER OF THE AFRICAN PEOPLE'S SOCIALIST PARTY, C. 2020. (DAVID LANCE, CREATIVE COMMONS LICENSE.)

Waller was charged and convicted of disorderly conduct and damaging city property. Sentenced to five years in July 1967, he was released after serving only two. While imprisoned, he founded the Junta of Militant Organizations (JOMO) in 1968, an organization like Oakland's Black Panther Party, and adopted the African name Omali Yeshitela, meaning "umbrella for a thousand people" in the Ethiopian language Amharic.

As the FBI's COINTELPRO program intensified its assault on the Black Power movement in 1972, Yeshitela understood that the freedom struggle required a party capable of advancing beyond protests and Black people striving for control over their own lives. In 1972 he aligned JOMO with the Black Rights Fighters and Black Study Group, both of whom were active in Florida and Kentucky. This alliance is what created the African People's Socialist Party (APSP) and shifted Yeshitela's focus from Black power to African Internationalism.[86] In 1976, the African People's Solidarity Committee (APSC) formed under the APSP's leadership to provide a space for whites as well as people not of African descent to "organize white reparations to African people" and materially support APSP.

In 1979, the APSP also launched the African National Prison Organization (ANPO) to raise awareness that imprisonment was increasingly becoming a tool of political repression. The APSP then relocated its headquarters to Oakland, California, in the 1980s. The 1982 Brooklyn tribunal advocating for African reparations led by the APSP and the 1984 Oakland housing-control ballot initiative were launched from their West Coast base. Oakland is where many of the party's ongoing economic institutions, such as Spear Graphics, Uhuru Bakery-Café, Uhuru Furniture, and Uhuru Foods, were established. Yeshitela then founded the International People's Democratic Uhuru Movement in Chicago in 1991.

The Uhuru House on 18th Avenue South in St. Petersburg became the party's headquarters again by 1993. *The Burning Spear*, which is the publication arm of the APSP, consistently portrayed African internationalism as the revolutionary, scientific, and materialist ideology of the

African working class. European actions—attacks, division, enslavement, scattering of Africans, and exploitative colonial and neocolonial systems within a capitalist structure—are presented in this theory as the root of Europe's wealth and Africa's impoverishment. The foundation of African internationalism was Garvey's Universal Negro Improvement Association (UNIA). Luwezi Kinshasa, the African Socialist International's secretary-general (an APSP offshoot), contended that the UNIA was the first international African liberation movement, yet it wasn't pan-Africanist.

Prior to Garvey and the UNIA, pan-Africanism lacked a precise definition. The application of colonial reform included people such as Henry Sylvester Williams, a lawyer of Trinidadian lineage and founder of the first Pan-African Conference. Various initiatives helped Africans return to their homeland from the Caribbean, Brazil, and the United States. Garvey then became a pioneer in forming a global organization for Black unity via the UNIA. It functioned among impoverished Black workers and peasants worldwide, aware of its mission for Black national liberation. However, Black-centered groups opposing the UNIA in the early twentieth-century like the National Association for the Advancement of Colored People, found a leader in W. E. B. Du Bois.

In his essay "African Internationalism Is Not Pan-Africanism," Yeshitela claims that

> *Pan-Africanism began as an assault on Marcus Garvey's movement. Pan-Africanism failed to equip the masses to confront white power disguised as Black authority. . . . Pan-Africanism is petty bourgeois (pun intended) intellectual opportunism, based on selfish class interests. To live off workers and poor peasants means that they cannot build a single organization, with a single discipline necessary to unify the African national liberation movement. The short-term Pan-Africanist fight for congressional seats, the nonviolence and no struggle with the State sacrificed the long-term struggle for revolution."*[87]

African Internationalism as conceptualized by Yeshitela is more closely aligned with the legal scholar Jeffery M. Brown's version of Black internationalism, contextualized as the liberation and empowerment of African-Americans intersecting with those of the African diaspora around the globe. Brown argues that Black internationalism's foundation, much like that of African internationalism, is rooted in the principles laid out in the UNIA. Garvey and the UNIA are considered the originators of the concept of economically grounded Black internationalism. Garveyism's emphasis on global racial economic empowerment provided a valuable model for Black global-empowerment efforts. Such an approach was particularly suited to addressing persistent problems of racial subordination.[88] Despite organizational shortcomings, Garveyism highlighted the importance of engaging working-class Blacks for a truly effective Black internationalism. Brown argues that an instructive example of Black internationalism in practice was the Free South Africa Movement (FSAM) that African Americans led in the mid-1980s.

Analysis of the FSAM reveals the potential and limitations of its economically focused Black internationalism on national and global scales. The oppressive apartheid regime in South Africa led to the formation of the FSAM. Brown noted the three key points of the domestic FSAM: (1) the dismantling of the apartheid system; (2) the release of all political prisoners, including Nelson Mandela, from South African prisons; and (3) the divestiture of all U.S. financial holdings in South Africa by our government, major colleges and universities, and corporations.

Three African American leaders—Randall Robinson, Walter Fauntroy, and Mary Frances Berry—peacefully occupied the South African embassy in Washington, D.C., on November 21, 1984. Until the South African government freed all political prisoners and dismantled apartheid, the protestors vowed to remain at the embassy. The efforts of the FSAM resulted in Mandela being freed years later.

Although Black internationalism has many similarities with the APSP's African Internationalism as it pertains to the unification of the Black working class internationally for liberation, there are major differences. For example, Brown argues that Black internationalism is a progression from pan-Africanism. Meanwhile, the APSP rejected pan-Africanism because of its Du Boisian origin in upper-class circles and its lack of an economic or revolutionary agenda. Meanwhile, the APSP's African internationalism advocates economic cooperation, based on socialism, among people of African descent worldwide, as well as propagating revolutionary change to systemic institutions. This is contrary to pan-Africanism, which, in the APSP view, promotes the political unity of Black people within oppressive systems without challenge.

According to Brown, contemporary Black internationalism embraces an idealistic view of pan-African unity, prioritizing a romanticized notion of shared interests among African Americans, Africans, and Afro-Caribbean peoples over practical political and economic realities. Black internationalism, as interpreted by Brown, is incapable of addressing the substantial and multifaceted obstacles presented by economic globalization, nor can it adequately support the very real material expectations of the most impoverished African Americans. Brown says his version of effective Black internationalism represents a departure from the traditional rights-based and pan-Africanist approaches, which focus on racial justice and pan-African unity. Black empowerment—economically grounded and efficient responsiveness to the developing global economy—is central to his version of Black internationalism. Again, this closely aligns with African internationalism in that it prioritizes the economic needs of the Black (African) working class the world over. However, a major difference is that African internationalism asserts that Marxism is the best way to improve the collective lives of the Black working class while Brown argues that capitalism is more effective.

An economically grounded Black internationalism would, at a minimum, stress three core objectives: (1) overt economic empowerment, (2) greater Black influence in shaping domestic and foreign policy initiatives on matters like free trade and third world development, and (3)

Black institutional capacity building, by which the goals identified under (1) and (2) above might be more effectively pursued. More pragmatically, Black internationalism would invigorate traditional efforts to ensure racial justice, both domestically and globally, by creating a more influential economic and institutional platform from which to promote and defend Black interests. Brown's arguments for using capitalist principles to empower Black people the world over was based on his observations that traditional Black internationalists like Du Bois did not have a program for short-term economic upliftment of Blacks. He also suggests that Black leaders remain torn between economic empowerment and civil rights advocacy as goals.

Black internationalism's ideological attachment to 1960s-era pan-African solidarity hinders its ability to understand and respond to short-term economic disruptions caused by global capitalism. Over fifty years have passed, and society must find new solutions in the form of an economically grounded paradigm that identifies how globalization of workforces and the international movement of capital directly affect African American communities and respond with Black-focused initiatives.

A key goal for any economic plan is recognizing globalization's negative short-term impact (U.S. job losses from capital outflows) and creating effective responses. Second, Black internationalism's failure to adopt an economically focused approach has left many in the Black community unclear on the difference between economic and institutional progress on the one hand and, on the other, the fight for civil rights at home.[89] For example, Congressman Jesse Jackson, Jr., opposed the African Growth and Opportunity Act (AGOA), claiming that multinational corporations would be the biggest winners under a trade agreement, in the manner of the North American Free Trade Agreement (NAFTA), which drew fire for favoring corporate needs over social justice.

Both Jesse and his father, the Rev. Jesse Jackson, Sr., have advocated for Black corporate employees to gain better opportunities in high-level positions within primarily-white corporate leadership. Brown's concluding argument on NAFTA ironically highlights the strong support for free trade agreements (such as NAFTA and the African Trade Bill) from the very corporations that Jesse Jackson, Jr., opposed. The positions held by the Jacksons reveal deep divisions in Black leadership and America concerning the definition and role of Black economic participation.

On the other hand, the African People's Socialist Party routinely criticizes capitalism and extolls the virtues of socialism and Marxism in its constitution and publications and in Yeshitela's speeches. The group often describes capitalism as "parasitic" and the United States as an imperial colonial power that thrives off the African working class not only domestically but also internationally. Their constitution serves as the foundation for their ideology:

> 3.1— *The aims and objectives of the APSP-USA are to lead the struggle of the African working class and oppressed masses against U.S. capitalist-colonialist domination and all the manifestations of oppression and exploitation that result from this relationship. The Party recognizes that the particular character of the oppression of African people within U.S. borders is domestic or internal colonialism. Leading the struggle to end the system of domestic colonialism and smash the U.S. capitalist-colonialist state is the immediate task of the African People's Socialist Party-USA and the African working class in the U.S.*
>
> 3.2— *The Party aims to advance the genuine liberation and unification of Africa and African people through its work as the U.S. Front of the worldwide African Revolution, and from this political vantage point fight for the creation of a single All-African Socialist State which will advance the development of a classless, communist society organized around the principle of, from each according to her or his ability and to each according to her or his needs.*

> *3.3— The Party works for the emancipation of the laboring masses of the world in every country in the contest against national oppression and capitalist exploitation and to advance the solidarity of all peoples in the relentless battle against imperialism and for the victory of world socialism.*
>
> *3.4— The Party aims to establish a formidable working alliance with progressive parties or forums that subscribe to the goals of the liberation and unification of Africa and African people under the leadership of the African working class and the toiling masses in general.*

Their party platform also makes several arguments for socialist programs for the purposes of uplifting persons of African descent worldwide. The last point of their platform is taken from Ghana's first prime minister and president, Kwame Nkrumah, and explicitly demands a socialist framework for a united socialist government of African people:

> *We believe that the total liberation and unification of Africa under an All-African socialist government must be the primary objective of all Black revolutionaries throughout the world. It is an objective which, when achieved, will bring about the fulfillment of the aspirations of Africans and people of African descent everywhere. It will at the same time advance the triumph of the international socialist revolution, and the onward progress toward communism, under which every society is ordered on the principle of—from each according to his (her) ability, to each according to his (her) needs.*

Yeshitela makes the case for a socialist agenda to unite and liberate African people worldwide by overthrowing "parasitic capitalism" and Black people moving toward a more socialist agenda for their empowerment:

> *Finance capital, the export of capital, monopoly, etc., are all articulations of a political economy rooted in parasitism and based on the historically brutal subjugation of most of humanity. Unlike Marx and Lenin, we African Internationalists deny that there has ever been anything progressive about capitalism. Capitalism was born parasitic. Without slavery North America, the most progressive of countries would be transformed into a patriarchal country. Wipe North America off the map of the world, and you will have anarchy—the complete decay of modern commerce and civilization. Cause slavery to disappear and you will have wiped America off the map of nations. What an excellent formula for the overthrow of capitalism!*

He then proposed a set of strategies in 1984 to implement these ideals of uniting and liberating African people by advocating for political independence:

> 1 *Our first and most important objective should be to win Black people to the position of political independence.*
>
> 2 *A second and related strategic objective for winning liberation is to establish the leadership of the pro-Independence movement.*
>
> 3 *Win support for the Independence position within current U.S. borders. The Party's pursuit of this objective has contributed to the creation of a North American (white) solidarity committee and the various committees which work under its leadership.*
>
> 4 *Another element of the Party's general strategy for liberation is the creation of dual, or competing, or contending, governmental powers. That is to say, to the degree possible, the Party and the general*

pro-independence movement must assume the real and actual responsibilities of government for our people.

5 *Another objective of the Party's general strategy is to expose the oppressive nature of the U.S. government, thereby constantly undermining it within and without the current U.S. borders.*

6 *The Party's general strategy also calls for winning international support for our independence position, thereby contributing to the international diplomatic encirclement of the U.S.*

7 *The seventh in our general strategy calls for the building of an African People's Liberation Army. In order for this to happen, the people must be schooled through their own struggles under the leadership of the APSP.* [90]

The African Socialist International (ASI) resolution advances Yeshitela's vision for an international program to liberate Africans. For the liberation and unification of Africa into one socialist nation, the African People's Socialist Party calls for all African revolutionaries worldwide to collaborate in establishing a united pan-African socialist organization. The party also believes that it can provide a unified direction, coordination, and support for African revolutionary movements aligned with international socialist goals. Their vision allows them to consolidate African identity for all Africans, fighting against oppression and exploitation caused by imperial forces across the globe.

The ASI would establish an international division of labor to serve the African Liberation movement in all its political and geographic aspects and benefit the Black diaspora worldwide. The benefit of a liberation base for Black people globally is that it allows for a global revolutionary party based on African working-class principles regardless of their economic standing on a global scale. The Revolutionary

National Democratic Program (RNDP) is the party's vehicle for enacting the goals of the ASI. The RNDP sets apart the goals of Black Americans from those of the U.S. power structure. Politically, the RNDP is frequently associated with Marxist movements aiming for liberation from colonial rule. The APSP believes that their version of an RNDP will defeat capitalism and therefore be replaced with a social system in which everyone in society owns the means of production. In other words, an RNDP will replace capitalism with socialism. The APSP's advocacy centers on working-class ownership and control of production, along with the political power to promote their interests and social progress.

There are fifty action items outlined in the InPDUM's RNDP. Guided by the APSP, each RNDP committee implements each item through various approaches. Overall, the InPDUM, the African People's Solidarity Committee, and the African National Women's Organization purport to work in conjunction toward achieving reparations, community sovereignty, and self-government for Black people worldwide. Their stated focus is also on organizing, solidarity, and addressing issues such as gentrification, police brutality, and the special oppression faced by Black women due to being both Black and female. Black Star Industries (BSI), also a part of the APSP, plays a significant economic role in realizing these goals.

BSI itself is a corporation that was created to centralize all economic development activities of the APSP and produce partnership opportunities for the community. According to its website, it supports the APSP by providing funds for economic development initiatives, aiming for organizational independence. The APSP economic organizations are therefore also accessible to InPDUM nonprofits, which creates collaboration for business development among Black people.[91]

The African People's Education and Defense Fund (APEDF) was established in 1994 to "develop and institutionalize programs to defend the human and civil rights of the African community, and to address the grave disparities in education, health, healthcare, and economic development faced by African people." Since the coronavirus pandemic, one of the more effective programs created from the APEDF and BSI is the Black Power Blueprint:

Black Power Blueprint is a joint program of the APEDF and BSI, transforming North St. Louis through renovation, economic development, and political power by and for the Black community. Led by Ona Zené Yeshitela, president of the APEDF and BSI, the Black Power Blueprint was launched in 2017 on the North Side of St. Louis, the most impoverished area of the city. The Black Power Blueprint is buying abandoned, dilapidated buildings, initiating a rapid process of restoration or demolition and re-allocation of land to create community-generated self-reliance programs that uplift the residents and engage them socially, politically, and economically in the future of our community.

In 2017, the Census Bureau released data showing that only 16% of African American millennials (ages 21 to 36) owned homes, less than a third of the figure for whites.[92] To address these daunting statistics, in 2020 four women, three of whom are from the community, created the Building Black Bed-Stuy (BBB) fundraising initiative to support African Americans in the Bedford-Stuyvesant neighborhood of Brooklyn, New York.

The founding members of the initiative are Kai Avent-Deleon, owner of the concept store Sincerely, located in Bed-Stuy; Nana Yaa Asare-Boadu, a performing artist and designer; Rajni Jacques, the fashion director at Allure; and Dana Arbib, a creative director and designer. The initiative began with a series of online fundraisers. Each Sunday, they hosted an outdoor marketplace and block party in front of Avent-Deleon's Sincerely Tommy and Eat & Stay, showcasing local talent and businesses. The women stated that the Bed-Stuy neighborhood was an historically proud Black neighborhood now suffering not only from gentrification but also from COVID-19. The effects of gentrification and the COVID-19 pandemic have closed businesses, triggering a cycle of vacant buildings, depressed property values, and finally large corporate developers buying vacant building at depressed prices, then redeveloping them into high-end housing and retail spaces, forcing the long-time African American residents to seek housing elsewhere. Funds are raised exclusively in the community and redistributed to three organizations in the community, representing the mission of Building Black Bed-Stuy, which is self-sufficiency and liberation. The Watoto Free School was one of the organizations that received funding from the BBB funding initiative.

The Watoto School states that it is an arts- and culture-based learning space for elementary-aged children. The founder of the school, affectionately called Mama Umi, created a curriculum based on Afrocentricity. The students learn languages such as French and Swahili, as well as agriculture and yoga. On Freedom Fighter Fridays, students celebrate different Black freedom fighters. Another organization that the BBB donated to was the Black Power Blueprint, which is a St. Louis–based organization with satellite offices in Bed-Stuy:

> *The Black Power Blueprint is actually based in St. Louis, but their work is so powerful we could not pass up the opportunity to help them. The organization is under the African People's Socialist Party led by Omali Yeshitela, one of the great Black leaders of our time. They've built a community from the ground up, complete with a community center, furniture store, bakery, farm, and CSA. The community is completely run by the Black community.*[93]

The APSP being recognized nationally since the election of Trump by Black grassroots organizations such as the Building Black Bed-Stuy initiative shows that they are relevant both as an ideology and as a party. And with the topic of reparations becoming more of a political focal point in Black political discourse since the election of Trump, it is not out of the realm of possibility for the APSP to be a leading advocacy group in a modern international reparations movement for people of African descent, whether it be a diaspora group in a predominantly-white country or a majority-Black country that is still affected by its former white colonizers. The APSP's inclusion of reparations in their platform solidifies their expertise on the subject and goes back to the early 1980s. From 1982 to 2003, the APSP convened twelve World Tribunals on Reparations for African People. The party has also written extensively about what reparations would entail:

> *We want the U.S. and the international European ruling class and states to pay Africa and African people for the centuries of genocide, oppression, and enslavement of our people. We believe that Africa and African people are due reparations, just economic compensation, billions of dollars which must be paid to the Organization of African Unity or any other legitimate international organization of African people, for equitable distribution for the development of Africa. We also believe that reparations must be distributed to the various independent African states dispersed throughout the world, and to the legitimate representatives of African people forcibly dispersed throughout the world who have not yet won liberation.*

In addition to an international reparations movement, stateside their Black Power Blueprint economic program is a modern Black nationalist framework in action. The various programs supported economically by Black Star Industries—including Uhuru Foods and Pies, Uhuru Design Studios, Burning Spear Publications, and Uhuru Furniture and Collectibles—align specifically with the economic principles of Black nationalism by creating industry in the predominantly-Black neighborhoods that they serve.

The most effective institution on the APSP platform that can be efficiently replicated in Black communities across the country with the support of Black grassroots organizations, Black businesses, and local Black politicians is Black Star Industries. However, in order for this to be even remotely possible, an organization that is either a chapter of the APSP itself or another predominantly-Black local grassroots organization will have to lead the efforts in spearheading alliances involving Black businesses in the predominant industry of that area, Black-owned secondary schools, Black-owned nonprofits, a banking institution that has favorable relationships with local Black-owned businesses, and finally local Black political candidates that have a history, whether in politics or in their private lives, of supporting Black people and Black interests.

Just as Black Star Industries serves as the financial arm of APSP institutions, the now-local Black conglomerate would also develop a funding platform in conjunction with local banks. This would provide either grants or low-interest loans with a mission to provide products and services in Black communities. The money made from these local businesses, with guidance from the Black conglomerate, can then be reinvested in the Black conglomerate to fund local secondary-education institutions geared toward career programs that will benefit local Black businesses. Once the relationship between local Black businesses and Black-owned educational institutions is established by the local Black conglomerate that helps fund them, the conglomerate can search for the candidate for targeted political offices, ideally city councils, commissioners, and mayors, that will serve the local Black population's interests.

The search for and vetting of candidates to support, no matter their race, will be done by the local Black conglomerate to ensure that they have an aligned vision of implementing the local Black conglomerate's platform. Once it is decided who will be supported, the Black conglomerate, which will by this point double as a political action committee, fund that candidate's campaign for office. And once in office, the politician will regularly update the conglomerate as well as their constituents on the progress of the implementation of said platform.

The conglomerate's PAC will regularly search for and vet individuals for political positions as they arise and use this as leverage to ensure that the politician that they are funding and supporting is held accountable for their performance. The local Black conglomerate within the same vein as the APSP, tangibly leading the local economic, educational, and political activities in predominantly-Black communities, is the ideal APSP model. This cycle of support between businesses, educational institutions, and politicians at the local level not only creates jobs for Black people but also moves the local community forward to self-reliance, which in turn brings them closer to the APSP's vision of self-governance and ultimately liberation from oppressive political, economic, and social conditions that were created by the American system of white supremacy.

CHAPTER SEVEN

KILLING WHITE SUPREMACY

Black nationalism continues to play a central role in the opposition and resistance to anti-Black racism and white supremacy in politics, economics, and education in America. To that end, the philosopher and author Neely Fuller, Jr., once said, "If you don't understand white supremacy, what it is and how it works, everything else will confuse you." On January 6, 2021, the nation itself was in a state of confusion as white supremacy was front and center in the mainstream news and social media. As paramilitary and affiliated groups descended on Washington, D.C., a confused nation watched in horror as these groups sought to prevent the certification of the transfer of power from Donald Trump to Joseph Biden. The white supremacist and fascist-leaning groups involved in the invasion included the Three Percenters, the Oath Keepers, the Proud Boys, and the Texas Freedom Force. Although many of these groups include working-class people, elite white supremacists who did not directly participate in the insurrection played a significant role in its development.

The genesis of the insurrection was in 2016, when the Republican lobbyist and convicted felon Roger Stone created the "Stop the Steal" website, claiming that Trump's opponents, first Jeb Bush and then Hillary Clinton, were

JANUARY 6, 2021, ATTACK ON THE UNITED STATES CAPITOL BY WHITE SUPREMACIST RIOTERS.
(TYLER MERBLER, CREATIVE COMMONS LICENSE.)

trying to steal the election from him. In each instance, the website emphatically announced, "If this election is close, THEY WILL STEAL IT." The former Trump advisor and convicted felon Steve Bannon, on the day after the 2020 election, declared on his podcasts, "We're calling it a fraud or we're calling it a steal—stop the steal." He created a Facebook group called Stop the Steal, which, along with similar groups on Facebook and platforms like Reddit, attracted millions of likes, comments, mentions, and followers.

Many of those who participated in the insurrection got their information from these online spaces. From the moment the election was called for Biden, these online groups organized and did reconnaissance on the nation's capital. They officially mobilized on January 6, 2021, into a full-fledged militia traveling thousands of miles from all over the United States into Washington. They wreaked havoc on the Capitol, burning effigies, breaking into government buildings, and even killing one United States Capitol Police officer, Brian Sicknick.

One could argue that the actions of these groups was a unique instance that just happened to occur during the ending of Trump's first presidency and that America itself is not an inherently racist nation. On the contrary, January 6th was a mirror reflecting the depths of ugliness in an America steeped in racism and hegemonic white supremacy. It also showed that, at a moment's notice, citizens who subscribe to white supremacy can bring the United States to a political standstill through calculated organizing with the purpose of inflicting violence on those who stand in the way of their beliefs and preventing democratic processes from taking place. Their ability to voice their displeasure with their violent version of the March on Washington illustrates the power these groups have always had, the power to use force when not satisfied with a political outcome. As soon as Trump lost to Biden, suspected white supremacists, whether the elites who coordinated the march or the marchers themselves, felt powerless and out of control. To regain control, these groups organized a coup against the office of the president. However, they also organized at the state and local level to elect politicians who fit their right-wing ideology.

Today's political landscape resembles the early Obama era, with Tea Party activists, including government officials and lobbyists suspected to be right-wing extremists, opposing leftist policies such as Obamacare and the Troubled Asset Relief Program. The success of the 2010 anti-Obama backlash built up to the election of Trump in 2016. This pattern, of a right-wing backlash in a mid-term election against a Democratic president, repeated itself in 2024 with "Make America Great Again" or "MAGA" politicians opposing leftist policies of the Biden–Harris administration, such as parole programs that allowed unauthorized immigrants from Cuba, Venezuela, Nicaragua, and Haiti to enter the United States and student loan forgiveness for millions of borrowers. MAGA politicians and Trump himself railed daily against these policies and ultimately defeated Vice President Kamala Harris for the presidency. As white supremacist and extreme right-wing organizations flex their muscles in the wake of this victory, it is important for the Black community—using Black nationalist principles—to gain economic control of their communities and leverage that dollar power to become serious contenders for political power.

Power in the hands of the Black community would not mean subjugation of other ethnic groups as it has during four hundred years of white supremacy. What power means for Black people in America is that Blacks would have more autonomy and not be forced to beg other groups for basic needs and survival. Economic and political power go hand in hand. A community without a powerful economic base will not be in control politically, even if they are the majority. A community without an economic base can only produce elected politicians who are Black or purport to be Black but ignore harmful policies or fail to enact policies that economically uplift Blacks. Black politicians, especially in major metropolitan areas, tend to support policies that are in the best interest, particularly the economic interest, of whites—especially the whites who fund their elections—in that city. This leads to the appearance that the Black community is well off, while the reality is wide wealth disparities between

Blacks and whites. A community where only a rare few Black people attain wealth is not "Black Success." Black nationalism in action would result in most Black citizens, especially in predominantly-Black municipalities, becoming more economically secure. Atlanta is a prime example of a majority-Black municipality with wide economic disparities and no Black nationalist ideology. Atlanta is 51% Black and 40% white and has had consecutive Black mayors since Maynard Jackson's first term in 1974 well into the twenty-first century. However, just 2% of white households in Atlanta live below the poverty line, compared to 29% of Black households. Also, Black households in the city are twice as likely as white households to have zero net worth, meaning no savings or property ownership.

At the base of white supremacist control is the reinforcement, for both Blacks and whites, either through formal education or informally in the home, of the idea that white power is the ruling power.

H. Rap Brown, in a speech titled "The Politics of Education," stated,

> *Whatever you don't control can be used as a weapon against you, anything that you don't control can be used as a weapon against you. Education has been used as a weapon against Black people because Black people have been trained to think a certain way. See we do not control politics so politics as it's known in this country is a weapon against Black people. Once we examine what politics is we find out that it is the apex of white cultural aggression. When a man tells you that you can only become free through voting, he is restricting your mobility and freedom. You were born free!*

Indeed, since Brown made these arguments, despite well-intentioned initiatives and laws and regardless of who is president, white supremacy has continued to evolve as a lethal weapon to subjugate Black people as servants to white-owned and -operated interests. In 2008, the president of Morehouse College, Robert Franklin, said if (then candidate) Obama won the presidency it would "raise the ceiling for everyone." Unfortunately, the ceiling has not been raised for Black America when it comes to economics and education. In fact, the wealth and educational outcomes in K-12 public education has significantly declined while Obama occupied the White House and since he left. Brown addressed this kind of thing in the 1960s, saying,

> *Politics does not mean Democratic or Republican. Politics goes into what happens to your life every day. . . . It wouldn't make a difference as it pertains to Black people occupying offices. When you begin to understand the type of system that operates in this country then you understand that it is not the individual who manipulates the system, it's the system who manipulates that individual. If Eldridge Cleaver or Dick Gregory had become President in this country, it would make absolutely no difference, because America would still be in war in Vietnam. Because the country operates off military industrial complex which says that war is profitable. Which says that US Steel must make steel for tanks because over 70% of people in this country are either directly or indirectly employed by the military. I am as much against a Black cat oppressing people around the world as I am a white cat oppressing people around the world. If all the white folks were to die and black folks took the political seats and assumed those positions and business went on as usual, then Vietnam would continue.*

The 1960s was also a turbulent crossroads for Black America as the two predominant movements, Black Power and Civil Rights, fought for the hearts and minds of citizens over what would be the best way forward to advance the interest of Black people in America. The Council for United Civil Rights Leadership, comprising six prominent organizations, spearheaded the civil rights movement.

To uplift Black communities socially and economically, these groups determined that integration was the best approach. However, Black Power movements led by Stokely Carmichael (Lowndes County Freedom Organization), Huey P. Newton and Bobby Seale (Black Panther Party for Self-Defense), Ernest Thomas, H. Rap Brown (SNCC, after 1965), Frederick Kilpatrick (Deacons for Defense), and Malcom X (Nation of Islam) countered the ideology of the civil rights organizations by not promoting nonviolence as a method to achieve civil rights. They also advocated for Black nationalism as well as "Human Rights" as the foundation for economic and social advancement of Black people. Ultimately, the civil rights ideology of integration and working within the structural confines of the system became the prevailing blueprint for both Blacks and whites in America to follow when analyzing the socio-economic standing of Black people. The Big Six's strategic approach to organized protests served as a template for Black political leadership and influenced white perceptions of advocacy and demonstrations. The methods are pronounced when civil rights groups advocate for a specific issue concerning the plight of Black people, whether it be politics, social norms, economics, education, or criminal justice.

The end of the "separate but equal" doctrine in with the 1954 *Brown v. Board of Education* decision established a precedent that ultimately ended Jim Crow laws, thanks also to relentless advocacy by prominent civil rights organizations. However, the philosopher Derrick Bell notes that the white elimination of Jim Crow laws was more sinister than benevolent.

Bell argues that the *Brown* decision's departure from precedent is inexplicable without acknowledging its benefits for white people. The ruling wasn't just about the views of some whites; it was about the immorality of racial inequality and the fact that some white policymakers could see the economic and political benefits of ending segregation. For one thing, the decision enhanced America's credibility in its fight against communism, particularly among developing nations, and it reassured Black Americans that the ideals of equality and freedom, emphasized during World War II, could finally be realized in their own country. Some whites realized that the South could only tap its potential and enter the lucrative Sunbelt economy after it gave up its fight for segregation. In other words, they realized that the segregation they fought so hard to hold onto was a roadblock to the South's economic progress.

Bell has also argued that the court in *Brown* should have upheld *Plessy v. Ferguson*, the 1896 ruling that mandated separate but equal facilities for Black and white Americans. Bell acknowledges the unfair treatment of Black children in segregated schools but believes the court should have focused on upholding the "separate but equal" doctrine's "equal" part, often ignored. A Black nationalist standpoint agrees with Bell's and H. Rap Brown's assessment of the public education system. Black people did not need the integration of public schools. The suggestion by the Big Six civil rights coalition that an integrated education with whites was necessary for a good education not only was misguided but also fed into white supremacist talking points that education by Blacks and for Blacks was and is inferior. What was ultimately needed was "separate but equal" being enforced to the extent of what "equal" means.

For example, whatever state funding the University of Florida receives as an appropriation from the state should also be received by Florida A & M University, Florida's only public historically Black university. The same would apply to K-12 education in which schools in predominantly-Black neighborhoods would receive the same funds as predominantly-white schools in suburban areas. The harmful idea that Black education is substandard, unfortunately promoted by both whites and Blacks, has dire consequences.

If whites and, by proxy, African Americans think that a predominantly-Black education, especially if it is African-centered, is inferior, how then would they be able to create and support other Black-owned institutions and businesses? How would they also be able to successfully defend themselves against the encroachment of non-Black businesses and residents into Black neighborhoods? Both issues are crippling for Black communities as they are tied directly to the attainment of wealth.

Throughout the latter half of the twentieth century and into the twenty-first, the United States has been involved in various wars and conflicts in different countries. In the era of Trump (which also encompasses Biden's presidency), these wars included the War on Terror in Iraq, Afghanistan, and Syria; trade wars against China and sanctions against Russia; and the clandestine operation in the United States against Black people conceptualized as the War on Drugs. These conflicts and wars were started before Trump took office, continue during his presidency, and will still be active after it. To counter the war against the upliftment of Blacks and eventually kill white supremacy, Black people must exercise a robust Black nationalist program. Amos Wilson suggests that Black nationalists must organize a national political party with a solid, well-trained, informed, and well-organized base of grassroots organization on local, state, regional, national, and international levels.

At these various levels, especially at the national and international levels, the Black nationalists must replace the assimilationist and neoconservative organizations as the primary and legitimate leaders of the African American community. They must provide the community with a viable, workable plan for economic development, based on a mixed economy of primarily cooperative and self-help economic institutions, collective enterprises, and corporate and proprietary businesses. Wilson argues that a Black nationalist party's legitimacy would depend on defining vital socioeconomic interests shared by the African American community and proving its ability to achieve those goals through its organizational skills. To gain legitimacy, a Black nationalist party needs to portray its rivals as ineffective representatives of the people.

The rival to a Black nationalist party would naturally be the Democratic Party, which since Lyndon Johnson has received undying support from African Americans. The Democrats have earned at least 80% of the Black vote in every election since Johnson signed the Civil Rights and Voting Rights Acts into law. However, in the Black nationalist view, the Democratic Party benignly neglects African Americans. The neglect starts with representation. The Democratic Party has done a masterful job at ensuring that African Americans are well represented in their party. Esteemed politicians such as Adam Clayton Powell, Jr., Shirley Chisholm, Obama, and Harris have done wonders in ensuring that African American politics are synonymous with the Democratic Party. Laws such as the Civil Rights Act, the Voting Rights Act, the Fair Housing Act, and the Fair Sentencing Act give the perception of addressing the condition of African Americans. While these laws may have improved certain aspects of quality of life for African Americans, they have not corrected the widening economic or education gap between African Americans and whites. This is where a Black nationalist party could contend for Black attention and ultimately votes. It would have to overcome the marketing, branding, celebrity, and historic ties that the Democratic Party has built with the African American community over several generations to ask them the question of the millennium: are you better off economically and educationally now than you were in 1964?

Wilson's conception of a Black Nationalist Party would be most appropriate in the era of Trump and beyond to counter Black America's education and economic last-place standing in America. Black Americans are still at the bottom of American society, forced to accommodate themselves to the primary goals and advancement of white people and white-owned interests. While in this position, they continue a pattern of economic and educational regression devoid of any major political institutional apparatus to aggressively address these issues.

To address this, Black people will have to deploy nationalistic ideas and behaviors that move them toward African-centered education, group economics, and political sovereignty. They will also have to create a Black nationalist party that can centralize the main goals of Black nationalism and form them into a coherent platform. There may be a few who suggest that a Black nationalist agenda could be advanced within existing political parties, akin to how the Tea Party funded right-wing candidates to promote Republican ideals of limited government.

Ultimately the grassroots efforts of the Tea Party led to 138 politicians who identified with their platform in the 2010 mid-term elections. Of these, forty-four went on to win major national seats, including Rand Paul, Mike Lee, Marco Rubio, Pat Toomey, and Ron Johnson. Their ideology influenced the rhetoric of Trump, which he used to defeat Rubio for the Republican nomination in 2016.

It is not suggested that a Black Nationalist Party attempt to take over a major political party as the Tea Party did the Republicans, since the basis of the Tea Party was Republican talking points of limited government. Tea Party candidates elected in 2010, who remained active after Obama's presidency, secured their seats by criticizing Republicans they believed had strayed from the core limited-government ideology, specifically objecting to their support for TARP and Obamacare. Tea Party candidates claimed that their opponents' support for these policies, which in their view ran up the deficit to record numbers, showed a lack of Republican credentials, claiming their Tea Party ideology was more consistent with the party's traditional limited-government stance. But the goal of both the Tea Party and mainstream Republicans was to maintain the system of white supremacy so that whites can continue to be the dominant group domestically and internationally. A theoretical Black nationalist takeover of the national Democratic Party would be not only impractical but also impossible because the overarching goal of the Democratic Party is to maintain a system of white supremacy in which white Americans and non-whites who practice anti-Black racism continue to dominate African Americans politically, economically, educationally, and culturally.

The main concern of a Black nationalist party would be the political and economic interests of Black people. The national Democratic platform has no goals or programs focused on the liberation of African Americans. Their platform is centered on placating African Americans, offering policies that on the surface appear to provide incremental remedies to certain problems, but in the end the policies end up benefiting non-Blacks a great deal more and ultimately keeping African Americans in servitude to whites. Creating a Black nationalist party that puts the interests of African Americans first would need to galvanize grassroots Black-centered organizations that have a national profile and are not tied to white-owned interests. Then, funding from Black elites and the working class will be essential for operationalizing the platform. After that, the party should engage in mass training on the importance of Black nationalism, economic cooperatives, and African-centered education.

Eventually, the party will be ready to engage in local, state, and national politics. Issues that would be a part of the party platform for each level of government would include tax policies that are beneficial to the great majority of the Black working class, education policies that are favorable to an Afrocentric curriculum in public, private, and charter schools, and reparations that benefit specifically those of African descent whose ancestry in America originates from the American plantation. Reparations are important not only to right the wrongs of slavery but also to compensate for the massacres and theft of property of African Americans by white people with the aid of state and local governments. The descendants of the Ocoee and Tulsa massacres would greatly benefit from this part of the platform as it would give them the policy tools to fight for the economic remedies that are owed to them. They would be able to make the case that state and local governments and officials played a central role in stealing the property of their forefathers by way of manipulation of taxes, falsifying records, and stacking the courts with white supremacists.

These crimes robbed the descendants of those massacres of an equal chance to build generational wealth, contributing to the wide economic disparity between whites and Blacks. As this hypothetical Black nationalist party continues to advocate for reparations at each level of government, a broader narrative of economic cooperation among the Black masses

WOMEN RAISING FISTS IN BLACK POWER SALUTE, C. 1968. (NATIONAL MUSEUM OF AFRICAN AMERICAN HISTORY AND CULTURE.)

in America would emerge. This would send the message that, while African Americans vehemently advocate for and demand reparations for redress, they will not sit back and do nothing while demanding it. A Black nationalist party would work with Black-centered economists and Black-centered economic organizations such as local African American chambers of commerce, the Black Economic Alliance, and the Center for Black Equity to craft personalized economic blueprints for Black communities. These economic cooperatives would work in conjunction with Black-centered political action committees and lobbying organizations to build and cement a unified economic base.

A cohesive economic base to complement the political goals of the liberation of Black Americans is the lynchpin for killing white supremacy not only in education, politics, and economics but also in the form of the psychological damage inflicted upon Black Americans, who have come to think of themselves not as a nation within a nation but as individual people who have to actively participate in their own domination to survive. If a Black Nationalist Party with the basic tenets of nationalism is not established with the end goal of killing white supremacy, the devolution of African Americans into second-class citizenship in perpetuity will be the bleak reality for future generations.

NOTES

1—Malcolm X, "The Ballot or the Bullet," April 12, 1964.

2—K. L. Sanger, "Slave Resistance and Rhetorical Self-Definition: Spirituals as a Strategy." *Western Journal of Communication* 59(3) (1995): 177–192.

3—David Walker, *David Walker's Appeal, in Four Articles, Together with a Preamble, to the Coloured Citizens of the World, but in Particular, and very Expressly, to those of the United States of America* (New York: Hill and Wang, 1965).

4—William Garrison, "Walker's Appeal." *Liberator* (1831).

5—Theresa A. Martinez, "Storytelling as Oppositional Culture: Race, Class, and Gender in the Borderlands." *Race, Gender and Class* 6(3) (1999): 33–51.

6—Malcolm X, "Message to the Grassroots," November 10, 1963.

7—Edmund S. Morgan, "Slavery and Freedom: The American Paradox." *Journal of American History* 59(1) (1972): 5–29.

8—Elizabeth A. Martinez, "What Is White Supremacy?" (2017).

9—Amos Wilson, *Blueprint for Black Power: A Moral, Political, and Economic Imperative for the Twenty-First Century* (New York: Afrikan World Infosystems, 1998).

10—Herman J. Blake, "Black Nationalism." *Annals of the American Academy of Political and Social Science* 382 (1969): 15–25.

11—Robert Steven Levine (ed.), *Martin R. Delany: A Documentary Reader* (Chapel Hill: University of North Carolina Press, 2003), pp. 107-108.

12—Dorothy C. Broaddus, *Genteel Rhetoric: Writing High Culture in Nineteenth-Century Boston* (Columbia: University of South Carolina Press, 1999).

13—Martin Delany, *The Condition, Elevation, Emigration, and Destiny of the Colored People of the United States* (Baltimore: Black Classics Press, 1993).

14—Booker T. Washington, , Susan B Anthony, Cotton States Exposition, Daniel Murray Pamphlet Collection, and Susan B. Anthony Collection. "Address of Booker T. Washington, Principal of the Tuskegee Normal and Industrial Institute, Tuskegee, Alabama: Delivered at the Opening of the Cotton States and International Exposition, at Atlanta, Ga., with a Letter of Congratulation from the President of the United States."

15—W. E. B. Du Bois, *The Souls of Black Folk* (Oxford: Oxford University Press, 2008).

16—Booker T. Washington, *Up from Slavery: An Autobiography* (Garden City, N.Y.: Doubleday, 1963).

17—C. Vann Woodward, *The Strange Career of Jim Crow* (New York: Oxford University Press, 1966).

18—Jarvis R. Givens, "'There Would Be No Lynching If It Did Not Start in the Schoolroom': Carter G. Woodson and the Occasion of Negro History Week, 1926-1950." *American Educational Research Journal* 56(4) (2019): 1457–94.

19—Carter G. Woodson, *The Mis-Education of the Negro* (Trenton, N.J.: Africa World Press, 1933).

20—Marcus Garvey, *The Marcus Garvey and Universal Negro Improvement Association Papers, Volume XI: The Caribbean Diaspora, 1910–1920* (Durham: University of North Carolina Press, 2011).

21—Marcus Garvey, *Aims and Objects of Movement for Solution of Negro Problem Outlined* (Mansfield Centre, Conn.: Martino Fine Books, 2024 [originally 1924]).

22—Marcus Garvey, *Philosophy and Opinions of Marcus Garvey* (Journal of Pan African Studies eBook, 2009 [originally 1918]).

23—*The Black Panther Party Program Platform* (Black Panthers, 1972).

24—Huey P. Newton "Intercommunalism: A Higher Level of Consciousness" (1970). Unpublished manuscript, Dr. Huey P. Newton Foundation, Inc., collection, Mo864, Department of Special Collections, Stanford University Libraries, Stanford, Calif.

25—Dan Berger, "'Free the Land!': Fifty Years of the Republic of New Afrika." Black Perspectives blog (https://www.aaihs.org/free-the-land-fifty-years-of-the-republic-of-new-afrika/).

26—Robert L. Tsai, *America's Forgotten Constitutions* (Boston: Harvard University Press, 2014).

27—Philip Nicols, *Sir Francis Drake Revived* (London: William Stansby, 1628).

28—R. C. Schwaller, "Contested Conquests: African Maroons and the Incomplete Conquest of Hispaniola, 1519–1620." *Americas* 75(4) (2018): 609-638.

29—Canter Brown, Jr., "Tales of Angola: Free Blacks, Red Stick Creeks, and International Intrigue in Spanish Southwest Florida, 1812-1821." in *Go Sound the Trumpet! Selections in Florida's African American History*, ed. by David H. Jackson, Jr., and Canter Brown, Jr. (Tampa, Fla.: University of Tampa Press, 2005), pp 5–21.

30—President Andrew Jackson's Message to Congress "On Indian Removal," Dec. 6, 1830; Presidential Messages, 1789 - 1875; Records of the U.S. Senate, Record Group 46; National Archives Building, Washington, D.C.

31—Thomas Sidney Jesup, "Negros, &c., Captured from Indians in Florida," letter from Secretary of War Doc. No. 225. House of Representatives War Dept February 27, 1839.

32—Charles Crowe (ed.), *The Age of Civil War and Reconstruction, 1830-1900: A Book of Interpretative Essays* (Homewood, Ill.: Dorsey Press, 1966).

33—The importation of Africans for the purpose of enslavement was banned by the U.S. Congress in 1808. Researchers estimate that at the time of the enactment of the law, there were one million enslaved people of African descent living in the United States. The white powers allowed the law to be enacted because the very nature of chattel slavery meant that there was already a population in place to be bred and sold like cattle.

34—Sylviane A. Diouf, *Dreams of Africa in Alabama: The Slave Ship Clotilda and the Story of the Last Africans Brought to America* (New York: Oxford

University Press, 2007).

35—M. E. J. Parrish, *Events of the Tulsa Disaster* (Tulsa, Okla.: Tulsa Historical Press, 1923).

36— Etamaze Nkiri, "What Was Lost: Greenwood Was the Heart of Black Tulsa, Oklahoma." *American History* 56(5) (2021): 46-48.

37—Lauren Grubb, "Williams Dreamland Theatre," *Cinema Treasures* (https://cinematreasures.org/theaters/12823).

38—Chris M. Messer, Thomas E. Shriver, and Alison E. Adams, "The Destruction of Black Wall Street: Tulsa's 1921 Riot and the Eradication of Accumulated Wealth." *American Journal of Economics and Sociology* 77(3/4) (2018): 789–819.

39—Walter White, "More than Two Hundred White and Colored Men, Women and Children Were Killed in the Bloody or Horrible Race Riots at Tulsa, Okla." *Broad Ax* (Salt Lake City, Utah), June 18, 1921.

40—Messer *et al., op. cit.*

41—Jenifer Jenkins, "A White Mob Unleashed the Worst Election Day Violence in U.S. History in Florida a Century Ago." *Seattle Times*, Nov. 2, 2020.

42—Carlee Hoffmann and Claire Strom, "A Perfect Storm: The Ocoee Riot of 1920," *Florida Historical Quarterly* 93(1) (2014): 25-43.

43—Jerald Podair, "For One Survivor, the Election Day 1920 Massacre in Florida Was 'the Night the Devil Got Loose.'" *Conversation*, Nov. 1, 2024 (https://theconversation.com/for-one-survivor-the-1920-election-day-massacre-in-florida-was-the-night-the-devil-got-loose-241545).

44—R. Thomas Dye, "Rosewood, Florida: The Destruction of an African American community." *Historian* 58(3), (1996): 605-622.

45—Son of Sarah Carrier and cousin to Aaron Carrier.

46—Ocean Hill–Brownsville parents organized through notices like this in spring 1968. Source: UFT Photo Collection, Robert F. Wagner Labor Archives, New York University.

47—Bayard Rustin 1964 interview with Robert Penn Warren. Recording tape three, accessed via Robert Penn Warren Center for the Humanities at Vanderbilt University, courtesy of the University of Kentucky.

48—Manning Marable and Leith Mullings (eds.), *Let Nobody Turn Us Around: An African American Anthology: Voices of Resistance, Reform, and Renewal* (Lanham, Md.: Rowman and Littlefield, 2009).

49—Gail L. Thompson and Tawannah G. Allen, "Four Effects of the High-Stakes Testing Movement on African American K-12 Students." *Journal of Negro Education* 81(3) (2012): 218-227, 301-302.

50—Gary Fineout, "Race and Gender Identity Clash as School Vouchers Divide Florida Democrats." Politico, Feb. 5, 2020 (https://www.politico.com/states/florida/story/2020/02/04/race-and-gender-identity-clash-as-school-vouchers-divide-florida-democrats-1258782).

51—Eliza Shapiro. "'I Love My Skin!' Why Black Parents Are Turning to Afrocentric Schools." *New York Times*, Jan. 8, 2019.

52—Amos N. Wilson and Sababu N. Plata., *Awakening the Natural Genius of Black Children* (New York: Afrikan World InfoSystems, 1992).

53—Amos N. Wilson, *Blueprint for Black Power: A Moral, Political, and Economic Imperative for the Twenty-First Century* (New York: Afrikan World InfoSystems, 2011).

54—Reparations Poll conducted in May 2014 by YouGov.

55—Ashley V. Reichelmann and Matthew O. Hunt, "How We Repair It: White Americans' Attitudes toward Reparations." *Brookings*, Dec. 8, 2021 (https://www.brookings.edu/articles/how-we-repair-it-white-americans-attitudes -toward -reparations/).

56—"Negroes of Savannah." *New-York Daily Tribune*, 13 February 1865, Consolidated Correspondence File, ser. 225, Central Records, Quartermaster General, Record Group 92, National Archives; from *Freedmen and Southern Society Project*.

57—William A. Gladstone Afro-American Military Collection: Special Field Orders, No. 15, Headquarters, Military Division of the Mississippi, by Major General W. T. Sherman, re "young and able bodied negroes must be encouraged to enlist," mentions bounties paid and locations for settlement of freed Negr. 1865. Manuscript/Mixed Material.

58—Henry and Berry, supra note 15 and 17, at 34–47.

59—Miranda Booker Perry, "No Pensions for Ex-Slaves: How Federal Agencies Suppressed Movement to Aid Freedpeople." *Prologue Magazine* 42(2) (2010) (https://www.archives.gov/publications/prologue/2010/summer/slave-pension.html).

60—J. Herman Blake, "Black Nationalism." *Annals of the American Academy of Political and Social Science* 382 (1969): 15–25.

61—David J. Garrow, *Protest at Selma: Martin Luther King, Jr., and the Voting Rights Act of 1965* (New Haven, Conn.: Yale University Press, 1978).

62—"Candidates, Committees Report $28.3 Million Spent In 1960; Actual Spending Far Greater." In *CQ Almanac 1961*, 17th ed. (Washington, D.C.: Congressional Quarterly, 1961), pp. 1077-78.

63—Dorothy I. Height, *Open Wide the Freedom Gates: A Memoir* (PublicAffairs Books, 2005), p. 140; "We Wanted the Voice of a Woman to Be Heard," in *Sisters in the Struggle: African American Women in the Civil Rights–Black Power Movement*, ed. by Bettye Collier-Thomas and V. P. Franklin (New York: New York University Press, 2001), pp. 83-92.

64—Evan Faulkenbury, "'An Uncommon Meeting of Minds': The Council for United Civil Rights Leadership in the Black Freedom Struggle, 1963–1967." *Journal of African American History* 104(3) (2019): 392–414.

65—Bradley R. Rice, "Maynard Jackson." *New Georgia Encyclopedia*, 2004 (https://www.georgiaencyclopedia.org/articles/government-politics/maynard-jackson-1938-2003/).

66—Phyllis B. Gerstenfeld, *Crime and Punishment in the United States* (Hackensack, N.J.: Salem Press, 2008).

67—Department of Justice Office of the Inspector General, "The CIA–Contra–Crack Cocaine Controversy: A Review of the Justice Department's Investigations and Prosecutions," 1997 (https://oig.justice.gov/sites/default/files/archive/special/9712/ch01p1.htm).

68—Bruce Western and Christopher Wildeman, "The Black Family and Mass Incarceration." *Annals of the American Academy of Political and Social Science* 621 (2009): 221–42.

69—*Population Representation in the Military Services, Fiscal Year 2004.*

70—Distributional Financial Accounts and Institute for Economic Equity calculations. Federal Reserve Bank of St. Louis.

71—Julia Hirschfeld Davis and Matt Apuzzo. "President Obama Condemns Both the Baltimore Riots and the 'Slow-Rolling Crisis.'" *New York Times*, Apr. 28, 2015.

72—United States General Accounting Office, Report to Congressional Committee, "Federal Lobbying: Differences in Lobbying Definitions and Their Impact," April 1999, p. 2.

73—J Street, "Tell Congress: Respect the Green Line—and the First Amendment" (undated petition) (https://act.jstreet.org/sign/stop-israel-anti-boycott-act/).

74—Cristy Mendoza and Salma Elakbawy, "Black 4zomen's Equal Pay Day 2023: No Matter What State They Live in, Black Women Make Less than White Men" (undated article), Institute for Women's Policy Research (https://iwpr.org/black-womens-equal-pay-day-2023-no-matter-what-state-they-live-in-black-women-make-less-than-white-men/).

75—*Lewis v. City of St. Petersburg*, 98 F. Supp. 2d 1344 (M.D. Fla. 2000). U.S. District Court for the Middle District of Florida—98 F. Supp. 2d 1344 (M.D. Fla. 2000), May 3, 2000.

76—"Decision in St. Petersburg Riot Case Sparks New Clashes." *Los Angeles Times*, Nov. 14, 1996.

77—Michael A. Fletcher, "Arrests of Fringe Separatists May Have Sparked St. Petersburg Disturbance." *Washington Post*, Nov. 16, 1996.

78—"Uhuru Movement's Lawsuit against City of St. Pete for Attack on Headquarters Goes to Court." *Burning Spear*, April 30, 2005 (https://theburning-spear.com/uhuru-movements-lawsuit-against-city-of-stpete-for-attack-on-headquarters -goes-to-court/).

79—Leonora LaPeter, "Gym Will Carry Name of Man Slain by Police." *Tampa Bay Times*. June 7, 2001.

80—Olivia Steen, "St. Pete Community Rallies Together on 25th Death Anniversary of Tyron Lewis," Oct. 25, (https://www.wfla.com/news/pinellas-county/st-pete-community -rallies -together -on -25th -death -anniversary WFLA. 2021-of-tyron-lewis/).

81—Marvin L. Simner, "Racial Segregation in the Rise and Fall of 22nd Street South: The Unfolding Story of the Historic Black Business Recreational District in St. Petersburg, Florida." *Psychology Publications, Psychology Department, Western University* (2017), p. 4 (https://ir.lib.uwo.ca/cgi/viewcontent.cgi?article=1111&context=psychologypub).

82—Kathlyn Gay (ed.), *American Dissidents: An Encyclopedia of Activists, Subversives, and Prisoners of Conscience* (Santa Barbara, Calif.: ABC-Clio, 2012).

83—Sue Landry and David Rogers, "A Long Road of Rage," *Tampa Bay Times*, Dec. 14, 1996.

84—Omali Yeshitela, interview by author, June 23, 2009; Anita Richway Cutting, "From Joe Waller to Omali Yeshitela: How a Controversial Mural Changed a Man" (unpublished undergraduate honors thesis, University of South Florida, 2000), p. 17.

85—Bill DeYoung, "Vintage St. Pete: George Snow Hill and 'Pass-a-Grille,'" *St. Pete Catalyst*, June 8, 2020.

86—Zizwe Poe, "African People's Socialist Party". *The Sage Encyclopedia of African Cultural Heritage in North America*, ed. by Mwalimu J. Shujaa and Kenya J. Shujaa (Thousand Oaks, Calif.: Sage Publications, 2015), pp. 131-32.

87—"African Internationalism Is Not Pan-Africanism! African Internationalism Is the Theory of the African Working Class!", African People's Socialist Party website, June 14, 2016 (https://apspuhuru.org/2016/06/14/african-internationalism-is-not-pan-africanism-african-internationalism-is-the-theory-of-the-african-working-class/).

88—Jeffery M. Brown, "Black Internationalism: Embracing an Economic Paradigm," *Michigan Journal of International Law* 23(4) (2002) (https://repository.law.umich.edu/mjil/vol23/iss4/2/).

89—Gary Chartier, "Civil Rights and Economic Democracy," *Washburn Law Journal* 40(2) (2001): 267-287.

90—"African People's Socialist Party: Our Standards of Party Life," *Burning Spear*, Oct. 4, 2019 (https://theburningspear.com/our-standards-of-party-life-who-are-the-members-of-the-african-peoples-socialist-party/).

91—"Introducing the Economic Future for African People" (undated article), African People's Socialist Party website (https://apspuhuru.org/about/black-star-industries/).

92—Peter Mateyka and Christopher Mazur, "Homeownership in the United States: 2005 to 2019," March 25, 2021, United States Census Bureau website (https://www.census .gov/library/publications/2021/acs/acsbr-010.html).

93—Brooke Bobb, "The Vibe Is about Celebrating Blackness: Meet the Women behind Building Black Bed-Stuy," *Vogue*, Oct. 13, 2020 (https://www.vogue.com/slideshow/building-black-bedstuy).

THANK YOU AND ACKNOWLEDGEMENT

248

This book is a thank you to all who inspired, supported, and believed in me on this journey.

To Andrea, Riley, Zuri, and Aria—you all's steadfast love and support were essential to this book's completion.

To my Mu Epsilon chapter family—your listening, challenges, and cheers helped me find my voice.

To Christina and Adeyemi, your wisdom, patience, and guidance helped me overcome obstacles in the face of uncertainty.

And to my readers—your curiosity and passion are what make this important work matter. This book serves as the pinnacle of my learned experience as an African American man attempting to navigate this world daily. Thank you for being a part of that experience.

With gratitude,
Dr. Vincent Edward Oluwole Adejumo